see it, say it, symbolize it

Teaching the Big Ideas in Elementary Mathematics

Patrick L. Sullivan

Solution Tree | Press

555 North Morton Street
Bloomington, IN 47404
800.733.6786 (toll free) / 812.336.7700
FAX: 812.336.7790

email: info@SolutionTree.com
SolutionTree.com

Visit **go.SolutionTree.com/mathematics** to download the free reproducibles in this book.

Printed in the United States of America

Library of Congress Cataloging-in-Publication Data

Names: Sullivan, Patrick L., author.
Title: See it, say it, symbolize it : teaching the big ideas in elementary mathematics / Patrick L. Sullivan.
Description: Bloomington, IN : Solution Tree Press, 2024. | Includes bibliographical references and index.
Identifiers: LCCN 2023055101 (print) | LCCN 2023055102 (ebook) | ISBN 9781960574503 (paperback) | ISBN 9781960574510 (ebook)
Subjects: LCSH: Mathematics--Study and teaching (Elementary) | Mathematics teachers--Training of.
Classification: LCC QA135.6 .S846 2024 (print) | LCC QA135.6 (ebook) | DDC 372.7--dc23/eng/20240310
LC record available at https://lccn.loc.gov/2023055101
LC ebook record available at https://lccn.loc.gov/2023055102

GROWING THE MATHEMATICIAN IN EVERY STUDENT COLLECTION

Consulting Editors: Cathy L. Seeley and Jennifer M. Bay-Williams

No student should feel they're "just not good at math" or "can't do math"!

Growing the Mathematician in Every Student is a collection of books that brings a joyful positivity to a wide range of topics in mathematics learning and teaching. Written by leading educators who believe that every student can become a mathematical thinker and doer, the collection showcases effective teaching practices that have been shown to promote students' growth across a blend of proficiencies, including conceptual development, computational fluency, problem-solving skills, and mathematical thinking. These engaging books offer preK–12 teachers and those who support them inspiration as well as accessible, on-the-ground strategies that bridge theory and research to the classroom.

Consulting Editors

Cathy L. Seeley, PhD, has been a teacher, a district mathematics coordinator, and a state mathematics director for Texas public schools, with a lifelong commitment to helping every student become a mathematical thinker and problem solver. From 1999 to 2001, she taught in Burkina Faso as a Peace Corps volunteer. Upon her return to the United States, she served as president of the National Council of Teachers of Mathematics (NCTM) from 2004 to 2006 before going back to her position as senior fellow for the Dana Center at The University of Texas. Her books include *Faster Isn't Smarter* and its partner volume, *Smarter Than We Think*, as well as two short books copublished by ASCD, NCTM, and NCSM: (1) *Making Sense of Math* and (2) *Building a Math-Positive Culture*. Cathy is a consulting author for McGraw Hill's *Reveal Math* secondary textbook series.

Jennifer M. Bay-Williams, PhD, a professor at the University of Louisville since 2006, teaches courses related to mathematics instruction and frequently works in elementary schools to support mathematics teaching. Prior to arriving at the University of Louisville, she taught in Kansas, Missouri, and Peru. A prolific author, popular speaker, and internationally respected mathematics educator, Jenny has focused her work on ways to ensure every student understands mathematics and develops a positive mathematics identity. Her books on fluency and on mathematics coaching are bestsellers, as is her textbook *Elementary and Middle School Mathematics: Teaching Developmentally*. Highlights of her service contributions over the past twenty years include serving as president of the Association of Mathematics Teacher Education, serving on the board of directors for the National Council of Teachers of Mathematics and TODOS: Mathematics for ALL, and serving on the education advisory board for Mathkind Global.

Acknowledgments

All the glory to God for giving me the wisdom to write this book. Many years ago He planted in my heart that the best way to glorify Him was to become a mathematics teacher. This has always been my calling! He has paved the way for me to receive many blessings, none of which I am worthy. I am thankful for the many early-morning awakenings that stirred my heart and provided the wisdom to put words on paper. Philippians 4:13: "I can do all things through Christ who gives me strength!"

This book is dedicated to my grandmother, Edna Sullivan, who passed away in the midst of my writing of this book. She taught me many years ago that there is always a path to understanding mathematics if you begin with what you already know.

A special thanks to my mentor, Kurt Killion, and my colleagues, Joann Barnett, Adam Harbaugh, and Gay Ragan. My writing has been greatly inspired by the many basement conversations we have had about student learning and how to best teach many mathematical ideas! We all know that "you can't miss class in the basement!"

Thanks to the many students I have had the opportunity to teach and the teachers who let me into their classrooms. It is their stories, thinking, and struggles that have inspired this book. I would not have the wisdom I have without their willingness to share their understanding of mathematics with me. They have inspired me to think hard to become a better teacher and explain ideas in a way that made sense to them.

I also want to thank those who encouraged me, edited my words, and walked this journey with me. A few of these include Albert Otto, Cheryl Lubinski, Kathy Reddy, and Kimberly Van Ornum.

Last, but definitely not least, I want to thank my family. To my wife, Dawn, for her unwavering support and willingness to allow me to bounce "math-y" ideas off her even long after her bedtime! You are my rock! And to my three daughters: Emma, who brings pictures to my words and sometimes helps with illustrations; Lily, for always pushing the envelope and challenging me to question my assumptions; and Gwen, for willingly testing out ideas in this book and being an active participant to help me "see it," "say it," and "symbolize it" in several of my classes.

Solution Tree Press would like to thank the following reviewers:

Lindsey Bingley
Literacy and Numeracy Lead
Foothills Academy Society
Calgary, Alberta, Canada

Kelly Hilliard
Mathematics Teacher
McQueen High School
Reno, Nevada

Erin Kruckenberg
Fifth-Grade Teacher
Jefferson Elementary
Harvard, Illinois

Molly A. Riddle
Assistant Professor of Elementary Mathematics Education
Indiana University Southeast School of Education
New Albany, Indiana

Katie Saunders
Kindergarten Teacher
Bath Community School
Bath, New Brunswick, Canada

Rea Smith
Mathematics Facilitator
Fairview Elementary
Rogers, Arkansas

Visit **go.SolutionTree.com/mathematics** to download the free reproducibles in this book.

Table of Contents

Reproducibles are in italics.

About the Author

Patrick L. Sullivan, PhD, is an associate professor of mathematics at Missouri State University. He is a former principal and mathematics teacher at Grace Prep High School in State College, Pennsylvania, an institution that under his leadership was recognized as one of the top 1 percent of all private schools in the state. Before that, Dr. Sullivan was the mathematics department head at De Soto High School and Mill Valley High School in Kansas. In his current role at Missouri State University, he teaches content and methods courses to preservice teachers as well as graduate courses that involve strategies for implementing the Standards for Mathematical Practice across mathematical content areas. He is a champion of all students, especially those who have lost hope in understanding mathematics. In the fall of 2022, he led an initiative to redesign a developmental mathematics course, coupled with improving the pedagogical training of graduate teaching assistants, that has already led to significant increases in the percentage of students achieving success.

Dr. Sullivan is the current president-elect of the Missouri Council of Teachers of Mathematics. In 1999, he received the Presidential Award for Excellence in Mathematics and Science Teaching in the state of Kansas, and in 2016, he was recognized as the

Missouri Teacher Educator of the Year. He has presented throughout the United States on best practical strategies for teaching mathematics, using technology to teach probability and statistics, and advancing students' understanding of fraction concepts. He is coauthor of the book *Foundations of Number and Operations for Teachers* and has published articles in several different journals, including *Mathematics Teacher: Learning and Teaching PK–12* and the *Australian Primary Mathematics Classroom*.

Dr. Sullivan received a bachelor of science in education from the University of Kansas, a master's degree in teaching and leadership from the University of Kansas, and a doctorate in curriculum and instruction from the Pennsylvania State University. He has a blog, *Not So Random Thoughts on Mathematics Education*, that can be found at sullycanmath.blogspot.com. He founded a company, Elevate to Excellence LLC, that is focused on providing parents and schools with the resources and tools to help every student stay in the mathematics game!

To book Patrick L. Sullivan for professional development, contact pd@SolutionTree.com.

Mathematics is not about numbers, equations, computations, or algorithms: it is about understanding.

—William Paul Thurston

INTRODUCTION

How Did I Get Here?

You know those moments in your development that seemed insignificant as they occurred but, years later, on further reflection, turned out to have played a critical role in charting the trajectory of your life? When I was a fourth grader, elementary school was personally a mixed bag. I was the awkward kid who wore cowboy boots, carried a big red handkerchief, spoke with a bit of a stutter, and struggled to read at the level of my peers. My saving grace was that I believed I was good at mathematics. Or at least I *thought* I was, until my experience with two-digit multiplication.

My mathematics identity started to slip when I couldn't figure out this specific operation. No matter how hard I tried, I could *not* wrap my head around what I was supposed to "carry" and why I needed to "add a zero." While this experience is nearly fifty years old, I vividly remember those feelings of not getting it, and with other aspects of school not going well at the time, I began to feel like school just wasn't my thing. On one particular day I had to stay in for recess, my favorite subject, because I, like a few of my peers, was not understanding two-digit multiplication. Our teacher thought that with a little more practice we would understand. It did not help. I left school that day even more frustrated. That night, I went to my grandma Edna's house in tears because I was struggling to figure out two-digit multiplication. And what I experienced that night became a significant moment in my life, changing my understanding of two-digit multiplication and, most importantly, the trajectory of my life.

Grandma Edna sat me down, and we went to work. What's amazing is I remember the exact problem she wrote on a three-by-five-inch index card: 24 × 35.

"Do you know what five times four is?" she asked.

"Yes, it's twenty."

"Do you know what five times twenty is?"

"Yes, it's a hundred."

She continued asking me the answers to 30 times 4 and 30 times 20. I replied 120 and 600, respectively.

"If you know the answers to these four problems," she said, "then you know how to solve twenty-four times thirty-five!"

Wait—what?

She spent the next few hours explaining to me how two-digit numbers, such as 24 and 35, were composed of two different units, tens and ones; why we "carried"; and why we "added a zero." We tackled many more problems until she was convinced that I understood the meaning of all the steps of two-digit multiplication.

I went to school the next day equipped with what felt like a *superpower*. Not only could I quickly and efficiently compute two-digit multiplication problems, but I knew the *why* behind the answer and how I'd arrived at it. That same day, several of my peers—also jail mates in the two-digit multiplication prison, meaning no recess—came to me wanting to know how my grandmother had taught me two-digit multiplication. It was then that I unknowingly taught my first mathematics lesson, but not my last. Fortunately, over the next few days, all of us were released from multiplication prison. My teacher, seeing the success of the other students, had me explain my method to the rest of the class because she had never seen it done that way. While my grandmother's method—which I would much later learn is called the *partial product algorithm*—wasn't the same one my teacher was using, it made sense to me and to my peers. I still use it to this day; it's how I *see* multiplication. That one night changed the way I think about multiplication, and I'm thankful for that experience. Many years later, when I asked my grandmother where she'd learned that method, she told me her father had taught her that way because "there were days the horse couldn't get [her] to school," and since he was "good with numbers," he taught her mathematics while she was home. An invaluable and perhaps unlikely lesson that reverberated across generations.

This early experience of mine is no slight on my fourth-grade teacher. She was only sharing what she knew about two-digit multiplication. As I've discovered many times myself, you can't teach something you don't know. In retrospect, my fourth-grade teacher showed a great deal of humility by giving a struggling fourth grader a platform because she wanted to learn more about what I knew. She was willing to give me the floor because she saw my peers understanding two-digit multiplication in a different way—a way that helped my peers and me understand the why behind it. This experience rekindled my passion and love for school and, more than likely, cultivated a love for helping others learn mathematics that has driven me throughout my adult life.

Of course, I wouldn't be sharing my story today without various elementary teachers: from Ms. Beets in first grade, who in a moment of exasperation with my inattentiveness during a mathematics lesson handed me the book and said, "Since you obviously know how to do this, why don't you come up and teach the rest of the class?" (see—look what she started!); to my fourth-grade teacher, Ms. M., who gave me a platform to share my thinking; to Ms. Feuerborn, who poured her love and wisdom into all of us sixth graders, making us believe that we could be more than we thought we could be. I am forever grateful for their loving corrections, wisdom, and nudges along the way. I needed every one of them!

Unfortunately, many students do not experience the sort of critical moment necessary to keep them in the mathematics game. In fact, I'm sure that I myself have contributed to a few students not experiencing those moments. It always broke me when students didn't get it even though I was doing everything I knew how to do to help them. I realized I needed to grow in my understanding of elementary mathematics and be a better listener. I needed to understand how students were making sense of the important ideas of mathematics so that I could better understand the why behind their struggle. Regardless of whether I was teaching high school algebra, college-level mathematics, or elementary mathematics methods or researching elementary and middle students' understanding of mathematics, what I've learned is that most students' difficulties are grounded in how they've made sense of a few essential elementary mathematics concepts—fractions, multiplication, division, ratios, and so on.

Beginning in 2014, as I listened to the stories of the students I teach in both preservice content courses and developmental mathematics courses (the lowest level of mathematics course one can take at a university), a theme emerged. There seemed to be a triggering event, like mine, in elementary school that they vividly remembered took them out of the mathematics game. Sometimes, this event was a personal one, such as the death of a family member, parents' divorce, a family move, or a test score that placed them in a mathematics class lower than that of their peer group. One student recounted how she'd been displaced from her peer group after a poor mathematics placement score in fifth grade: "It hurt being placed into 'bridge math,' which my friends, who were in the higher class, called 'stupid math.' I was good at other subjects, so I just started living up to the expectations others had for me." Another student shared, "At the beginning of fifth grade, I took a test, didn't pay attention to it, and got put into a lower-level class. I was in fifth grade! I didn't need to miss out on learning higher levels of math the rest of my life because of a stupid test in fifth grade! Who does that to a fifth grader?"

Other times, as in my case, the traumatic experience involved a specific facet of mathematics, such as working too slowly through timed multiplication tests, struggling to master two-digit multiplication or long division at the pace of the class, or being unable to make sense of fraction concepts. Whether it was a life or mathematical event, there was a specific moment that students remembered when they started to feel that being good at mathematics was no longer part of their identity. And once they were on the "I'm not good at math" train, they were never given the opportunity to get off! The following email I received from one of my college students ahead of the semester exemplifies the heart of this struggle and how many students see themselves.

I am currently enrolled in your Math 101 class. This is going to be my third try at this class. I've always struggled with math courses because I'm not good with mental math and often will end up making multiple small mistakes that I know I shouldn't have. I am not sharp on my multiplication tables and will mix up numbers easily. In the past, I've struggled to ask for help in math because I don't like to seem stupid for not understanding such an easy level of math. Goals I've mapped out for this semester include passing this class, and I hope you will be able to help me accomplish this goal.

This book is the result of my personal quest to create Grandma Edna trajectory-changing moments for more students and to help other teachers do the same for their students. As I suggested earlier, this book has been shaped by my listening to not only how younger students reason about the big ideas of elementary mathematics but also how the preservice elementary and secondary mathematics teachers I've taught, as well as the college-level developmental mathematics students, reason about those same ideas. It's important to note that developmental mathematics students are typically freshmen with an ACT mathematics score that requires them to take a noncredit mathematics course before they can take a mathematics course that satisfies their degree requirement. In other words, I've listened to students' understanding of these elementary mathematics concepts almost immediately after their first experiences with these concepts as well as adult learners who are far removed from their initial experiences learning these same concepts. A theme that emerged across these groups is that, for many, their struggles with mathematics were anchored in a fixed and disconnected understanding of number concepts. While many expressed to me that they had a way to get an answer, they often had no idea why that answer made sense. They lacked the ability to do anything beyond mimicking a nonmathematical procedure or mnemonic (for example, "get a common denominator" or "keep, change, flip") that they'd been taught. Most importantly, they didn't have a way through when they didn't know what to do.

The focus of this book is to provide you with tools you can employ to create more Grandma Edna moments for your elementary students. These tools will support your efforts to develop in your students a dynamic and flexible view of numbers across all four operations that will unleash their inner mathematics superpowers. This book will challenge you to keep an open mind while engaging in what professor of mathematics education Jo Boaler (2022) refers to as a *mathematical mindset.* A mathematical mindset provides opportunities for you to see patterns and relationships between numbers and operations in new, exciting ways and to make connections that you may have never thought of. It denotes a willingness to imagine different possibilities and to objectively weigh what you're learning against what you already know. It involves transforming your thinking and questioning your assumptions. And, in this book, it means acquainting yourself with potentially unfamiliar language that will help you communicate mathematics concepts in a more student-brain-friendly way.

On that note, to begin engaging us in the work required of a mathematical mindset, I'd like to first draw your attention to a set of addition problems that we're going to revisit throughout the introduction. Moving forward, we'll explore the enlightened approach to mathematics we'll take in this book, examine the three critical elements that compose this approach, get candid about the differences between our 21st century students and ourselves, take a look at what you can expect from each of the book's chapters, and touch on the key points of this introduction that will help orient you as we dive into chapter 1.

See It–Say It–Symbolize It Approach

Please take a moment to reflect on the addition problems shown in figure I.1 represented using standard mathematical notation. What do you see when you look through these problems? What mathematical language do you associate with solving each of these problems?

1 267 + 3,580

2 0.267 + 0.0358

3 $\frac{1}{2} + \frac{3}{8}$

Figure I.1: Three addition problems written in standard notation.

Now consider the same problems represented in a slightly different form, as shown in figure I.2. This form is what I like to refer to as *numeral-unit-name* notation. What do you see when you look through these problems? What mathematical language do you associate with solving them?

1	+		**2** hundreds	**6** tens	**7** ones
		3 thousands	**5** hundreds	**8** tens	**0** ones
2	+	**2** tenths	**6** hundredths	**7** thousandths	**0** ten-thousandths
		0 tenths	**3** hundredths	**5** thousandths	**8** ten-thousandths
3		**1** half + **3** eighths			

Figure I.2: Three addition problems written in numeral-unit-name notation.

Did you think about each set of problems the same way? Did you see the same ideas in both sets? Did the same language come to mind? More than likely, the first set of problems cued you to think about a known solving process that involved your using language such as "need to carry the one," "need to line up the decimals," and "need to get a common denominator." Did the representation of those same problems in numeral-unit-name notation cause you to think differently or change the focus of your attention? Would the language you'd use to communicate your understanding be the same or different? Can you now see connections that you were unable to see when the problems were represented as shown in figure I.1? The differences between these sets have everything to do with tapping into a mathematical mindset and empowering all elementary students with transformative understandings that will keep them in the mathematics game.

The two preceding sets shed light on the approach to mathematics teaching and learning that we'll rely on throughout this book—one comprising three crucial elements: (1) see it, (2) say it, and (3) symbolize it. For a given mathematical concept, we educators must be intentional in the use of the concrete and pictorial representations we present to students ("see it"), the language we expect students to use to communicate their understandings of those representations ("say it"), and what we ask students to do to meaningfully engage with those representations ("symbolize it"). As shown in figure I.3, each related element represents an opportunity or entry point for fostering in students *conceptual consistency* among the other elements.

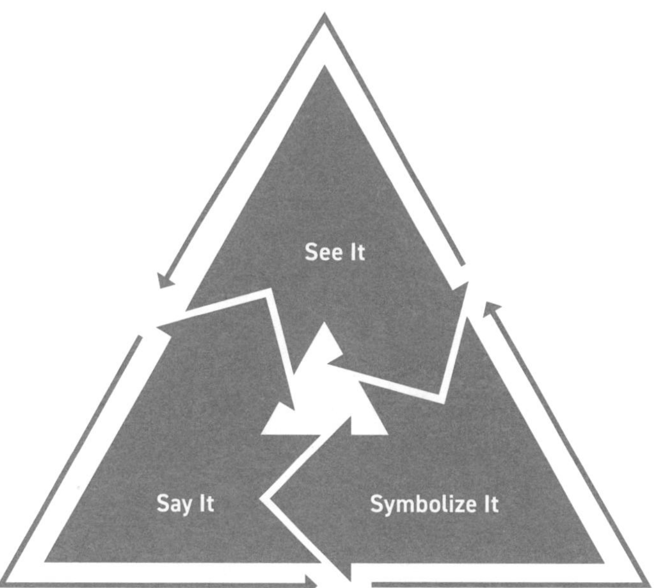

Figure I.3: See it–say it–symbolize it approach.

Adam Harbaugh, a colleague at Missouri State University, introduced the construct of conceptual consistency to me (personal communication, June 6, 2023). His conception of conceptual consistency is about alignment and connectedness among what is seen, said, and symbolized. For example, consider the array of squares shown in figure I.4. What do you "see"? How do you "say" it? How do you "symbolize" it?

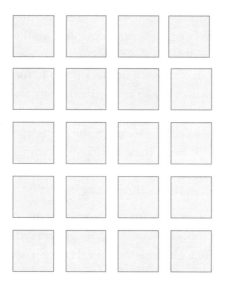

Figure I.4: An example of see it–say it–symbolize it.

More than likely, you saw a rectangular array of 5 rows of 4, or 5 "groups of" 4, which represents the symbolized multiplication problem 5 × 4. As we will discuss in much greater detail in chapter 7 (page 147), my desire is for students to "see" multiplication (that is, repeated groups of the same size of group) as they look through an array; "say" what they are "seeing" using "groups of" language while also communicating that the number of columns signify the number of groups and the number of columns signify the size of the group, or multiplicative unit; and "symbolize" what they are "seeing" and "saying" (that is, 5 × 4). A student with a conceptually consistent understanding of multiplication is able to "see" a symbolized problem (for example, 5 × 4), form mental images of pictorial and/or concrete representations consistent with this symbolized problem, and use language that binds together what is "seen" and "symbolized" (for example, 5 groups of 4 or 5 units of 4).

This approach is a blend of both foundational and emergent research, such as that of mathematics educators David Tall and Shlomo Vinner (1981), who put forth the idea of the concept image, or the cognitive structure in a student's mind that's associated with a given concept (or a representation of that concept). See it–say it–symbolize it also makes use of what Yew Hoong Leong, Weng Kin Ho, and Lu Pien Cheng (2015) of Singapore's National Institute of Education describe as the concrete-pictorial-abstract sequence that guides representational flow—which has its roots in psychologist Jerome S. Bruner's (1966) conception of the enactive, iconic, and symbolic modes of representation. And, finally, the approach we'll use throughout this book incorporates psychologist Jean Piaget's (1977) perspective on viewing students' mathematical reasoning through the lens of their mental actions and the language they use to communicate what they are seeing.

Instruction with the see it–say it–symbolize it approach involves teaching the foundational understandings of a concept by having students perform actions using concrete objects, seeing those same actions in pictorial models, and using symbols and language to record both physically modeled and seen actions. The instructional focus is on illuminating important features of those foundational understandings across each representational form so that students' initial concept images reflect rich and powerful understandings while also providing opportunities for them to make connections so that they can flex their superpower muscles.

Imagine a concept image as a file cabinet drawer full of experiences and understandings related to a topic. Have you ever found yourself in a position in which you needed an important document from a file cabinet drawer but weren't able to find it, either because it wasn't there or because it was hidden behind a bunch of other papers? The same thing happens to our students. For example, as we'll discuss in chapter 4 (page 73), many experienced mathematics students mistakenly conceive of fractions not as numbers but as relationships between the two numerals of the fractions (Sullivan, Barnett, & Killion, 2023). This concept image is a product of their past experiences with representations of fractions and the mental activities they engaged in while learning fraction concepts. Unfortunately, this enduring initial concept image of fractions often leads many students to struggle in future coursework as well as with their own mathematics identities. The overarching goal of the see it–say it–symbolize it approach, then, is develop a conceptually consistent understanding of foundational mathematical ideas that meshes together what is seen, what is said, and what is represented symbolically so that more students develop a rich and meaningful understanding of critical concepts.

As an adult learner, you're already living in the symbolic, or abstract, world because you've already had experiences with solving problems such as 267 + 3,580. In the context of our approach to mathematics, think about what you *see*—that is, what you think about—when you look through this problem. Whatever you're thinking about is part of the concept image that you've come to associate with this symbol string. You already know that each of the numerals in the symbol string is associated with a particular place value and that the + signifies the operation of addition. It's also likely that you've come to associate specific terms, actions, and possibly other representational forms with this symbol string. Think about what you would *say* to someone else to explain how to solve this problem. I asked my wife, who is not a mathematics teacher, how she would describe this process to another person. Figure I.5 shows her recorded actions and the language she associated with those actions. Would you say or do anything different if you were explaining this problem to someone else?

		1		
	3	5	8	0
+		2	6	7
	3	8	4	7

1. Place the same unit in each column.
2. Add 0 and 7. Bring 7 down.
3. Add 8 and 6, bring 4 down, and carry the 1.
4. Add 1 and 5 and 2. Bring 8 down.
5. Bring 3 down.

Figure I.5: My wife's explanation for how to solve 267 + 3,580.

Think about this particular explanation from the perspective of someone first learning this operation. You can probably imagine an inquisitive student asking a question like "Why are we 'bringing the 4 down' and 'carrying the 1'?" There are a few reasons why we *don't* want our students' first experience with addition to involve the "bringing down" and "carrying" language. One is that it doesn't speak the *why* of these actions, and it doesn't lend itself to conceptual consistency across all the mathematical entities (for example, fractions and algebraic expressions) in which we combine quantities of units. The other issue, as mathematics educators Dolores D. Pesek and David Kirshner (2000) explain, is that once students' concept image involves a standard algorithm to solve problems of a particular type, it's difficult to push them to develop a deeper conceptual meaning because they believe that they have what they need and that they understand the concept.

However, hidden in my wife's recorded actions and explanation are also the three foundational ideas that we *want* to place at the front of students' addition file cabinet drawer. First, we want students to see that *numbers* are a collection of quantities (represented by the numeral) and sizes of units (represented by the unit name). For example, the number 267 is 2 hundreds, 6 tens, and 7 ones. Second, the action of addition involves combining quantities of the same size of unit (for example, 8 *tens* + 6 *tens* = 14 *tens*). Third, because we're working within the decimal number system, when there's a quantity of 10 of a particular size of unit, the quantity of that unit can be *equally exchanged* for 1 of the next greater size of unit (for example, 10 *tens* are equally exchanged for 1 *hundred*). The intentional focus on these three foundational ideas influences the representations that we use to teach addition, the activities in which we engage students to learn addition, and the language we expect students to use to communicate their understanding of addition. Let's now briefly examine in a little more detail the distinct elements of the see it–say it–symbolize it approach.

SEE IT

The *see it* element of our approach to mathematics involves either (1) purposefully illuminating an aspect of a concept so there's a better chance students will see that aspect and understand it conceptually or (2) using a representation that simply makes an idea more visible. At the very start of their book *How Learning Works*, educators Marsha C. Lovett, Michael W. Bridges, Michele DiPietro, Susan A. Ambrose, and Marie K. Norman (2023) provide an apt quote that's also one of my favorites, attributed to "one of the founders of the field of cognitive science," Herbert A. Simon: "Learning results from what the student does and thinks and only from what the student does and thinks. The teacher can advance learning only by influencing what the student does to learn" (p. 1). As with students' doing and thinking, what students are able to see matters tremendously—and we can influence what they see, and in turn digest, by being thoughtful about the nature of the learning activities we place before them. Consider the same addition problem I gave my wife, 267+ 3,580, but with the size of the unit made explicit as shown in figure I.6. Moving forward, I refer to this as a *numeral-unit-name chart*.

		2 hundreds	**6** tens	**7** ones
+	**3** thousands	**5** hundreds	**8** tens	**0** ones

Figure I.6: Numeral-unit-name chart for addition.

The purpose of writing the unit name is to focus students' attention on the unifying concept of adding whole numbers, decimals, and fractions—*the action of addition involves combining quantities of the same size of unit*. Writing out the unit name is a purposeful choice meant to make the size of the unit explicit. We want all students, when they're first learning the concept of addition, to *see* that every numeral in a number represents the quantity of a size of unit. Another benefit of writing out the size of the unit is that we provide students with a clear opportunity to reckon with the situation in which we have a quantity of 10 or more of a particular size of unit. That is, as shown in figure I.7, the 14 tens resulting from combining 6 tens and 8 tens can be equally exchanged for 1 hundred and 4 tens.

		1 hundred		
		2 hundreds	**6** tens	**7** ones
+	**3** thousands	**5** hundreds	**8** tens	**0** ones
		hundreds	~~**14** tens~~	
	3 thousands	**8** hundreds	**4** tens	**7** ones

Figure I.7: Making the equal exchange of 14 tens for 1 hundred and 4 tens explicit.

Illuminating unit names to ignite understanding in the immediate context of addition also sets students up for success later on, when we're ready to introduce more universally challenging concepts, such as fractions. In fact, the one reason why fractions are often so difficult for students to understand has to do with an important caveat with regard to the idea that every numeral in a number represents *the quantity of a size of unit.* Consider one of the fractions from our original problem set, written in standard notation: 3⁄8. With fractions, numerals can represent both a quantity *and* a size of a unit. In this instance, the 3 signifies the quantity of a size of unit, eighths, signified by the 8. Much more on fractions later!

SAY IT

This leads into the second element of our mathematical approach, *say it.* Often overlooked, this element involves the development of the conceptual language we want students to not only associate with a given concept but utilize in written and verbal communication to demonstrate their understanding. The use of mathematical language, however, is challenging for many students, as mathematics educator David Pimm (1987) has shown in his foundational *Speaking Mathematically: Communication in Mathematics Classrooms.* One of the challenges relates to the concept image that students associate with words and phrases that we often use in mathematics. For example, consider what comes to your mind when you see the words *numerator* and *denominator.* What understandings have you come to associate with these terms? How do you utilize these understandings to make sense of mathematics? If you're like many of my students, perhaps you associate these terms with the placement of numerals in a fraction without truly understanding what they symbolize. In other instances, the language students associate with a mathematical idea serves as a cue to perform a procedure that carries no meaning. For example, students often commit to memory the phrase "carry the one" without understanding conceptually what that phrase means. The *say it* element is about condensing and employing age-appropriate language to make connections and build a consistent conceptual meaning. For example, the conceptually consistent language that unifies all three addition problems from our original problem set is that, as shown in figure I.8, the operation of addition, regardless of the type of number (that is, whole, fraction, or decimal), involves combining quantities of the same size of unit.

Figure I.8: Focusing attention on the size of unit to solve the three addition problems.

Instead of using disconnected, procedural language (for example, "lining up decimals" or "getting a common denominator") to communicate addition, students need to understand and utilize one conceptually consistent idea (for example, combining quantities of the same size of unit) that connects adding whole numbers through adding algebraic expressions. Likewise, rather than using the procedural language "carrying the one," students are more likely to *connect ideas* if they have the age-appropriate, conceptual language that serves to communicate exactly what actions they're performing on a number (or quantity) and why (Peng et al., 2020; Purpura, Logan, Hassinger-Das, & Napoli, 2017; Vanluydt, Supply, Verschaffel, & Van Dooren, 2021). That's why, throughout the book, instead of using more formal mathematical terms for numbers and expressions, we'll be using their conceptually consistent equivalents. For example, as shown in figure I.8, since we use the decimal number system, when we reach 10 of a particular size of a unit, we can exchange that quantity for 1 of the next greater size of unit. In this instance, 10 tens can be *equally exchanged* for 1 hundred because both represent the same amount (that is, **10**0 or **1**00). Instead of having students "carry the one," we can challenge them to use the term *equal exchange* because it exemplifies conceptually what is happening and it connects with what they already know about money. We also challenge them to explicitly state the size of the units involved in the exchange (that is, "10 tens are equally exchanged for 1 hundred"). Three other equal exchanges are shown in the shading of problems 2 and 3 in figure I.8. Take a moment to determine what those equal exchanges would be.

SYMBOLIZE IT

The last element of our mathematical approach to teaching and learning, *symbolize it*, could represent either a utilizing activity or a creating activity, depending on where students are in the learning process of a given concept. That is, *symbolize it* involves either looking through known symbols (utilizing understandings already in the file cabinet drawer) in order to solve a problem or creating symbols (both mathematical and written language) to describe an understanding of a problem or idea. Piaget (1977) captures these modes of understanding in his distinction between *assimilation* (that is, a concept fits with something that's already in the file cabinet drawer) and *accommodation* (that is, an individual needs to make room in the file cabinet drawer to add something new). This element is probably the hardest for adult educators to conceptualize because we already have a lot in our file cabinet related to the concepts we teach and we have pulled from those files multiple times to teach this content. My hope is that the content of this book will add to what is already in your file drawers and give you a few more options when you open those drawers.

Think about the experience you had earlier with the addition problem 267 + 3,580: your addition file cabinet drawer was already full of ideas, images, and mental actions associated with this operation, though it's possible that in the last few pages you encountered something new or gained an insight that you added to the drawer (for example, equal exchanges). The *symbolize it* element is how students represent their thinking to make sense of a problem. It's not about how we use symbols (that is, pictures, words, and mathematical notation) during learning experiences but about how students internalize those learning experiences and the associations they make from them. The only evidence that we have of what students have internalized is what they say or record. For example, suppose you asked your class to solve the problem "Hot dogs come in packages of 8. You purchase 3 packages. How many hot dogs do you have?" Depending on the nature of your students' concept image, they may or may not see this as a multiplication problem. What they see the problem as influences the symbols they use to record their understanding of the problem. A few different examples of how students could symbolize it are shown in figure I.9.

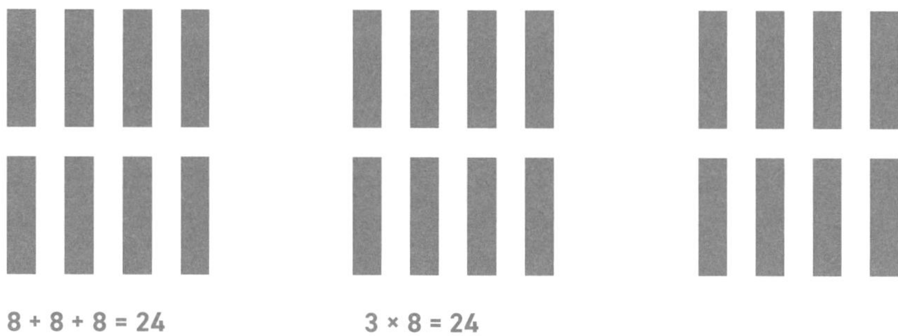

8 + 8 + 8 = 24 3 × 8 = 24

Figure I.9: Symbolizing 3 packages of 8 hot dogs.

As mentioned earlier, *symbolize it* includes the written recording of the language students use, *say it*, which opens a window into how they will *see it*. And the *it* could be any mathematical entity—such as a symbol string, concrete model, pictorial model, pattern relationship, or contextual problem—that the student is asked to reason. Once we as teachers are aware of how our students are seeing it, we'll know how to best help them move their thinking forward.

A Necessary Shift for Classrooms

Take a moment to reflect on what you thought about when you initially saw the standard-notation problem set shown in figure I.1 (page 5). What did you see? Did you think about connections among the three problems? Or what each of the numerals in the problems represented?

I suspect you saw three separate procedures. If that's the case, don't be too hard on yourself! This is how most of us have been trained to think. Remember to stay in a mathematical mindset while also giving yourself a little grace. Most of us, including myself, learned elementary mathematics this way. The phrases "get a common denominator," "carry the one," and "line up the decimals" are deeply rooted in us because that's how we were taught. These phrases cued the procedural steps that we were expected to follow. And many of us were quite good at learning mathematics this way. After all, many of us were told that we *had* to learn these procedures because we wouldn't be carrying around calculators all the time! Who knew, right? Of course, technology transforms the world and the classroom very quickly. The answer to a problem is no longer the destination—answers are readily accessible. In the 21st century classroom, the answers are in fact the starting point, and the why behind those answers is the destination.

Unfortunately, many of the traditions of teaching and learning elementary mathematics are grounded in a 1970s workforce mindset (Boaler, 2022; Ellis & Berry, 2005). The workplace of the 1970s demanded individuals to perform quick, efficient calculations because the technological means for producing those calculations weren't broadly accessible. Much like rubber cement, metal lunch boxes, and scratch-and-sniff stickers, this particular mindset speaks to our past but not to our students' present and future. As such, we must rethink our efforts.

Our students, unlike many of us when we were their age, carry devices that enable them to quickly and efficiently obtain answers to any of the addition problems of our initial problem set. A student might say to their preferred AI software, "What's ½ plus ⅜?" Within a few seconds, this device will deliver the answer. The adult world our students will enter is much different from the world most of us entered. The workforce and societal demands of mathematics for our students are different from the demands placed on us. We didn't have the same technology, or at least we didn't have it at our disposal every moment of the day. As a young student, I did many calculations in my head because I either was too lazy or couldn't quickly find my calculator. Our students don't have that issue, which necessarily means they have different mathematical demands. They need to know whether what they're entering into the technology is giving them a correct answer and, if not, how to program the technology so that it does. (Interestingly, when you ask Siri to add ½ and ⅜, she chimes, "point six" (0.6). See! Even Siri doesn't like fractions!) Arguably more than students and workers of prior generations, our students need to understand the why behind what they're doing—so they can do the type of thinking that their own world demands.

If students see only a procedure when given a problem like ½ + ⅜, their options for proceeding when they're unsure what to do next are limited. If students fail to recall the right rule or cue at the right time, they feel helpless and lost. I get it when they say, "This doesn't make any sense!" I want students to have more than what I had. I want them to not only be able to mentally compute ½ + ⅜ but also know why that answer makes sense so they have something to hang on to when they're uncertain. Thinking about the why behind the procedures gives students a way through—a way to reason about the problem without relying on a rule they might even misremember. If I had a penny for every time I had a student ask me, "Is this where I get a common denominator?" I would have a lot of pennies! As mentioned earlier, this book is about empowering you with a deeper, and different, understanding of mathematics that will help you keep more students in the mathematics game. While this book may challenge many assumptions that you might have about elementary mathematics, I'll provide a reasoned argument for why I'm challenging those assumptions, with an eye toward helping more students develop a love and appreciation of mathematics. I can assure you that you'll leave this book with a deeper and more connected understanding of the mathematics that you teach.

About This Book

Before we start our journey, let's take a few moments to explain important features of the book as well as how the book is organized. In each chapter, you'll encounter Pause and Ponder opportunities. The prompts in these boxes are meant to give you time to reflect on your own thinking or how you might tweak your own practices to incorporate ideas from the chapter in question. What follows is an example of this feature.

PAUSE AND PONDER

Take a moment to think about your own mathematics journey. Were there moments in which you felt that you were no longer part of the mathematics game? Was a specific topic or course the culprit?

Now reflect on your students—are there any individuals you can sense are feeling as though they're no longer part of the mathematics game? Do you feel like you have the tools to help them, and if not, what do you believe you'll need to learn to better assist them? Having read most of this introduction, consider, for example, what tweaks to your addition curriculum, lesson plans, or instructional practices you're willing to make.

Another aspect of this book is the Try It feature, which you'll also find in each chapter. The prompts in these boxes are meant to give you either an opportunity to engage with chapter concepts yourself so you can apply your understandings to your teaching or an opportunity to engage students in a task so you can explore their thinking. This feature is centered on elements of the see it–say it–symbolize it approach. Here's an example.

Using the numeral-unit-name notation, write out the following two addition problems and solve them: (1) 387 + 256 and (2) 0.387 + 0.256. What's the language you would use with students to illuminate the connections between these two problems?

How could you use the term *equal exchanges* to illuminate the conceptual meaning of the process of "carrying the one" when solving these problems?

Instead of using the phrase "get a common denominator," apply ideas from this introduction to explain to a student how to solve the problem $\frac{1}{4} + \frac{5}{8}$.

Now suppose individual parents question why you're teaching their children addition using an approach different from how they learned the operation. Using ideas from the introduction, what would be the three main points of your argument?

Additionally, each chapter will close with a reproducible guide featuring the key concepts covered along with ways to incorporate those practices into your teaching moving forward. You can also access online versions of all reproducibles in this book at its website (visit **go.SolutionTree.com/mathematics**).

The main concepts of the book are organized sequentially, or appear in accordance with when they're introduced in the customary mathematics curriculum. Each chapter involves a progressively deeper dive into each of these ideas so that you'll not only gain a deeper understanding of these ideas at your students' grade level but also see how the same conceptually consistent approach is applied to later grades. Chapter 1 (page 21) begins by exploring early number concepts and establishes why they're important. Here, for example, we take a look at the many ways that different students could see the same set of objects.

In chapter 2 (page 31), we consider the ways that the same numeral can carry different meanings and how the same string of numerals can represent multiple quantities and sizes of units. And it's here that we take a deeper dive into the first of what I like to refer to as *superpower understandings* in mathematics—transformative understandings that will help students conceptually understand and connect multiple mathematical ideas. In this case, chapter 2 focuses on two superpower understandings that I touched on in this introduction: (1) seeing numbers in terms of *quantities* and *sizes of units* and (2) knowing how and when to make an *equal exchange*. We revisit these superpower understandings throughout the book and pick up a few more along the way.

In chapter 3 (page 47), we discuss why fractions are a difficult concept for students to understand, as well as why it's critical to illuminate—at least in students' initial experiences with them—that fractions represent numbers or measures.

Chapter 4 (page 73) begins our journey into operations. We revisit addition, reinforcing the ideas that numbers can be combined only when the sizes of the units are the same and that equal exchanges can be performed to make this happen. We also familiarize ourselves with *analogous problems*, using this lens to see connections between and among problems that we perhaps may never have realized.

In chapter 5 (page 91), we leverage our knowledge of addition to explore how to see and say subtraction in a conceptually consistent way.

In chapter 6 (page 111), we explore the complexities of teaching multiplication and why the topic is challenging for so many students. As with the previous two operations, we illuminate the conceptual language of multiplication while also providing concrete examples that support the conceptual development of the important ideas related to multiplication and how those ideas are connected to the early number understandings discussed in chapter 1. We also explore a different interpretation of a fraction—as an action.

We'll conclude our journey through the operations in chapter 7 (page 147) as we unpack the important aspects of division. In this chapter, we look at the two contextual forms of division—(1) sharing and (2) measurement—while also employing the language necessary for helping students develop a strong conceptual understanding of division. As with chapter 6, we also explore another interpretation of a fraction—as division.

Finally, in chapter 8 (page 175), we consider ratios, percentages, and proportions. In this chapter, as with the previous two chapters, we explore how a ratio involves a completely different interpretation of a fraction and why it's essential to illuminate the multiplicative relationships that exist between and within measured spaces of equivalent ratios. As you learn and engage with the concepts throughout these chapters, please make use of the extensive glossary I provide at the end of the book.

Are you ready for more? I'm excited to take you on this journey over the next eight chapters. This book will challenge you to see the mathematics that you teach in a different light. You'll learn to see and say many of the topics that you teach in a way that enables you to make connections between ideas that may have felt disjointed before. My hope is that you'll leave this book with ideas that'll help you create more Grandma Edna–style life-changing moments for your own students—equipping them with understandings that not only have them believing they're still in the mathematics game but make them feel like they have mathematical superpowers.

Key Points

Before proceeding with chapter 1 (page 21), please take a moment to review the following takeaways from this introduction.

- The mathematical demands of the students we teach are much different from the mathematical demands we encountered at their age. Most of our students carry a piece of technology that, when prompted, automatically performs accurate, efficient calculations for them. Our students need to understand the why behind these calculations so that they know whether what they're entering into the technology is correct, as well as how to adjust the technology so that it provides correct answers.
- In our approach to the teaching and learning of mathematics, we must always attend to three elements: (1) see it, (2) say it, and (3) symbolize it. *See it* involves deliberately illuminating aspects of a concept to ensure that students think about those aspects. For example, writing a number using the unit name—for example, 267 is 2 hundreds, 6 tens, and 7 ones—illuminates the size of the unit, forcing students to think about its meaning. *Say it* involves illuminating the conceptual language that we desire for students to associate with the concept and utilize in communicating their understanding of the concept. For example, in the addition problem 27 + 36, the 7 ones and 6 ones are combined to form 13 ones, which can be equally exchanged for 1 ten and 3 ones, which underpins why the procedural language of "carrying the one" fits (that is, the 1 is carried to the next greater size of unit, tens). The last element, *symbolize it*, is how students utilize symbols to describe their thinking and what they see as they look through a symbol string. Of course, we want students to solve an addition problem such as 27 + 36 quickly, but we also want them to see *more than a procedure* when they look through this symbol string. In this case, for example, we want them to see the size of unit that each numeral represents, what equal exchanges are and when they're needed, and how any problem with a similar structure (for example, 0.27 + 0.36 or 2.7 + 3.6) can be solved using the same steps on different sizes of units.
- Superpower understandings are transformative understandings that will help students conceptually understand and connect multiple mathematical ideas. One superpower understanding is seeing numbers as quantities of different sizes of units. That is, the same numerals can have completely different meanings depending on the nature of the number. For example, the numerals 3 and 8 in the whole number 38 represent a quantity of tens and ones, respectively. In the decimal 0.38, those same numerals represent the same quantities, but with different sizes of units, tenths and hundredths. And in the fraction $3/8$, one of the numerals, 3, represents a quantity, while the other numeral, 8, represents a size of a unit, eighths.

God made the natural numbers,

all the rest is the work of man.

—Leopold Kronecker

CHAPTER 1

Early Number Concepts

While early number sense is not a significant focus of this book, it's crucial to explore the understandings that support students' reasoning about number concepts and operations. For example, imagine the power of a student who is able to solve the addition problem 7 + 8 by "breaking apart" the 8 into the 5 and 3 and "seeing" the problem 7 + 8 as having the same answer as 10 + 5 instead of having to count on from 7 (that is, "eight, nine, ten, . . . fifteen"). Or consider another student who is able to "see" a visual representation of the multiplication problem 7 × 3 as the sum of two multiplication problems, 5 × 3 and 2 × 3. "Seeing" both of these problems in the ways described is underpinned by flexibility with early number concepts. Many conversations I've had with my mentor, Kurt Killion, a professor of mathematics education, have greatly influenced the thinking captured in this brief chapter, and much of the content is also supported by the work of mathematics educators Doug Clements and Julie Sarama (2020). If you're interested in learning more about their number research and related classroom resources, you can find a compilation at the Learning Trajectories website (https://learningtrajectories.org).

In this chapter, I zero in on the early number concepts that I return to throughout the book to make connections. These concepts are an essential part of the dynamic view of numbers that we want to nurture in students. In the pages that follow, we examine all these concepts in the context of a specific domino representation that can help to illuminate student thinking. Then, we close out the chapter by reflecting on just how essential these foundational understandings are to students staying in the mathematics game long-term. Let's get started!

Foundational Concepts as Captured in Student Thinking

Take a moment to think about how you would determine the total number of dots shown in figure 1.1.

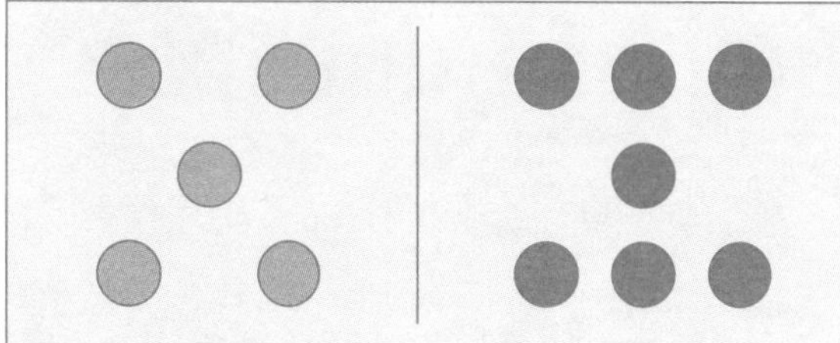

Figure 1.1: Domino showing 5 dots and 7 dots.

Recall from the book's introduction (page 1) that reasoning begins with what you see when you look through what is shared with you. More than likely, as an adult learner with some experience playing dominoes, after reviewing figure 1.1, you determined the total number of dots without counting each dot. That is, you didn't *need* to count each dot. You probably recognized a pattern in the arrangement of dots that enabled you to quickly identify that there are 5 light blue dots and 7 dark blue dots. This is called *perceptual subitizing*.

Typically, perceptual subitizing is associated with a small number of objects—think fewer than 10. Second, you engaged in *conceptual subitizing*. That is, you combined the two quantities, 5 and 7, and used a memorized fact, 5 + 7, or a part-whole relationship, to determine that there are 12 dots. According to educational psychologist and mathematics educator Arthur J. Baroody (1987), *subitizing*, an essential skill that students need to develop to reason dynamically about numbers, means that students can see the quantity of a set of objects without having to count each object in the set.

As adult learners, we already have well-developed early number reasoning strategies, which sometimes makes it difficult for us to imagine the different strategies a student might use to solve this problem. Depending on the nature of their understanding of numbers, students might use any number of strategies to determine how many dots are shown in figure 1.1. The key for us is to observe students' thinking so that we can better understand what they see when we give them a visual image like this one or another set of objects arranged in a similar manner.

Of course, not every student will see the same thing. Uncovering what individuals see gives us insight into how to best move their thinking forward. Remember from the introduction (page 1) that we can use any element of the see it–say it–symbolize approach as a starting point for uncovering or introducing or advancing understandings. With early number concepts, what a student *says* sheds light on how they are *seeing* these concepts. By showcasing students' written responses, figure 1.2 provides an example of four different ways students commonly think about the total number of dots.

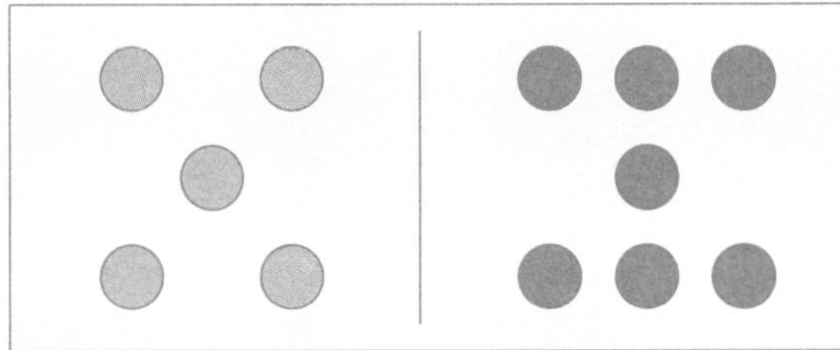

Student A

"There are one, two, three, four, five, six, seven, eight, nine, ten, eleven, twelve total dots [pointing to and counting each dot]."

Student B

"I see seven dots [pointing at dark blue dots] and eight, nine, ten, eleven, and twelve total dots [pointing to and counting each of the light blue dots]."

Student C

"There are seven dark blue dots. Add three light blue dots to make ten, then two more light blue dots to total twelve dots."

Student D

"I see five dots and seven dots, which makes a total of twelve dots."

Figure 1.2: Student work exemplifying different early number concepts.

Let's examine these four different ways of thinking to tease out the early number concepts at their core and what can we glean from them.

Student A's thinking is demonstrating a *one-to-one correspondence* because they're assigning the correct number name to each dot that's counted. They're also demonstrating *cardinality*, a concept closely related to one-to-one correspondence because they know the last number name used, "twelve," corresponds with the number of objects in the set.

Inherent in student B's thinking is a *counting-on* strategy. They subitized the larger set when they said "seven" without counting each dot, and then they individually counted the rest of the dots, using their one-to-one correspondence strategy, to determine the total number of dots.

Student C's thinking reflects a *make-a-ten* strategy. As mathematics educators John A. Van de Walle, Karen S. Karp, and Jennifer M. Bay-Williams (2023) point out, a student utilizing this strategy is demonstrating a *part-part-whole* understanding, seeing one of the most critical relationships involving numbers. That is, the student sees that a number of objects consists of *subsets* of that number of objects. For example, as further illustrated in figure 1.3, student C is able see a quantity of 5 dots as a subset of 2 dots and 3 dots or 4 dots and 1 dot.

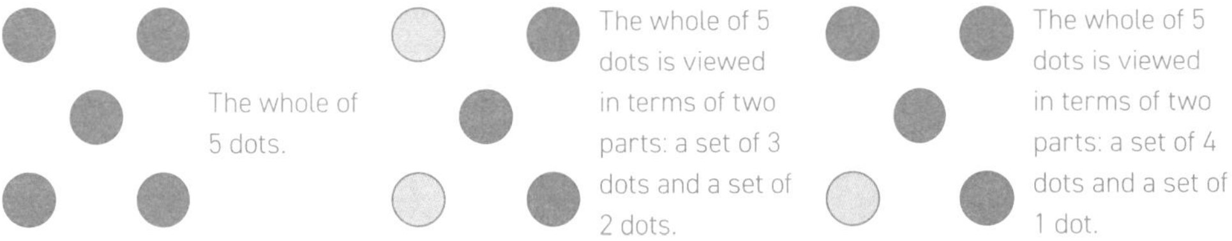

The whole of 5 dots.
The whole of 5 dots is viewed in terms of two parts: a set of 3 dots and a set of 2 dots.
The whole of 5 dots is viewed in terms of two parts: a set of 4 dots and a set of 1 dot.

Figure 1.3: Different part-part-whole relationships of the whole of 5 dots.

The work of cognitive scientist Karen C. Fuson (1992), as well as that of mathematics educator Leslie P. Steffe and philosopher and researcher Ernst von Glasersfeld (1988), confirms that additive thinking (a construct we'll discuss in greater detail in later chapters) isn't fully developed until a student can simultaneously think about the whole and the part-part relationships within the whole.

Making a ten involves a strategic choice of a part-part-whole relationship by the student. For example, in student C's reasoning, as shown in figure 1.4, the part of 3 dots is combined with 7 dots to create a set-of-10 object, or 1 unit of ten. The remaining subset of 2 dots is combined with the 1 ten to determine the total number of dots (that is, 10 + 2 = 12).

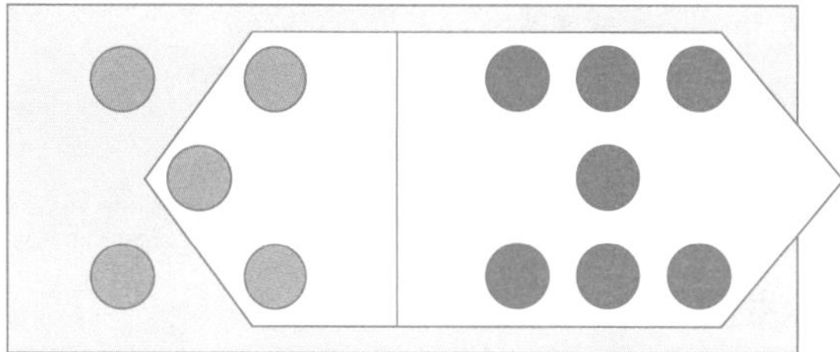

Student C

"There are seven black dots. Add three gray dots to make ten, then two more gray dots to total twelve."

Figure 1.4: Student making a ten to reason about the number of dots.

The make-a-ten strategy is difficult to see visually unless students have physical objects that they can manipulate in a way that sheds light on the nature of their reasoning. Students who make a ten are creating a composed unit—that is, a quantity of 10 units of one becomes 1 unit of ten, or 1 ten. Being able to create a composed unit and knowing when to do so demonstrate a significant advancement in a student's thinking.

As conveyed in the book's introduction (page 1), a composed unit of 1 ten is an abstract idea born of the fact that we operate in the decimal, or base 10, number system—that is, with only ten numerals, 0–9. If we operated in a different number system, such as the dozenal or the hexadecimal number system, the bundling or composing of quantities to create a quantity of a different size of unit would occur at a quantity of twelve or sixteen, not at a quantity of ten of those units. Students are making not a twelve or a sixteen but a ten. Subtly, a student employing the make-a-ten strategy is becoming familiar with a foundational concept of our number system, place value.

Finally, student D exemplifies thinking indicative of many adults. The student has subitized both sets and, more than likely, combined them using a known number fact (in this case, 7 + 5 = 12). The student could be using a part-part-whole relationship or another strategy, but we just don't know unless we ask.

PAUSE AND PONDER

Think about common games that you play with dice, cards, or dominoes. In what ways do these games support the development of early number concepts?

At the grade level that you teach, are you aware of the early number concepts that your students are utilizing to solve problems? If not, what's one thing you're going to implement in your classroom to become more aware?

If you're a K–2 teacher, what are two ideas that you can share with parents to help them develop their own children's early number sense?

Mathematical Superpowers for Elementary and Beyond

These early number understandings play a significant role in students' capacity to develop a dynamic view of numbers. A dynamic view of numbers requires a flexible view of part-part-whole relationships and composed units. Many of the young adults that I work with in my classes show elements of part-part-whole relationships as they reason about addition problems, but not with multiplication problems. For example, I'll ask students in these classes to describe to me how they think about solving a problem like 9 + 6 or 68 + 28. With 9 + 6, I watch as students slide their hands under the table and raise a finger, signifying the making of a ten, before they then state an answer of 15. A similar thing happens with 68 + 28, except two fingers are raised and the response is 96. Maybe without being aware, students are using the make-a-ten strategy to create problems that are mentally easier to solve (that is, 10 + 5 and 70 + 26).

Unfortunately, what I observe with addition problems doesn't transfer to multiplication. To assess whether students have an inkling of a dynamic view of multiplication, I ask them to mentally compute 13 × 8. Frequently I get a shrug of the shoulders or a shake of the head indicating that they can't do so. I follow up by asking them whether they can tell me what 10 times 8 is. Almost 100 percent of the time they confidently tell me 80. I then ask them whether they can tell me the answer to 3 × 8. Again, most students confidently tell me it's 24. I ask them to add the products together—104—and then tell them they just mentally computed 13 × 8.

The typical student response that exemplifies this more static view of numbers is "I didn't know you could do that!" What this means is that students aren't *seeing* the number 13 in terms of a part-part-whole relationship (that is, a part of 10 and a part of 3 is the same as a whole of 13). There is more complexity to mentally computing 13 × 8 using a part-part-whole relationship—more on that in chapter 6 (page 111).

As mentioned in the introduction (page 1), this book is about helping students develop a dynamic view of numbers across all four operations to support the unleashing of their mathematics superpowers. Unfortunately, many of the students I teach at the undergraduate level, in both developmental mathematics courses and content courses for teachers, have a static view of numbers. That is, they have only one dominant conception. Many individuals see numbers, and operations involving numbers, as fixed ideas, leaving them unable to reason beyond a known procedure or one interpretation of a number. The ideas from this book will give you the tools to help your students develop a dynamic view of numbers. And as this chapter has shown, it all begins with seeing and saying foundational early number concepts.

Place an array of dots on the whiteboard (for example, 2 × 6). Ask students to write down what they see. Have students share the different ways in which they are seeing the same array of dots.

Ask your students to mentally compute a grade-level-appropriate addition problem. Have them share the strategies they used to determine the answer. What surprised you? How does what you learned inform your instruction?

Key Points

Before proceeding, please take a moment to review the following takeaways from this chapter.

- The decimal, or base 10, number system means that we can utilize only ten numerals (0–9) to represent numbers and that consecutive place values (that is, sizes of units) increase or decrease by a factor of 10. For example, 1 tenth is ten times greater than 1 hundredth.
- That a student says the number names in correct order from one to one hundred doesn't mean that the student understands the quantity of objects (100) or the different units that are associated with that quantity. For example, a student may be able to count to 15 (for example, "one, two, three, . . . fourteen, fifteen") but may not understand that each counted number is assigned to one object and that the last object counted implies the total number of objects or that "fifteen" represents 1 unit of *ten* and 5 units of *one*.
- There is a progression of early number understandings a student must develop to have a dynamic view of numbers. For example, making a ten involves the student creating a composed unit. This is a foundational understanding that underpins much of the work students will do as they learn place value concepts.
- A dynamic and flexible view of numbers is also grounded in student's ability to see different part-part-whole relationships in the same number and compose different quantities and sizes of units that represent the same amount. For example, the number 10 can be thought of in terms of 1 ten, 10 ones, 6 ones and 4 ones, or 5 ones and 5 ones. Likewise, the number 100 can be thought of in terms of 1 hundred, 10 tens, 100 ones, 90 tens and 10 ones, or 70 tens and 30 ones. There are many part-part-whole relationships within a composed number, so it's important that students first recognize the possibilities so that they can later choose those part-part-whole relationships that will make solving a problem easier.

The key points in this chapter focus on those early number understandings that underpin a dynamic and flexible understanding of numbers and operations. The questions in the following application guide are related to those key points and are intended to help you assess and advance your own students' understanding of these early number concepts.

Chapter 1 Application Guide

Chapter Concepts	How Can I Incorporate This Into My Teaching Practice Moving Forward?
One-to-One Correspondence Cardinality Counting On Subitizing	1. Place an array of counters (<10) in front of a student and ask how many counters there are. Observe how the student determines the number of counters. 2. Increase the number of counters to see whether the student's thinking reveals changes in strategy from subitizing to counting on to one-to-one correspondence.
Part-Part-Whole Relationships	1. Place an array of counters in front of a student and ask how many counters there are. 2. Separate the counters into two piles. Cover one of the piles with a hand or a sheet of paper and ask how many counters must be in the other pile. 3. Repeat for a greater number of counters. 4. Once the student is proficient with steps 1–3, have the student record the number sentence that corresponds with the actions performed with the number cubes (for example, 4 + 2 = 6).
Make a Ten	1. Provide a student with two arrays of number cubes (ideally a representation that can be formed into 1 unit of ten) with a total greater than 10. 2. Have the student physically create a unit of 1 ten with the number cubes. Ask the student to describe the quantity of tens and the quantity of ones. 3. Once the student is proficient with steps 1–2, have the student record the number sentence that corresponds with the actions performed with the number cubes (for example, 7 + 5 = 10 + 2 = 12).

Without mathematics,

there's nothing you can do.

Everything around you is mathematics.

Everything around you is numbers.

—Shakuntala Devi

CHAPTER 2

Same Numeral, Different Meanings

Now that we've explored the early number concepts that form the basis of a student's dynamic understanding of numbers, we can begin our dive into the nuances of numbers, considering both the ways that a given numeral can carry different meanings and how a given string of numerals can in fact represent multiple quantities and sizes of units. Being able to see numbers in terms of both quantities and sizes of units is a superpower understanding that will propel student thinking and keep learners in the mathematics game. This ability goes hand in hand with another superpower understanding: knowing how and when to make an equal exchange. In this chapter, we explore these and related concepts, touching on potential impediments to students' understanding as well as leveraging visuals and terminology that illuminate what we *want* students to see. First, we'll take a closer look at sizes of units and place value, explore equal exchanges that use the same string of numerals, and consider the choice of number names to guide student thinking about unit size. Then, we'll transition to equal exchanges in the context of part-part-whole relationships before moving on to decimal units; use of the number line; and the difference between seeing additive versus multiplicative relationships.

Sizes of Units and Place Value

Recall from chapter 1 (page 21) that we use the decimal, or base 10, number system, which restricts the numerals (0–9) we can use to represent numbers. This has implications for not only the numerals that we use to represent numbers but also the sizes of the units denoting the different place values. Let's start by thinking about this idea in terms of money. How many times greater is 1 ten-dollar bill than 1 one-dollar bill? How many times greater is 1 one-dollar bill than 1 dime? Now think about this idea in terms of place value, as illustrated in figure 2.1.

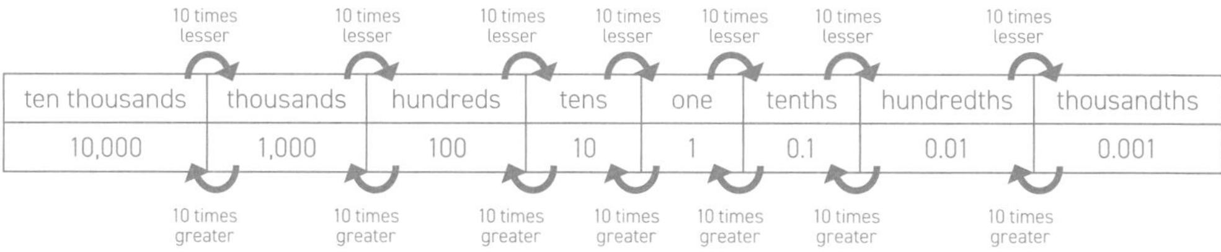

Figure 2.1: Consecutive sizes of units are 10 times greater or lesser.

Moving from right to left, with a lesser size of units on the right, the size of a unit is 10 times greater than the size of the unit to its right. For example, 1 hundred is 10 times greater than 1 ten, and 1 tenth is 10 times greater than 1 hundredth.

Answer the following questions. (If it's helpful, think about them in terms of money.)

How many times greater is 1 ten than 1 tenth?

How many times greater is 1 hundred than 1 hundredth?

Very early in students' mathematical journeys, they are challenged to see these ten familiar numerals in different ways. The moment that students make a ten, they begin to experience the multiple meanings of the same string of numerals. Remember from chapter 1, for example, the reasoning student C demonstrated when using 3 dots from a set of 5 dots to ultimately create a set of 10 dots (see figure 1.4, page 24). I want to take a moment to reflect on the complexity of what a student first learning these ideas must navigate to have a dynamic view of numbers. Everything is smooth sailing counting 9 objects or fewer, but once 10 objects are reached, everything changes. Numerals are the same, but now the use of the 1 means something different. No longer does the numeral 1 strictly signify oneness (that is, 1 object). Now the 1 in the string of numerals 10 represents the quantity of 1 of a different size of unit, 1 *ten*. This is a new place value—tens. The numeral 10 is the first instance students experience in which the same string of numerals has multiple meanings of quantities and sizes of units. For example, the string of numerals 10 can represent either 1 *ten* (**1**0) or 10 *ones* (**10**). Likewise, the string of numerals 100 can signify 1 unit of a *hundred* (**1**00), 10 units of *ten* (**10**0), or 100 units of *one* (**100**).

Equal Exchanges: Same String, Different Quantity and Size of Unit

Depending on our students' life experiences, they may come to us already with some experience with this type of thinking. Consider the superpower understanding of equal exchanges. A dynamic view of place value involves students seeing and utilizing different combinations of quantities and sizes of units within the same string of numerals. Students may not even be aware that they already have experiences with this type of thinking when they exchange denominations of money. As an example, consider some of the ways, using only one other size of unit, that 1 one-hundred-dollar bill can be equally exchanged. For example, 1 one-hundred-dollar bill can be equally exchanged for 10 ten-dollar bills or 100 one-dollar bills. As shown in figure 2.2, as the quantity increases by a factor of 10 (10 times greater), the size of the unit decreases by a factor of 10 (10 times lesser). This is an idea we will revisit in chapter 3 (page 47), in the context of equivalent fractions.

Increase the **quantity** of the unit by a factor of 10.

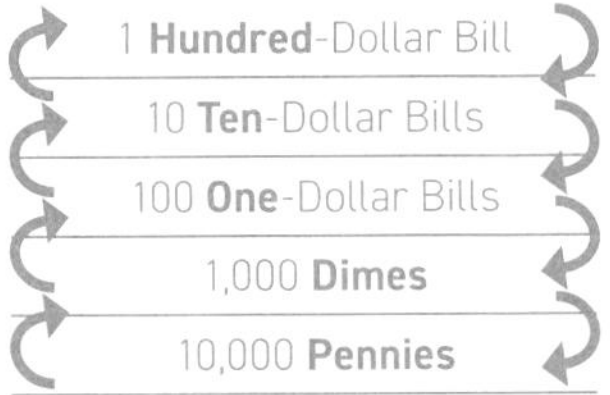

Decrease the **size of the unit** by a factor of 10.

Figure 2.2: Relationship between quantity and size of units in an equal exchange.

As students become comfortable creating equal exchanges using the same string of numerals, they'll begin to see the relationship between the quantity and size of unit. That is, moving from right to left, each place value increases the quantity of the size of the unit by a factor of 10 while, at the same time, decreasing the size of the unit by a factor of 10. For example, 100 one-dollar bills are an equal exchange for 1,000 dimes. The quantity increased by a factor of 10 (100 to 1,000), and the size of the unit decreased by the same factor (ones to tenths). Figure 2.3 makes the connection between monetary units and base 10 sizes of units and possible equal exchanges of the number 100.

1	0	0 .	0	0	
1	0	0	0	0	1 hundred
1	**0**	0	0	0	10 tens
1	**0**	**0**	0	0	100 ones
1	**0**	**0**	**0**	0	1,000 tenths (dimes)
1	**0**	**0**	**0**	**0**	10,000 hundredths (pennies)
Hundreds	Tens	Ones	Tenths	Hundredths	

Figure 2.3: Using free zeros to illuminate equal exchanges of 100.

What's amazing is that these equal exchanges, and many more, are right in front of us if we just add zeros. I love those free zeros—they make those equal exchanges pop out! For example, simply adding another 0 to the right of 100 means the last zero is in the tenths place (that is 100.0) so we can now see that 1 hundred (100) can be equally exchanged for 1,000 tenths (**100.0**). Adding another free zero to the right of 100.0 (**100.00**) means that 1 hundred is also an equal exchange for 10,000 hundredths.

TRY IT

What is the quantity and size of unit represented by the number 1,000?

What are three possible equal exchanges of this number that involve a quantity and size of unit that represents a place value? How about if the number was 0.1?

Word Names for Numbers Are Messy!

Remember our see it–say it–symbolize it approach. A significant part of the *see it* related to place value is students seeing that each numeral in a string of numerals represents a size of unit and that the same string of numerals can represent different equal exchanges. The difficulty is that certain number names muddy students' ability to explicitly see the size of the unit. There is greater complexity in the *say it* aspect of illuminating the quantity and size of unit than you might imagine. Take a moment to say aloud the following numbers: 10, 11, 12, 13, 14, 15, 16, 17, 18, 19, and 20.

The spoken word names *eleven* and *twelve* have no connection to quantity and size of unit. The teens (*thirteen*, *fourteen*, *fifteen*, and so on) are a little less muddy since the unit of ten is somewhat apparent in the number name, though the size of the largest unit (tens) is at the end of the number name. For example, in the number 13, or *thirteen*, the placement of the numerals signifies 1 ten and 3 ones, while the suffix *-teen*, signifying a larger unit, is at the end of the word, not the beginning. Number names become a little less muddy at *twenty*, but we still use a new variation of ten, *-ty*. The suffix *-ty* signifies tens, so *twenty* is 2 tens. Can you believe that to say those 11 numbers you used three different phrases to represent the size of the unit of ten (that is, *ten*, *-teen*, and *-ty*)? What I'm about to say will probably be a little controversial, but with an eye toward conceptual consistency (numerals represent quantities and sizes of units) between what is seen and said, I pose the following question: What if we, at least when students are first learning these ideas, used one of the two alternatives shown in figure 2.4 to represent these numbers?

	Standard	One Alternative (Sousa, 2016, p. 88)	Another Alternative (Siemon et al., 2020, p. 381)
10	ten	Ten	onety
11	eleven	ten-one	onety-one
12	twelve	ten-two	onety-two
13	thirteen	ten-three	onety-three
14	fourteen	ten-four	onety-four
15	fifteen	ten-five	onety-five
16	sixteen	ten-six	onety-six
17	seventeen	ten-seven	onety-seven
18	eighteen	ten-eight	onety-eight
19	nineteen	ten-nine	onety-nine
20	twenty	two-ten	twoty
21	twenty-one	two-ten-one	twoty-one
...			
30	thirty	three-ten	threety
31	thirty-one	three-ten-one	threety-one
...			
40	forty	four-ten	forty

Figure 2.4: Using different word names to say numbers.

The complexity of the language that U.S. students traditionally learn to use to count from 10 to 20 has implications. U.S. students need twenty-eight words to count from 1 to 100 while Chinese students need only eleven words. Given that U.S. students need more than twice the number of words to count from 1 to 100, it's not surprising that by age four, most Chinese learners can count to 40 while U.S. learners of the same age can generally count to 15 (Sousa, 2016).

Once we enter the twenties (for example, 21, 22, 23, 24, 25, and so on), the quantity and size of unit becomes more explicit. For example, the word name of the number 25 is *twenty-five*. The word *twenty* represents 2 tens, while the *five* represents 5 ones. We no longer have these issues once we move beyond the tens place value into the hundreds and thousands place values. For example, the word names for the numbers 100 and 2,000, *one hundred* and *two thousand*, seamlessly align with the quantity and size of the units, 1 hundred and 2 thousands. However, moving into higher place values, we don't always signify the size of the unit represented by every place value. For example, consider the numbers 13,000 and 320,000. We say not "1 ten thousand and 3 thousands" and "3 hundred thousands and 2 ten thousands" but "thirteen thousand" and "three hundred twenty thousand," respectively.

I often wonder whether something would be lost if we made it easier for our younger students to better see numbers in terms of quantities and sizes of units. What if, at least initially, we introduced the number name for 11 as *ten-one* or *onety-one* instead of *eleven*, or 16 as *ten-six* (Sousa, 2016) or *onety-six* (Siemon et al., 2020)? Would we be hurting our younger students if we did? I admit I'm probably biased, but I think it would help more students gain a deeper understanding of place value. I don't see many adults riding bikes with training wheels, but we support young children learning how to ride a bike by using them. In my mind, there is no difference here. Over time, the more common number names could be introduced, but not until students fully understand the quantity of the size of unit represented by each numeral of the number—that is, once students can "see" and "say" two-digit numbers in terms of their quantity. For example, once you are confident that the student "sees" and "says" 1 ten and 2 ones when they look through the numeral 12, it seems appropriate to introduce them to the standard numeral name (that is, *twelve*). Many students will come to your class already knowing traditional numeral names (for example, *twelve*), so it will be important to emphasize the size of the unit represented by each numeral even if they do use the traditional numeral names. I'm certain that you'd need to have a conversation with students' parents explaining your rationale for doing so. It's hard for adults to put themselves in the shoes of young students learning these ideas for the first time. A college student recently shared insight with me that captures this: "Be more patient and make it more obvious to us what we need to know. You have been learning this stuff for thirty years, but it is our first time."

PAUSE AND PONDER

Consider the two sets of alternative number names shown in figure 2.4 (page 35).

If you had a choice, which one would you be more comfortable introducing in your classroom?

What would you say to parents to explain your justification for using one of these alternatives?

Equal Exchanges: Part-Part-Whole Relationships

Before moving on from whole numbers, it's important to consider another, less explicit, form of equal exchange. Let's return to the number represented by the string of numerals 100. We already discussed that this could represent multiple equal exchanges (1 hundred, 10 tens, and 100 ones). Using our understanding of part-part-whole relationships, there are other possible equal exchanges. I want to introduce a word that I will use extensively in the next few chapters: *decompose*. Decomposing, an action associated with an equal exchange, involves breaking apart a size of unit to create another size of unit. This type of action is depicted three times in figure 2.5.

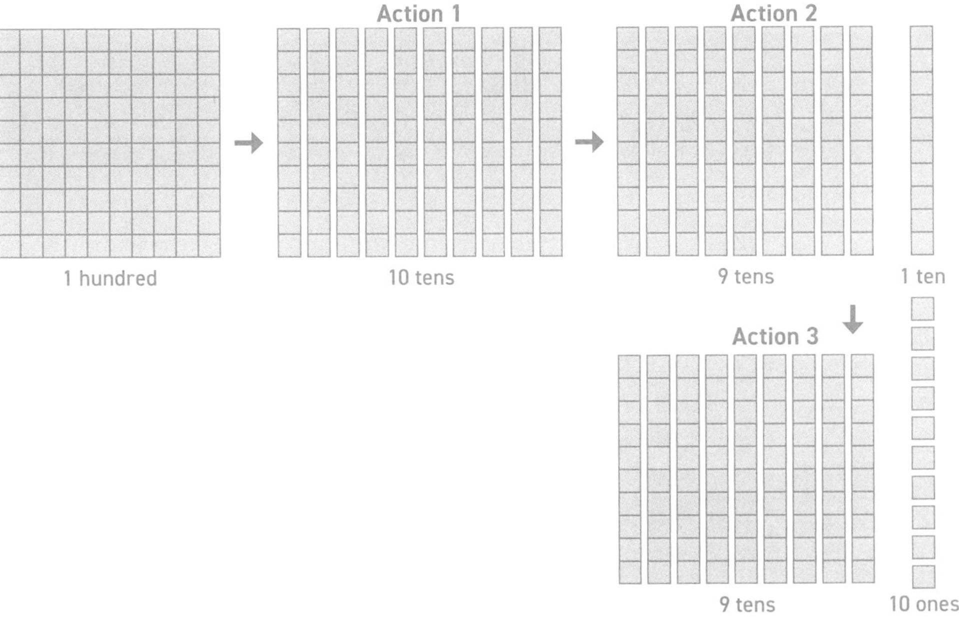

Figure 2.5: Different equal exchanges of 1 hundred.

Here, we can decompose 1 *hundred* into a different size of unit, 10 *tens*, which results in an equal exchange (action 1). Using a part-part-whole relationship, we can separate 10 *tens* into two sets, creating another equal exchange, 9 *tens* and 1 *ten* (action 2). Using another decomposing action, we can equally exchange the 1 *ten* for 10 *ones*, which results in another equal exchange, 1 *hundred* for 9 *tens* and 10 *ones* (action 3). Flexibility with these decomposing actions and an awareness of the different types of equal exchanges they create support a dynamic understanding of numbers.

Create three different equal exchanges of the number 120. Be sure to use both types of equal exchanges that we've already discussed.

Beyond Whole Numbers

Up to this point, the size of the unit we have discussed has been greater than 1. We will now consider instances in which the size of unit is less than one but greater than zero (that is, decimal units).

Focusing on the size of units less than one (for example, tenths and hundredths) provides a great opportunity to communicate how the use of the spoken language can either mask or illuminate important mathematical ideas. If possible, take a moment and ask Siri or Alexa, "What is 24,536 divided by 100?" More than likely, the response you receive is "two hundred forty-five point three six." The technology illuminates the quantity and size of the unit to the left of the decimal point ("two **hundred** forty-five") but hides the size of the units to the right of the decimal point ("point three six"). To illuminate the size of unit to the right of the decimal point, the technology might instead deliver the answer "two hundred forty-five and thirty-six hundredths." Notice there is a still a condensing of the size of the unit to one unit (hundredths). Depending on the nature of your students' understandings, it may be appropriate to communicate the quantity and size of each numeral—for example, "2 hundreds, 4 tens, 5 ones, 3 tenths, and 6 hundredths." That, however, becomes very cumbersome for numbers with multiple sizes of units.

I don't think I myself was aware of the decimal point issue until I asked, as part of a diagnostic assessment in a developmental mathematics class of more than a hundred students, what number was represented by the numeral string 0.1. Only about 20 percent of the students were able to correctly describe the quantity and size of the unit—"1 tenth." The rest of the class used the descriptive language of "point one" but were unable to tell me the size of the unit represented by this decimal value. This issue was further illuminated in a small-group setting in which I asked students to solve two addition problems involving the same numerals—(1) 245 + 378 and (2) 0.245 + 0.378—by making the quantity and size of the unit explicit. Students had no problem writing out the sizes of the units for the whole-number problem (hundreds, tens, and ones) but struggled to write out the sizes of the units for the decimal problem (tenths, hundredths, and thousandths).

This is another area in which we educators, though unintentionally, muddy the waters for students when they're first learning about place value. Technically, every number we use in mathematics is a decimal because we're operating in the base 10 number system. However, many classrooms feature curricula that separate content into numerals to the left of the decimal point (whole numbers) and numerals to right of the decimal point (decimal numbers). It's important to consider that this separation might be unnecessary, and even potentially harmful, to students' development of a dynamic view of numbers (Siegler, Thompson, & Schneider, 2011). It can be argued that there is no need to separate adding whole numbers and adding decimals because both involve the same idea: combining quantities of units of the same size. As a result of this separation, many students I've interviewed see the decimal point as a demarcation line that is interpreted differently depending on which side of the decimal point you are on. Think about this point (OK, pun intended!). As shown in figure 2.6, starting at the decimal point and moving to the left, the sizes of the units become increasingly greater (tens, hundreds, thousands, and so on), but moving to the right from the decimal point, the sizes of the units become increasingly lesser (tenths, hundredths, thousandths, and so on). The decimal point merely separates sizes of units greater than one and sizes of units lesser than one. Unfortunately, many students don't see the decimal point in this way.

size of unit increases ← decimal point → size of unit decreases

1 ten thousand	1 thousand	1 hundred	1 ten	one	1 tenth	1 hundredth	1 thousandth
10,000	1,000	100	10	1	0.1	0.01	0.001

Figure 2.6: Exemplifying the trouble with reasoning from the decimal point.

Think about the difference in meaning between a unit of 1 *ten* and a unit of 1 *tenth*. I had a student once tell me, "I just thought there were tens that went in both directions." Completely understandable! Given that I'm deaf in one ear, it's hard for me sometimes to distinguish among the spoken words *ten*, *tens*, and *tenths*. It's subtle, but there's a big difference. The *-ths* morpheme is helpful for understanding the meaning of ten*ths*, hundred*ths*, and thousand*ths*. We're prematurely dipping our toes into fraction waters, but we won't be there long! Imagine if I had 1 whole chocolate bar and decided to share 1 tenth with you. (I like my chocolate!) What would you do to determine how much you would receive?

As shown in figure 2.7, you would partition the whole candy bar into 10 equal parts (sizes of those parts are called *tenths*) and take 1 of those parts. The point I want to make is that the morpheme *-ths* can mean to equally *partition* 1 one, or 1 whole unit, into a given number of equal parts represented by the word before the morpheme (for example, **ten**ths, **hundred**ths).

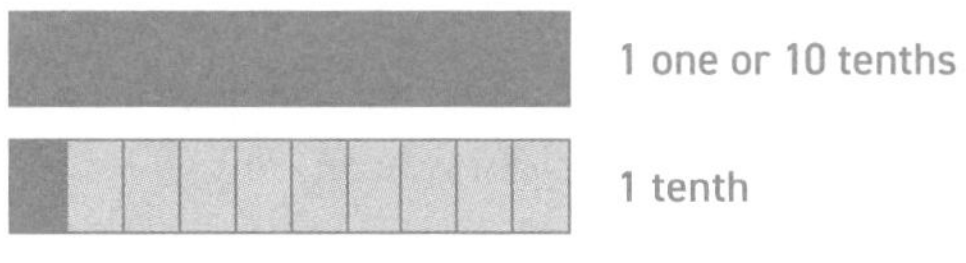

Figure 2.7: The meaning of *tenth*.

Many of our students are already familiar with size of units less than one before they enter our classrooms. Can you say, "Money, money, money"? Our currency system is great with helping students make connections to place value, but we must be careful how we use it. We have denominations that perfectly align with place values less than one (that is, dimes and pennies). Children in the late 1800s even had *mils* (thousandths). Can't buy much for a mil these days—or a penny, or a dime! What part of 1 one dollar is 1 dime? One penny? One mil?

There are other denominations of money, however, that don't align as well with sizes of units in the decimal number system. These include twenty-dollar bills, five-dollar bills, the novel two-dollar bills, quarters, and nickels. We just need to be mindful of how we use those denominations to help students make connections to place value concepts. One of the advantages of using denominations of money to model equal exchanges is that many students are familiar with it and the action involves physically exchanging quantities of denominations (that is, sizes of units).

Remember the overarching goal of this work is to help students develop a dynamic view of numbers. Inherent in this view is the flexible use of equal exchanges and a firm grasp of place value, which is underpinned by knowing the quantity and size of unit represented by each numeral. I would argue that you've been performing equal exchanges for years but calling them by different names. Depending on how old you are and the means by which you were taught mathematics, you may be familiar with any number of words that represent equal exchanges, such as *carrying*, *composing*, *borrowing*, and *decomposing*. The goal of using the term *equal exchange* is to condense the language we use to talk about many different mathematics concepts while also connecting those concepts and focusing attention on the quantity and size of the unit (that is, place value of the numeral).

Use of the Number Line to Represent and Compare Numbers

A number line is a powerful tool for making sense of the magnitude of numbers. The problem with many elementary curriculum resources is that they preclude the most important sensemaking opportunity by giving students a completed number line. I will pose two scenarios to illustrate this point. Imagine if I asked you to identify the location of 2 on the number line shown in figure 2.8 (page 41). Could you?

Figure 2.8: Number line with no unit established.

If you're confused, that's OK—you should be! This is part of a deductive reasoning game that I like to play with students called "What Do You Know?" The premise of the game is to give students as little information as possible and then ask them, "What do you know?" After students share their responses, I provide another piece of information and then again ask, "What do you know?" In this instance, since I gave them a number line marked only with 0, they should be able to tell me that 2 is to the right of 0—assuming I tell them that on a number line, numbers greater than 0 are plotted to the right of 0. And we educators need to be careful with those assumptions!

Now imagine if you were given the location of 1 on a number line, as shown in figure 2.9, and I again asked, "What do you know?"

Figure 2.9: Number line with unit length of one established.

Providing the location of 1 opens the floodgates because now the length of a unit of *one* is known! What is illuminated on a standard number line as shown in figure 2.9 is the location of the number (that is, 1), but what is not as obvious, but very important, is the unit length of *one*. Placement of other numbers on the number line is dependent on the given length, which in this instance is the distance from the number 0 to the number 1.

At this point, you would have no difficulty determining the location of 2 because it's 2 copies of a unit length of *one*. Or placing 4, or even ½, on the number line! Once the unit length of *one* is established, you can accurately place any whole number on a number line by *iterating* unit lengths of *one*. What I mean by *iterate* is that you know a length of a unit (that is, 1 unit of length one) and you are going to measure using that length of a unit multiple times to determine another length or location. This is captured in figure 2.10.

Figure 2.10: Iterating unit of length one 3 times to determine length of 3 units of one, or 1 unit of three.

For example, placing 3 on the number line would involving iterating the unit length of one (represented by the length of a block spanning from 0 to 1) 3 times since 3 is technically 3 units of *one*, or 3 copies of a unit length of *one*, or 1 copy of a unit length of *three*. Suppose now, as shown in figure 2.11 (page 42), that after giving you the location of 0, I give you the location of 2, instead of 1, and again ask, "What do you know?" Can you still determine the unit length of *one*?

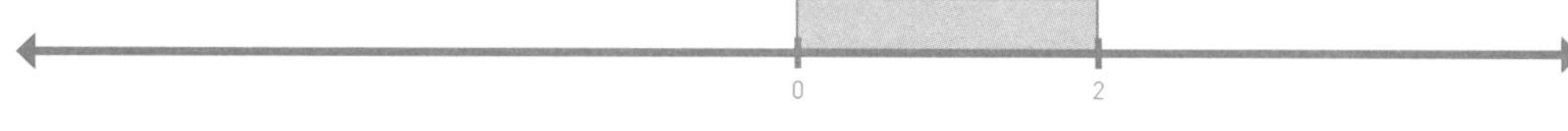

Figure 2.11: A length of 2 units of one.

In this instance, you would have to partition, or cut, in half the length of 2 units of *one*, which would give you the unit length of 1. In fact, you could also accurately determine the location of ½ by partitioning, or folding, the unit length of 1 in half, as shown in figure 2.12.

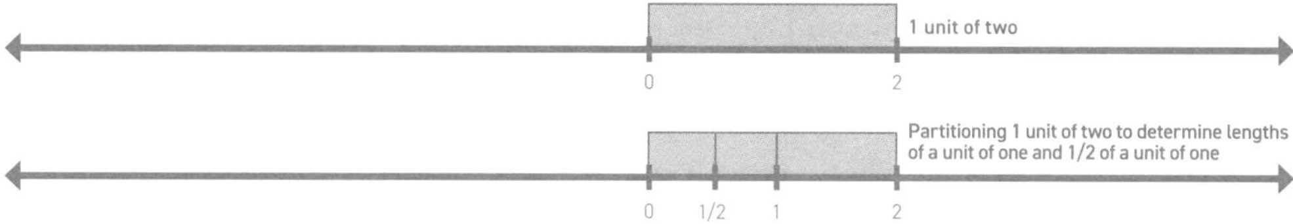

Figure 2.12: Partitioning the length of 2 units of one to determine lengths of a unit of one and ½ of a unit of one.

Mathematics educators Amy J. Hackenberg, Anderson Norton, and Robert J. Wright (2016) confirm that the actions of iterating and partitioning are powerful concepts that help students make sense of fraction concepts down the road. These same actions can be introduced to students before fractions by giving them opportunities to place whole numbers on a partially completed number line.

Given the location of the number 4 on the number line that follows, determine the location of the numbers 2, 1, ½, and 3.

Additive Versus Multiplicative Relationships

Since I'm introducing number lines, it's important that I make a distinction between two ways that students may see a comparison between the magnitude of two numbers: (1) additively and (2) multiplicatively. Number lines are a wonderful tool used to compare the magnitude of numbers, but the language students will use to communicate sheds light on which relationship they are seeing. Initially, additive relationships are easier to see because of students' prior experiences with part-part-whole relationships and addition. Mathematics educators Merlyn J. Behr, Guershon Harel, Thomas Post, and Richard Lesh (1994) explain that as students gain more experience in mathematics, we want to move them from seeing *additive relationships* to seeing *multiplicative relationships*. It's important to note that students could see either an additive or a multiplicative relationship between numbers. For example, consider the relationship between the numbers 1 and 3 and their location on the number line as shown in figure 2.13. We can see either that 3 is "two more" than 1 (1 + **2** = 3), an additive relationship, or that 3 is "three times greater" than 1 (**3** × 1 = 3), a multiplicative relationship.

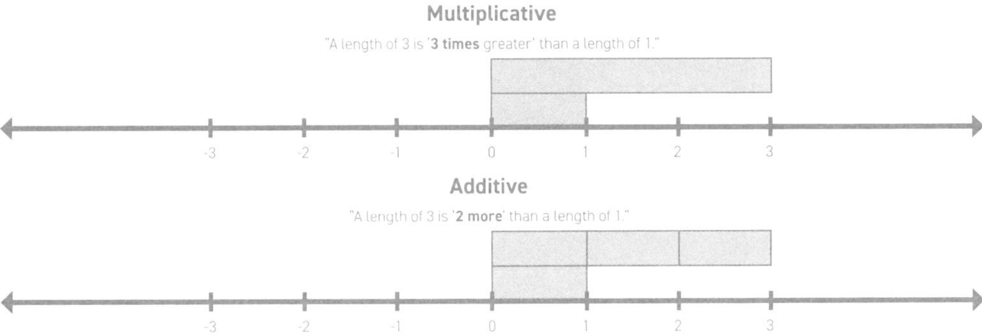

Figure 2.13: Seeing an additive relationship versus a multiplicative relationship.

Key Points

Before proceeding, please take a moment to review the following takeaways from this chapter.

- Woven throughout this chapter are two superpower understandings that support a dynamic and flexible conception of relationships and operations involving all types of numbers. The first superpower understanding is that all numbers can be expressed in terms of *a quantity and a size of unit*, and the same string of numerals can represent different quantities and sizes of units. For example, the whole number 134 is based on the placement of the numerals 1 hundred, 3 tens, and 4 ones, and the numerical string 134.0 can represent not just 1 hundred, 3 tens, and 4 ones but also 13 tens and 4 ones, 134 ones, or 1,340 tenths. The second superpower understanding is that a quantity and size of a unit can be *equally exchanged* for other quantities of different-sized units: 1 hundred can be equally exchanged for 10 tens or 9 tens and 10 ones.
- The same numeral can represent different sizes of units (that is, **3**0, **3**00, 0.**3**) depending on the place value (that is, size of unit), and in some cases, the numeral can represent the unit (that is, thirds). This is one of the reasons fractions are such a difficult concept.
- There are two types of equal exchanges involving numbers. The first type is based on the numerals representing the number. For example, the string of numerals 300.0 can be interpreted as 3 hundreds (**3**00.0), 30 tens (**30**0.0), 300 ones (**300**.0), 3,000 tenths (**300.0**), and so on. In this type of equal exchange, there is a relationship between the quantity and size of unit. As the quantity increases by a factor of 10, the size of the unit decreases by a factor of 10. For example, comparing 3 hundreds and 30 tens, the quantity increases by a factor of 10 (3 to 30), and the size of the unit decreases by a factor of 10 (1 *hundred* to 1 *ten*). The second type of equal exchanging involves decomposing numbers into multiple quantities and sizes of units. For example, 3 hundreds, using part-part-whole relationships, can be separated into 2 hundreds and 1 hundred, which can be equally exchanged for 2 hundreds and 10 tens by decomposing 1 hundred into 10 tens. Both types of equal exchanges are conceptually consistent with what students may already understand about money. That is, 1 hundred-dollar bill can be equally exchanged for 10 ten-dollar bills or 9 ten-dollar bills and 10 one-dollar bills.

The key points in this chapter emphasize the usage of numeral-unit-name notation to focus students' attention on the unit, helping students "see" equal exchanges, and using multiplicative language to "say" the relationships they are seeing between numbers. The application guide for this chapter provides suggestions as to how to incorporate these key points into your classroom instruction.

Chapter 2 Application Guide

Chapter Concepts	How Can I Incorporate This Into My Teaching Practice Moving Forward?
Seeing Size of Units	Use the numeral-unit-name notation when writing numbers (for example, 243 is 2 hundreds, 4 tens, and 3 ones), making the quantity and size of unit explicit.
Seeing Size of Units **Numeral-Unit-Name Notation**	Use conceptually consistent terms for number names to illuminate the quantity and size of unit and place the size of the unit in the correct order. For example, *twelve* is either *ten-two* or *onety-two*.
Seeing Equal Exchanges	Write a string of numerals on the board (for example, 120) and ask students to generate equal exchanges using both numeral-unit-name notation and monetary denominations. This is a topic that would make a great number talk.
Seeing Size of Units **Number Lines**	Provide students with a number line with the locations of 0 and another number (for example, 4). Ask them to describe the given length (that is, 4 units) to determine other lengths. Challenge them to use multiplicative language (for example, placing 2 on the number line, the student says, "2 is at this location because this length is one half the length of 4").

The advantage of growing up with siblings is that you become very good at fractions.

—Robert Brault

CHAPTER 3

Fractions: The *F* Word of Elementary Mathematics

Ah, fractions—the *F* word of elementary mathematics! I like to ask adults and college students to complete the following statement: "I stopped liking mathematics when . . . ." I would estimate that around 80 percent of the time, their responses involve fractions. They might even add, "I never understood fractions!" or "I *hate* fractions!" Frequently in my interviews with college students, they'll explicitly tell me they first started to feel like they were no longer part of the mathematics game when they started learning about fractions. Since 2014, several of my colleagues and I have spent extensive time researching how students at different levels of mathematics exposure (that is, elementary and middle school students, college students, and preservice teachers) understand fraction concepts. Fractions, depending on the situation, can be interpreted in several different ways—as a part-part-whole relationship, a ratio, an operator, division, or a measure (Behr, Harel, Post, & Lesh, 1992). The problem is, based on our research, many students leave their elementary mathematics experiences without a conceptual understanding of any of these different interpretations.

Fractions are such a critical concept that it's necessary to devote an entire chapter to it. After all, it's difficult for a student to have a dynamic understanding of numbers without a deep understanding of fraction concepts. The research of educational psychologist Julie L. Booth and mathematics educator Kristie J. Newton (2012) shows a clear relationship between students' knowledge of fractions and algebra readiness. Moreover, educational psychologists Robert S. Siegler, Clarissa A. Thompson, and Michael Schneider (2011) connect an understanding of fractions to overall performance in mathematics. Fraction concepts are that important—they're the gateway to success in future mathematics courses! Unfortunately, many elementary students are not seeing fractions in a way that supports this continued success (Booth, Newton, & Twiss-Garrity, 2014; Siegler & Pyke, 2013; Torbeyns, Schneider, Xin, & Siegler, 2015).

In this chapter, after offering another problem set for your review, I explain how many students are seeing fractions, or why fractions are so hard, and make a case for writing fractions in numeral-unit-name notation. After that, I discuss the power in seeing a fraction differently; the way to illuminate the size of the unit; the connective nature of the fraction-as-measure conception; equal exchanges as they relate to and unify several fraction concepts; concrete recommendations for cultivating a deep understanding of fractions among students; and decimals—those fractions in disguise.

Three Fraction Problems

Much like we did in the book's introduction (page 1), before we dive into the fraction concepts that make up this chapter, I'd like for you to take a few moments to review the following set of three problems, which we'll revisit moving forward. Instead of relying on procedures that you know, gear your thinking toward how *your students* might reason through these represented fractions. Feel free to jot down your ideas in the spaces provided. We'll use these three problems to explore why fractions are so challenging to understand.

1. Two pizzas are the same size. Carlos ate $\frac{1}{6}$ of one of the pizzas. Terrell ate $\frac{1}{8}$ of the other pizza. Who ate more pizza?

   ____

   ____

   ____

   ____

   ____

2. Two pizzas are the same size. Carlos ate $\frac{5}{6}$ of one of the pizzas. Terrell ate $\frac{7}{8}$ of the other pizza. Who ate more pizza?

   ____

   ____

   ____

   ____

   ____

3. Thomas ate ¾ of a whole medium pizza, and Lydia ate ⅝ of a whole medium pizza. Together they ate how much of a whole medium pizza?

____

____

____

____

____

Before we begin our discussion of fractions, let's remember two things: (1) we're still talking about numbers, and (2) as in previous chapters, it is important to emphasize the size of the unit.

Why Fractions Are So Hard

In interviews with students, from fourth graders, immediately after learning about fraction concepts; to seventh graders, a few years removed from their first exposure to these concepts; to college students and practicing teachers, who are many years removed from their first experience with these concepts, there are common themes that emerge. Based on research my colleagues and I have conducted (Sullivan et al., 2023), I'm convinced that the struggle with fractions is a result of the meaning that students initially associate with the numerals of a fraction written in traditional fraction notation (for example, ⅝).

When a student sees a fraction such as ⅝ for the first time, what have their prior experiences trained them to see? Yes, students see two numerals, 5 and 8, which, up to this point in their learning numerals, have *always* represented quantities. In fact, according to Sousa (2016), the human brain comprehends numerals first as quantities. Up to this point in students' prior experiences with numbers, a numeral such as 8 represented the quantity of a particular size of unit. For example, in the numbers 83, 800, and 0.8, the numeral 8 represents the quantity of a size of a unit called tens, hundreds, and tenths, respectively. In other words, students already have a lot of baggage associated with the numeral 8, and all that baggage is related to the numeral 8 representing a quantity. The same is true if the numerator of a fraction is an 8 (for example, 8⁄5). Those previous understandings are helpful and consistent when a numeral is represented in the numerator of a fraction. For example, the numeral 8 in the fraction 8⁄5 represents the quantity of a unit called *fifths* (that is, 8 *fifths*).

The difficulty comes when a numeral is the denominator of the fraction (for example, 5 eighths). Say the fraction out loud—"five eighths." Now a student is challenged with a new meaning of the numeral 8, one that sounds very similar to already familiar words (that is, *eight* and *eights*). No longer is the numeral the quantity; now it's a size of a unit, eighths. An *eighth* is an object describing a specific size of a unit. Creating eighths involves a specific action, partitioning the length of the whole unit into 8 equally sized lengths. Each of those 8 equal lengths represents a specific size of unit, 1 *eighth*. Beginning with fractions, students must now navigate situations in which the numeral could represent not only a quantity (for example, **8** fifths) but also a size of a unit (for example, 5 ***eighths***). This is problematic because intuitively, and further conditioned by all their schooling up to this point, students see numerals as quantities, not sizes of units. As a matter of fact, the only time a numeral represents a size of unit is when it is represented in the denominator of a fraction.

Let me re-emphasize that one of the main reasons that students struggle with fractions is that they don't see what each numeral of a fraction written in standard notation is supposed to signify. Introducing students to fractions using the standard adult notation (that is, ⅝) is one of the biggest mistakes that we make in elementary mathematics because the size of the unit, at least initially, is not made explicit. This is an example in which we approach young students' learning mathematics from an adult-brain perspective. I know this is going to be controversial, but hear me out in the following section. I'll let the reasoning of students trying to make sense of fraction concepts convince you.

A CASE FOR WRITING FRACTIONS USING NUMERAL-UNIT-NAME NOTATION

The written work shown in figure 3.1 is from a group of fifth-grade students comparing the fractions I asked you to reason about at the beginning of the chapter, ⅙ and ⅛.

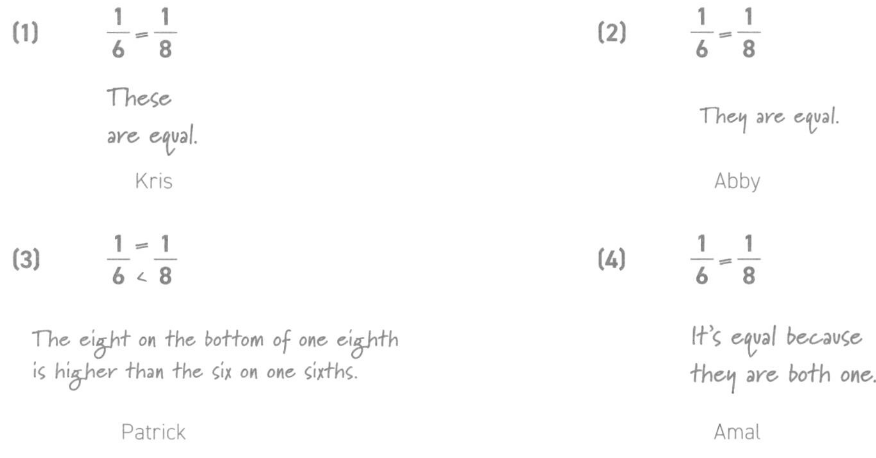

Figure 3.1: Comparing the fractions ⅙ and ⅛.

These student responses shed light on what they are seeing, or their concept image of fractions. Each student's reasoning involves comparing the numerals in the fraction. That is, the students are seeing fractions in terms of quantities without sizes of units. More specifically, the comparison strategies of Kris, Abby, and Amal simply involve comparing the magnitude of the numbers shown in the numerator, without considering the meaning of the different denominators. Meanwhile, Patrick's comparison strategy does involve the denominators, but it's based only on their magnitude as whole numbers (that is, 8 > 6), not what they represent in terms of the size of the unit (that is, eighths are smaller pieces than sixths).

Now consider the student work shown in figure 3.2 representing the second problem that I asked you to reason about earlier that involved comparing the fractions ⅚ and ⅞.

they are the same amount because each numerator is one away from the denominator

Figure 3.2: Student reasoning comparing eating ⅚ of a whole pizza to ⅞ of a whole pizza.

Consistent with students' reasoning shown in figure 3.1 comparing ⅙ and ⅛, the student in figure 3.2 is also seeing fractions as a comparison between quantities without consideration of the different sizes of units (that is, sixths and eighths). The student work shown in figure 3.3 reveals that part of his concept image to compare fractions involves making sure the whole unit (same-size rectangles) is the same and partitioning the whole unit into a quantity of equal parts (represented by the numeral in the denominator) and shading a quantity of parts (represented by the numeral in the numerator). However, his reasoning suggests that he is focusing on a quantity that is missing, not that there is a size of unit (that is, sixths and eighths) connected to each of those quantities.

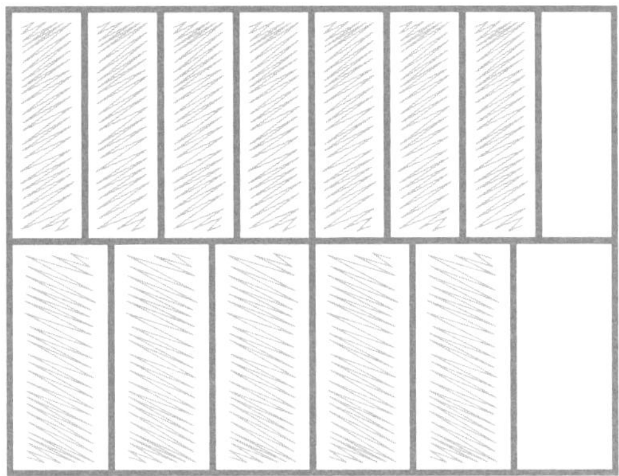

The top numbers matter, but if the top number is the same, look at the bottom; but in this case they ran the same. Why? They both have only one space not filled!

Figure 3.3: Another student's reasoning when comparing ⅚ and ⅞.

Interestingly, during the two-year period that I posed the same question to more than 1,000 college-level developmental mathematics students, more than 25 percent of them indicated that Carlos and Terrell ate the same amount! Why? Students who reason that ⅚ and ⅞ are equal are seeing fractions in terms of a missing addend problem (that is, 5 + ? = 6 and 7 + ? = 8). Students who have conceptualized fractions in this way will often indicate that any two fractions from the same benchmark (for example, 1) will be equal (for example, 5⁄4 and 4⁄3 are equal because 5 = 4 + ? and 4 = 3 + ?).

Recall from chapter 2 (page 31) that these students are essentially using additive reasoning in a situation in which it is not appropriate. Such a student approach, similar to the one shown in figure 3.2, reflects *gap reasoning* (Sullivan & Barnett, 2019)—also described by mathematics researchers Catherine Pearn and Max Stephens (2004) as *gap thinking* and by mathematics researchers Doug M. Clarke and Anne Roche (2009) as *benchmark-value distance*. A student using gap reasoning considers only the difference between the numerator and denominator, with no accounting for the difference of the size of the unit represented by the denominator. Students who use this reasoning have a concept image of a fraction that is merely a comparison between two numerals. It is important to note that students using this flawed reasoning would correctly answer every fraction comparison problem in which either the numerators or denominators of the two fractions are the same. A few examples of each type of problem are shown in figure 3.4.

For each fraction pair, circle the fraction that's greater.

Feature	Fraction Pair		Possible Flawed Reasoning
Same Numerator	1/4	1/6	1/4 is 3 away from whole, while 1/6 is 5 away from whole.
Same Numerator	1/8	1/6	The difference between 1 and 8 is 7, and the difference between 1 and 6 is 5.
Same Denominator	4/6	5/6	5/6 is 1 away from the whole, and 4/6 is 2 away from the whole.
Same Denominator	7/8	5/8	It takes 1 more to go from 7 to 8 and 3 more to go from 5 to 8.

Figure 3.4: Examples of correct answers with flawed reasoning.

Other students have a concept image of a fraction that enables them to create pictorial models to compare fractions, but there are still limitations in their reasoning. For example, consider the student reasoning related to one of the tasks from the beginning of the chapter (that is, comparing 5/6 and 7/8) shared in figure 3.3. This reasoning exemplifies a student who understands that the numeral of the denominator of the fraction is the quantity of equal parts the whole is partitioned into (for example, 8) and the numerator is the quantity of parts to shade. The gap in students' understanding is that there is no acknowledgment that the missing pieces are a different size of unit. The student sees only that there is just 1 unshaded region, not that those unshaded regions represent different sizes of units (eighths and sixths, respectively).

These results from our research are consistent with what others have found (Behr et al., 1992; Mitchell & Clarke, 2004; Simon, 2006; Simon, Placa, Avitzur, & Kara, 2018; Stafylidou & Vosniadou, 2004). Many students' initial concept image of a fraction is not as a number, which would require an understanding of a size of a unit, but as a part-whole relationship involving two quantities. As the student reasoning in figure 3.3 exemplifies, many students see this part-whole relationship as a comparison between a quantity of shaded parts (part) and a quantity of total parts (whole). The limitations of this part-whole conception of fractions are well documented (Simon et al., 2018). As we will discuss in chapter 8 (page 175), this limited part-whole understanding of fractions is more reflective of seeing a *fraction-as-ratio* (that is, interpreted as two quantities) and not *fraction-as-measure* (that is, interpreted as a quantity and a size of unit).

Take a moment to consider why many students develop a concept image of fractions as only a part-whole relationship. It's what's illuminated in many of the pictorial models that are utilized when students first learn fraction concepts. For example, look at the missing-piece model featured in figure 3.5 (page 53) and determine the fraction representing the shaded part of the circle. What you more than likely see is the quantity of shaded parts (7) and the remaining unshaded part (1) to determine the total parts (7 + 1 = 8). Less visible is the size of the unit represented by each of these pieces (that is, 1 *eighth*). Given these challenges, I avoid using missing-piece area models to represent fractions and instead use models that illuminate seeing the size of the unit.

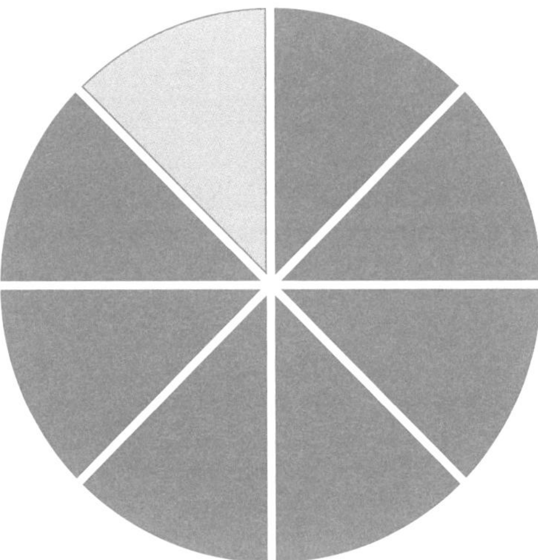

Figure 3.5: Seeing shaded parts and total parts.

THE ABILITY TO SEE A FRACTION DIFFERENTLY

It's critical that that students see fractions as numbers from the very beginning of their experiences with fractions. The third- and fourth-grade Common Core State Standards for mathematics emphasize seeing fractions as numbers and placing fractions on a number line (3.NF and 4.NBT; National Governors Association Center for Best Practices & Council of Chief State School Officers, 2010). Addressing these standards aligns with students developing *fraction-as-measure* conceptions or seeing fractions in terms of their magnitude (that is, a number; Hackenberg et al., 2016). A *fraction-as-measure* conception involves a student seeing a fraction as a quantity and size of unit. What I would like to scream from the rooftops is that with this goal in mind, the size of unit, as we discussed earlier with whole numbers, should be made explicit when students are first learning about fraction concepts. This means avoiding the usage of the standard fraction notation (for example, 7⁄8) and instead utilizing the *numeral-unit-name* notation (7 eighths) until you are confident students see fractions as numbers.

Before we get into why this fraction-as-measure conception is so important, let's take a brief detour into language. What words come to mind when you see a fraction written in standard notation (for example, 7⁄8)? I know that the two words I associate with a fraction are *numerator* and *denominator*. This is what I was taught, and I never questioned why those words were used.

Twenty-five years into my teaching, in a moment of curiosity, I researched the meaning of these two words. As with many mathematical words, their roots lie in the Latin language. The word *numerator* is derived from the Latin word *numerus*, which means "number," and the word *denominator* is derived from the Latin word *denomino*, which means "to name." In other words, the numerator represents the quantity, and the denominator represents the size of the unit.

Unfortunately, as stated earlier, many students don't associate the denominator of a fraction with the size of a unit. For many students, their concept image of the denominator of a fraction is either a whole number to be compared to the whole number of the numerator (see figures 3.1 and 3.2, pages 50 and 51) or a partitioning action on the whole unit (see figure 3.3, page 51). Again, the size of the unit would be more explicit if the numeral-unit-name notation (for example, 3 *eighths*) was used. What is wild is that this was a common practice in 19th-century textbooks (Brooks, 1873)! I'm not sure what happened that we got away from this practice. These are a few comments from my developmental mathematics students when we incorporated an intervention that involved writing fractions using the numeral-unit-name notation.

"I used to see $^4/_5$ as just a hard math problem. Now since we talked numerator (number) and denominator (name) I see it as 4 fifths, which is much easier when adding or subtracting fractions. I always struggled with fractions, but this new way is helping me out a ton."

"The greatest impact on me is using unit and quantity instead of numerator and denominator. I was taught from a young age numerator and denominator. I think quantity and unit is easier to remember, and I get less confused."

THE ILLUMINATION OF THE SIZE OF THE UNIT

The superpower understanding of fractions is seeing the unit fraction as a measure. Students can't see other fractions until they see the unit fraction and its relationship to a whole unit. Teachers often ask me, "What do we need to do to enable our students to see a fraction as a measure?" To answer this question, let's role-play for a moment. Suppose that I had a whole chocolate bar and I wanted to give you 1 eighth of that whole chocolate bar. (I still like chocolate!) You broke off a part of that chocolate bar. What would you do to convince me that you broke off 1 eighth of the whole chocolate bar? Consistent with my desire to help students build fraction-as-measure conceptions, I'm going to illustrate this work using a *bar–number line model.* The reason is that number lines are the best representational tool to support students seeing fractions as measures (Siegler et al., 2011), but the difficulty is that the number line hides the length of unit. The bar, representing a linear model, is added to make the length of the unit more explicit.

Suppose you broke off a piece of the whole chocolate bar as shown in figure 3.6 and wanted to check whether you'd broken off 1 eighth of the whole chocolate bar. Take a moment to think about what you would do.

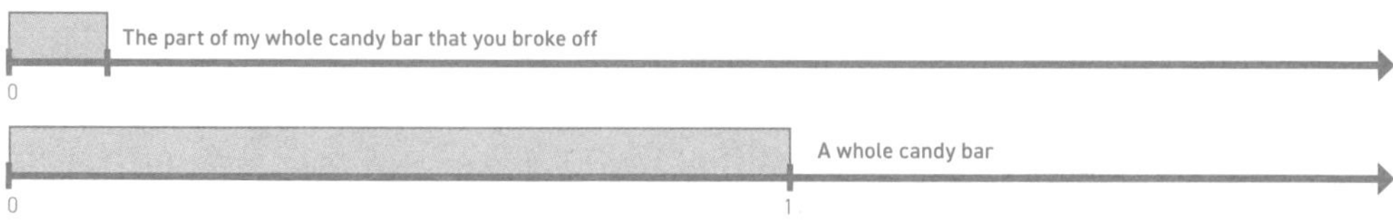

Figure 3.6: Testing to see whether the part represents 1 eighth of the whole.

More than likely, you would *iterate* your length of chocolate 8 times to determine whether the end of your 8th piece ended at the same length as the whole candy bar. If it didn't, your length doesn't represent 1 eighth of the whole (see figure 3.7). Sneaky you! You took more than 1 eighth of a whole candy bar!

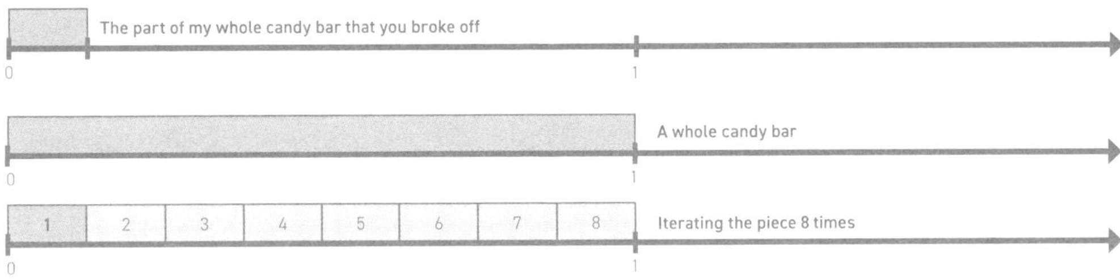

Figure 3.7: Iterating to determine whether your piece represents 1 eighth.

Being a little more strategic this time, you *partitioned* the whole candy bar into 8 equally sized lengths as shown in figure 3.8. This time you're certain your length is 1 eighth of the whole because it takes 8 of those lengths to create the whole candy bar (that is, 8 copies of a length of 1 eighth is 8 eighths or 1 whole). This is an implied multiplicative relationship, $8 \times \frac{1}{8} = 1$, but we'll save that discussion for a later time.

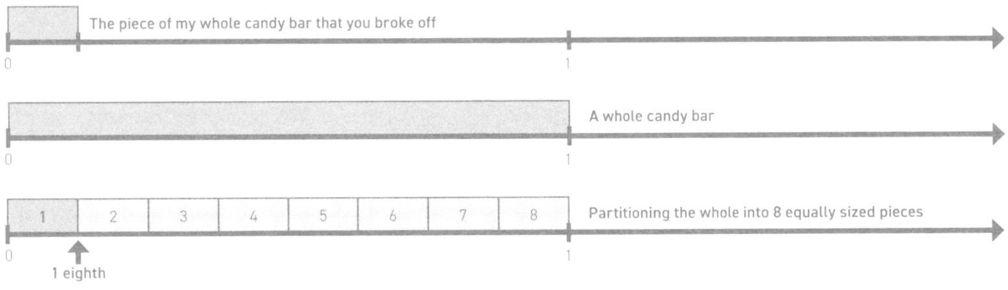

Figure 3.8: Partitioning to determine 1 eighth.

This contrived exchange illustrates what students need to see to conceptualize a fraction as a measure. The first concept that needs to be seen is the measure of a unit fraction (size of unit) and its relationship to the whole unit (Hackenberg et al., 2016). In this instance, the correct unit-size length of 1 eighth was determined when 8 of those unit-size lengths completed the whole. Generally, a unit size of 1 *n*th is determined when *n* copies of the unit-size length of 1 *n*th complete the whole (that is, $n \times \frac{1}{n} = 1$). For example, a length of 1 *fourth* of the whole is established when 4 copies of a length of 1 *fourth* are the same length as 1 *whole* unit; likewise, a length of 1 *sixth* of the whole is established when 6 copies of a length of 1 *sixth* are the same length as 1 whole unit.

As mentioned earlier, the ability to see fractions in terms of copies of the unit fraction, representing the size of the unit, is a superpower understanding. Seeing all fractions as quantities of unit fractions is like other superpowers (for example, equal exchanges). It's a transformative understanding because other fractions of the same size of unit are derived from the unit fraction. Consider how a length of 1 eighth of a whole unit is created. The whole unit is partitioned into 8 equally sized pieces. The length of each of those pieces is 1 eighth, and there are 8 distinct 1 eighths in 1 whole unit.

Determining a unit fraction, such as 1 eighth, requires students to navigate two different sizes of units. The first unit is the whole unit because the whole unit determines the size of each of the unit fractions (that is, 1 eighth). The second unit is the unit fraction because the unit fraction determines the length of multiple copies of the unit fraction. For example, 2 eighths are created by iterating the length of 1 eighth two times, 3 eighths iterating the length of 1 eighth three times. Thinking multiplicatively, 2 eighths is 2 times greater than 1 eighth, and 3 eighths is 3 times greater than 1 eighth. Once the unit-size length is determined, as shown in figure 3.9, creating copies of that unit-size length is straightforward.

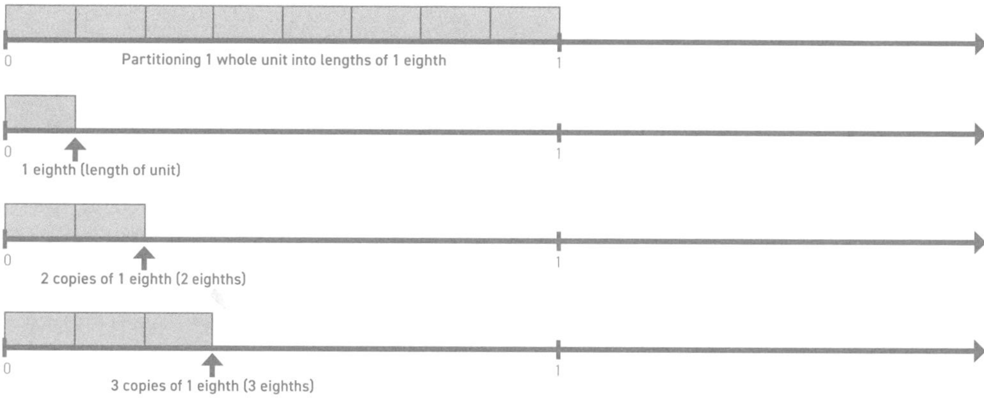

Figure 3.9: Making copies of 1 eighth.

In other words, once you know the unit length of 1 eighth, you know all the other lengths of copies of 1 eighth. This even extends beyond the whole unit. For example, if I asked you to do so, you could probably mark a length of 11 eighths on figure 3.9.

PAUSE AND PONDER

Suppose you asked your students to compare the fractions 1 sixth and 1 eighth. Based on what you have read, what would you want a student to say that would convince you that they understand why 1 sixth is greater than 1 eighth?

And in this case, the *see it* element opens a window on the *say it* element—there is one more reason why it's important to use the unit name when introducing fractions. Recall from chapter 2 (page 31) the morpheme *-ths*, which can serve as a cue to an action, partitioning the whole unit into an equal number of pieces. For example, the unit name eighths is a cue to partition the whole into 8 equally sized lengths or 8 copies of 1 eighth. This morpheme is not helpful for halves and thirds, but starting with fourths, the suffix *-ths* is a powerful language cue that signifies the quantity of equally sized lengths to partition the whole.

Part of saying it is being explicit about communicating the important aspects of the concept. For example, we challenge students to move beyond using the term *piece* because it doesn't speak to the size of the unit. Comparing the fractions $\frac{1}{6}$ and $\frac{1}{8}$, students will often say that $\frac{1}{6}$ is greater than $\frac{1}{8}$ because the "pieces are bigger." Our desire is for students to communicate both the quantity and the size of unit.

Depending on your grade level, ask your students to compare appropriate fraction pairs that would provide you insight into the nature of their thinking. For example, start with a unit fraction pair (for example, $\frac{1}{4}$ and $\frac{1}{6}$) and create a few that involve the same numerators and same denominators. Then, try one that has the potential to reveal gap reasoning (for example, $\frac{5}{6}$ and $\frac{7}{8}$).

Suppose that you were given the fraction measures represented on the bar-number lines in the figure that follows. What other fraction measures could you determine? (Hint: Start by determining the length of the whole unit.) Each problem will challenge you to think a little differently. Take note of your thinking on each problem.

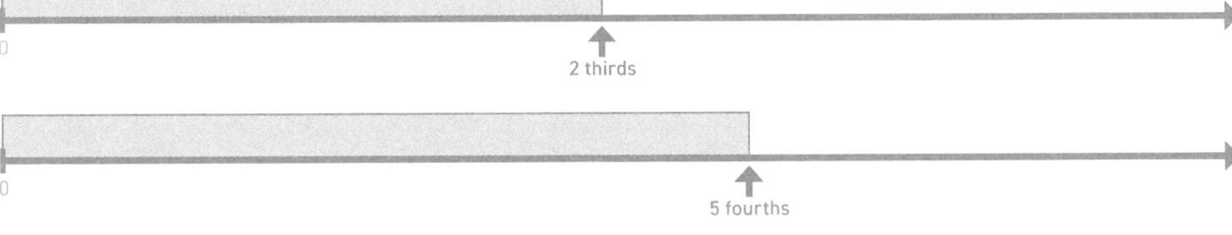

Consider the two fraction comparisons discussed earlier in the chapter (that is, 1/6 and 1/8 and 5/6 and 7/8). The fractions 1/6 and 1/8 are shown in figure 3.10.

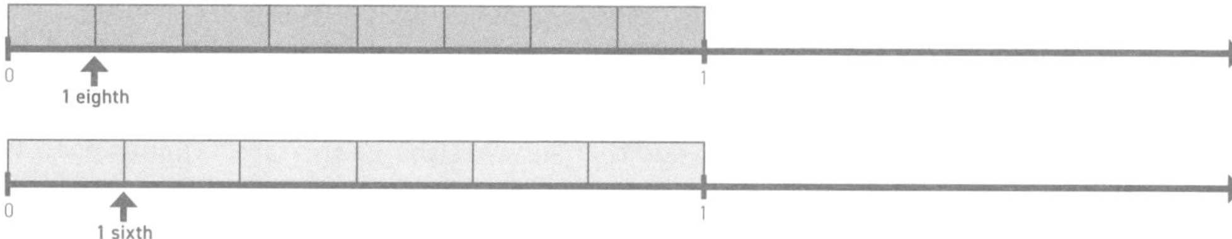

Figure 3.10: Comparing 1 eighth and 1 sixth.

The quantities are the same (1), but the greater size of unit is sixths since it takes 6 sixths (6 copies of 1 sixth) to make the whole, as compared to 8 eighths (8 copies of 1 eighth)—fewer lengths of 1 sixth to create the whole than lengths of 1 eighth. Student reasoning that exemplifies the language we desire for them to use when comparing unit fractions is shown in figure 3.11.

1/6 is greater than 1/8 because the quantity of each unit is the same, but sixths are greater-sized pieces than eighths because with sixths the whole unit has been partitioned into 6 equal sized pieces. The fewer pieces the whole unit has been partitioned into, the bigger the size of the unit. So 1 sixth, the larger unit, is greater than 1 of the smaller units, eighths.

Figure 3.11: Student reasoning exemplar comparing 1/6 and 1/8.

The fraction comparison 5/6 and 7/8 also involves reasoning about the unit fractions 1/6 and 1/8. In this instance, it's about comparing the remaining lengths to reach 1 whole unit. That is, 5/6 (5 sixths) is 1/6 from 1 whole unit, and 7/8 (7 eighths) is 1/8 from 1 whole unit. As shown in figure 3.12, the fraction with lesser remaining length (that is, 7 eighths) represents the greater length.

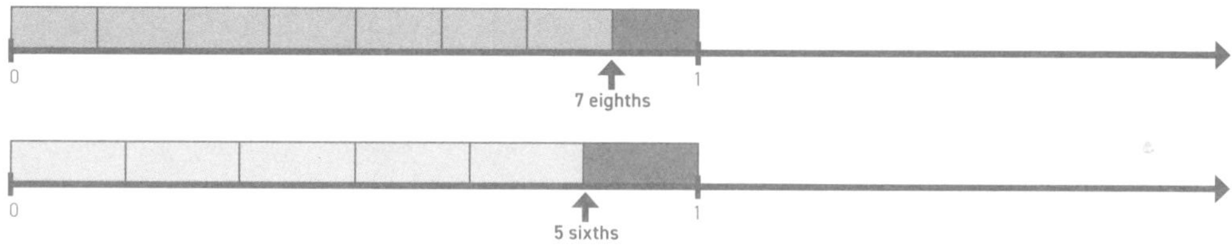

Figure 3.12: Comparing 7 eighths and 5 sixths.

Comparing fractions by reasoning from a whole unit, or another benchmark fraction, is called *residual reasoning* (Sullivan & Barnett, 2019). It's important that students have conceptual fraction comparison reasoning strategies, such as residual reasoning, because these strategies have been found to have an impact on students' overall mathematical achievement (Siegler et al., 2011; Siegler & Pyke, 2013). Student reasoning that exemplifies residual reasoning is shown figure 3.13 (page 59). Here, the student explicitly communicates the quantity and the size of unit missing from the whole unit and utilizes that reasoning to determine who ate more.

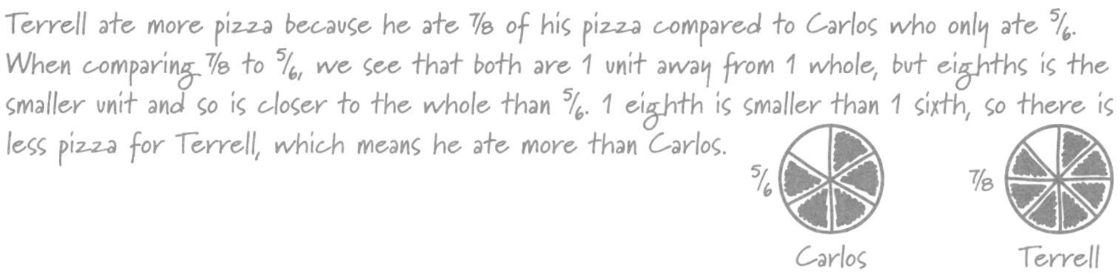

Terrell ate more pizza because he ate 7/8 of his pizza compared to Carlos who only ate 5/6. When comparing 7/8 to 5/6, we see that both are 1 unit away from 1 whole, but eighths is the smaller unit and so is closer to the whole than 5/6. 1 eighth is smaller than 1 sixth, so there is less pizza for Terrell, which means he ate more than Carlos.

5/6 Carlos

7/8 Terrell

Figure 3.13: Student reasoning exemplar comparing 5⁄6 and 7⁄8.

A Means to Connect the Dots

To drive home the importance of the fraction-as-measure superpower understanding, let's revisit the third problem that I posed at the beginning of this chapter: "Thomas ate 3⁄4 of a whole medium pizza, and Lydia ate 5⁄8 of a whole medium pizza. Together they ate how much of a whole medium pizza?" Over 50 percent of my developmental mathematics students on a diagnostic assessment reasoned that the answer would be 8⁄12, merely adding together the quantities represented by the numerator and denominator of each fraction (3 + 5 = 8) and (4 + 8 = 12). Please understand that I don't mean to diminish these students in any way—they are dear to my heart! But these results do tell a story that makes my heart ache. These students have navigated a significant amount of mathematics while missing an important understanding of fractions. How do you make sense of adding fractions without seeing fractions in terms of quantities and sizes of units?

The main point that I want to make is one that we are revisiting from the introduction (page 1). Recall the unifying understanding of addition—to perform the quantity-combining action of addition, the size of the unit of each number must be the same. This applies to adding fractions as well. To see a fraction as a number requires that students see the fraction as a measure that involves both a quantity and a size of unit. For example, as shown in figure 3.14, you cannot combine 3 *fourths* and 5 *eighths* because the size of unit is not the same, but you can combine 6 *eighths* and 5 *eighths*.

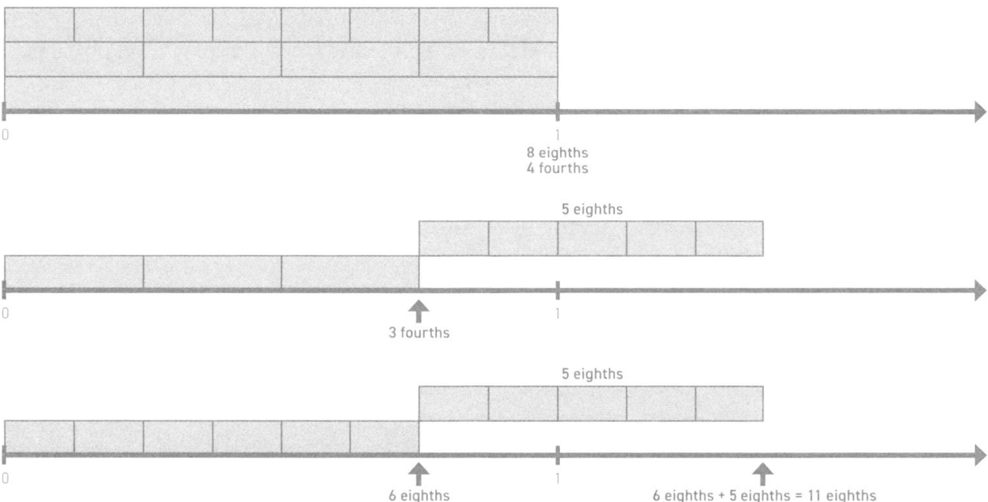

Figure 3.14: Creating fractions with same size of unit to perform addition.

Equal Exchanges Again!

I thought I snuck that one by you, but you're in that mathematical mindset mode, so you're probably saying, "Wait a minute!" How did you determine that 6 eighths are the same as 3 fourths? I am glad you asked! As with whole numbers, we can make equal exchanges of fractions. It just has a different feel to it. Recall from chapter 2 (page 31) that an amount of 1 hundred (100) could be equally exchanged for 10 tens (**10**0). As the quantity of the unit increased by a factor of 10, the size of the unit decreased by a factor of 10. Many unit exchanges of whole numbers involve increases and decreases of quantities and sizes of units of by a factor of 10. For example, an equal exchange of 1 hundred for 10 tens increases the quantity by a factor of 10 (1 to 10) but decreases the size of the unit by a factor of 10 (1 hundred to 1 ten).

Equal exchanges with fractions often involve sizes of units that are not decimal units (for example, fourths, sixths, eighths, and so on). These equal exchanges also depend on the relationship between the sizes of unit and the quantity needed to create a whole unit. Before reading any further, take a moment to cut several strips of paper that are the same length. Take one of those strips and fold it in half and fold it in half again. What size of unit did you create? Mark the length on the strip that would represent the length of 3 fourths. Take another strip and repeat the process but fold the strip in half three times. What size of unit did you create? As before, mark the length of the strip that would represent 6 eighths. Your work should look like what is shown in figure 3.15.

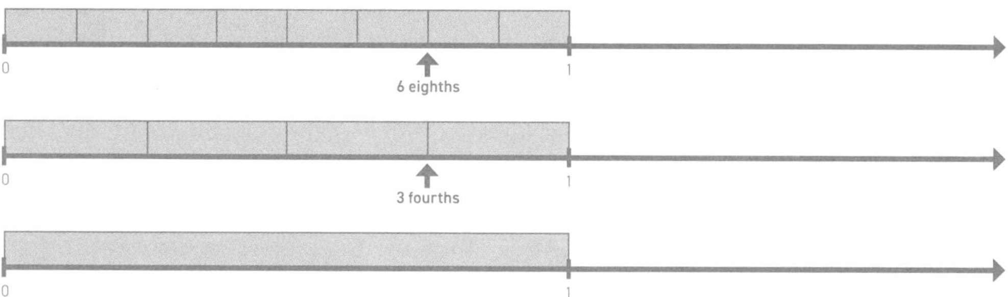

Figure 3.15: Showing that 3 fourths and 6 eighths are the same length/number.

As you can see in this equal exchange (3 fourths and 6 eighths), the quantity has doubled, or increased by a factor of 2, from 3 to 6, but the size of the unit has halved, or decreased by a factor of 2 (fourths to eighths). In other words, it takes 2 eighths to make 1 fourth.

Create several fraction strips to represent 1 whole unit. Fold one of the strips into fourths and another strip into twelfths. (Hint: Fold the fraction strips into thirds first and then perform the halving action.)

Convince yourself that 6 twelfths are an equal exchange of 2 fourths. In this equal exchange, what happens to the quantity? Size of unit?

EQUAL EXCHANGES AND THE EQUIVALENT FRACTIONS PROCEDURE

I want to take a moment to take you back to the way I learned to create equal exchanges, or what we commonly know as equivalent fractions. Let's consider the two fractions that I had you create in the preceding Try It. Now, does the symbolic work in figure 3.16 look familiar to you? The phrase "multiply the top and bottom by the same number" hides in plain sight the concept of equal exchange. The 3 in the numerator represents a tripling or multiplying of the quantity by a factor of 3 (2 to 6). The same numeral, 3, in the denominator, which is actually the number $\frac{1}{3}$, represents a multiplying of the size of the unit by a factor of $\frac{1}{3}$ ($\frac{1}{3} \times \frac{1}{4} = \frac{1}{12}$)—in other words, a thirding of 1 fourth to create 1 twelfth. I hope this makes you as giddy as it did me the first time I realized this! It's important to note that with fractions, the factor used to create an equal exchange can be any whole number.

takes **3** times as many twelfths to make same amount as 2 fourths

↓

$$\frac{2}{4} \times \left(\frac{3}{3}\right) = \frac{6}{12}$$

↑

partitioning each fourth into thirds to create twelfths

Figure 3.16: Making a connection between equal exchanges and the procedure for creating equivalent fractions.

EQUAL EXCHANGES AND THE RECOMPOSING FEATURE

Before ending our journey through fraction concepts, let's discuss one more type of equal exchange that's similar to the whole-number equal exchange involving multiple sizes of units. Remember from chapter 2 (page 31) the whole number of 1 hundred can be equally exchanged for 9 tens and 10 ones. This type of equal exchange is analogous to converting an improper fraction to a mixed number. That is, a quantity of one size of unit is being exchanged for quantities of multiple sizes of unit. Let's start with the improper fraction 13⁄6, or 13 sixths. Creating whole units from a quantity of sixths requires *recomposing*, not decomposing. That is, we're bundling together a quantity of smaller-sized units to create 1 of a larger-sized unit. As shown in figure 3.17, each group of 6 sixths is recomposed into 1 whole unit, creating an equal exchange. This action results in another equal exchange of 1 whole unit and 7 sixths, or 1 7⁄6. It may look a little different from what you're familiar with, but no mathematics rules were broken creating it! Since there are more than 6 sixths (that is, 7), we can recompose another 6 sixths into 1 whole unit, which results in another equal exchange, 2 whole units and 1 sixth, or 2 1⁄6. It's that simple. In other words, 13 sixths are an equal exchange for 1 whole and 7 sixths, which is an equal exchange for 2 whole units and 1 sixth. No tricks, no rules, just recomposing quantities of sixths into quantities of whole units and sixths. Same language, different type of numbers.

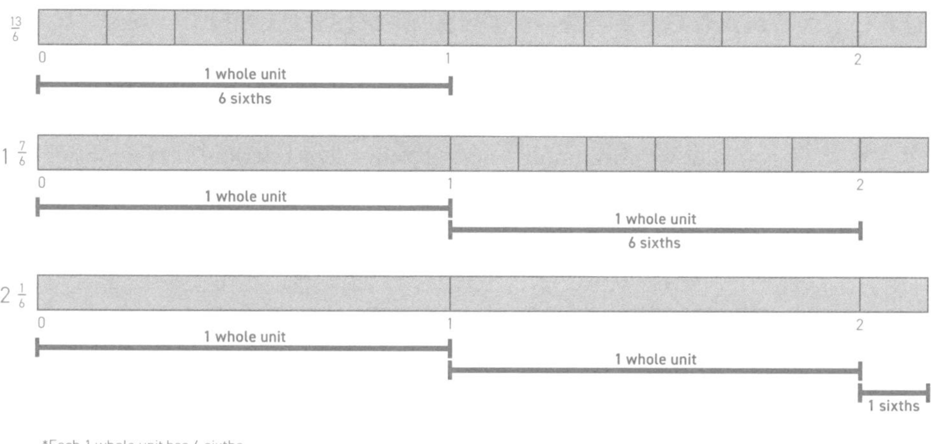

Figure 3.17: Creating equal exchanges from the improper fraction 13 sixths.

The same ideas apply when converting from a mixed number to an improper fraction. Once again, we're creating equal exchanges. Why do we call it a mixed number? Let's use the mixed number 3 1⁄4 as an example. You might remember the rule for converting mixed numbers to improper fractions—"multiply the number in front by the denominator and add the numerator, and then write the number over the denominator." Again, it's important to ask *why*. The conceptual connection between the rule most of us learned and the emphasis on size of unit is shown in figure 3.18 (page 63).

Standard Notation

$^{1}3\frac{^{2}1}{4} = \frac{^{3}13}{4}$

Traditional Procedural Steps

Step 1: Multiply 3 × 4 = 12

Step 2: Add 1 to 12 (13)

Step 3: Write the answer to step 2 with a denominator of 4.

Numeral-Unit-Name Notation With Connection to Procedural Steps

3 whole units and 1 fourth

How many 1 fourths are in each 1 whole unit? (4)

How many 1 fourths are in 3 whole units? (3 × 4 = 12)

12 fourths + 1 fourth = 13 fourths

Figure 3.18: Connecting procedure of converting a mixed number to an improper fraction to its conceptual underpinnings.

To see this connection, let's look at placing the fraction 3 ¼ on a bar–number line. The fraction 3 ¼ is considered a mixed number because it consists of two different-sized units—3 units of one and 1 fourth. Imagine placing the mixed number on the bar–number line. This would involve identifying the whole unit, finding the location of 3 whole units, partitioning the whole unit between 3 and 4 whole units into four equal parts, and identifying the length of one of those four equal parts (see top bar–number line in figure 3.19). Now imagine partitioning each whole unit into fourths (see bottom bar–number line in figure 3.19). How many fourths does it take to make 3 whole units? Each 1 whole is decomposed into 4 fourths, so 12 fourths is an equal exchange for 3 whole units. As figure 3.19 shows, 3 whole units (12 fourths) and 1 fourth is the same location, or length, as 13 fourths (3 ¼ = 1 ¾). In other words, 3 units of one and 1 unit of a fourth is the same number as 13 fourths. It is a single fraction greater than one, and there is nothing improper about it!

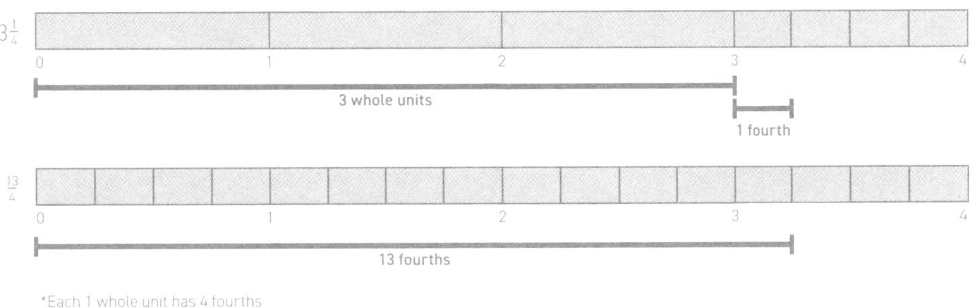

Figure 3.19: Showing that 3 whole units and 1 fourth is an equal exchange of 13 fourths.

Over the course of these sections on equal exchanges, we've connected fraction concepts that may have seemed disconnected in our minds. Thinking about our own concept image, we may find that these concepts have been in their own file cabinet drawers, separate from each other. Hopefully, now the ideas of equivalent fractions, the conversion of an improper fraction to a mixed number, and the conversion of a mixed number to an improper fraction are in the same file cabinet drawer, bound by the concept of an equal exchange. This is just one more reason why equal exchanges, much like the fraction-as-measurement conception, are a superpower understanding.

Similar to what I showed in figures 3.17 (page 62) and 3.19 (page 63), use bar-number lines to create your own depictions to convert the mixed number 2 ¾ to an improper fraction and convert the improper fraction ⁹⁄₅ to a mixed number. Take note of the equal exchanges involved in each of these problems.

The Common Denominator and Butterfly Strategies

As I did earlier with connecting the process of how we learned to create equivalent fractions and equal exchanges, it's important to connect conceptually with strategies commonly used to compare fractions. Two strategies often used to compare fractions are what's called the *butterfly method* and *common denominator* or, more conceptually, same size of unit. These strategies are shown in figure 3.20 to compare two common fractions, ¾ and ⁴⁄₅.

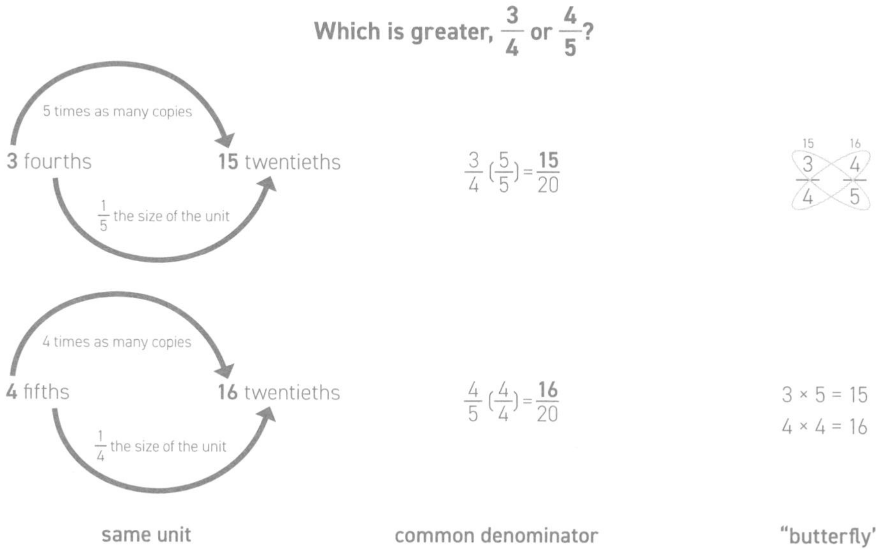

Figure 3.20: Common strategies to compare 3 fourths and 4 fifths.

I caution sharing either the common denominator or butterfly strategy with students until they have had extensive experiences making equal exchanges and comparing fractions using the other strategies that we've already discussed. Once students have strategies such as common denominator and butterfly as part of their concept image, they will stop reasoning about the relationship between the quantity and size of unit. Both strategies are fraction-relationship-reasoning killers because they yield correct answers without requiring students to think about the size of the unit. The butterfly strategy doesn't require students to engage with the meaning of the size of the unit, while the common denominator strategy does involve the size of the unit of each fraction, but they're the same, so they're often dismissed. The problem is that many elementary mathematics curricula introduce these strategies too early in students' fraction development. As with cell phones, once students have the concepts, it's hard to take them away! Think of these strategies like Kryptonite is to Superman—they actually weaken students' superpowers!

PAUSE AND PONDER

Considering what you've read in this chapter related to fraction concepts, ask yourself the following questions to reflect on your own curriculum.

- Is the curriculum emphasizing fraction-as-measure conceptions so that students see fractions as numbers?

- How are fractions represented? If missing-piece models are used, what do I need to do to focus students' attention on the quantity and size of unit represented? Are linear models (for example, paper strips and bar–number lines) used to reinforce fraction-as-measure conceptions?

- Are there places in which I need to delay exposing students to strategies (that is, common denominator and multiplying top and bottom by same number) that may hinder my students' ability to see unifying ideas (for example, equal exchanges)?

- How will my instruction practices related to teaching fractions shift as a result of my reading this chapter?

How to Turn a Hatred of Fractions Into a Love of Fractions

If I were charged with helping *all* students develop a deep understanding of fraction concepts, one in which as adults they would not associate the word *hate* with the concept, the following would be my five recommendations.

1. Begin fraction instruction by making sure the denominator of a fraction is represented using the name for the unit (for example, 3 eighths) so that fraction-as-measure conceptions take root. The size of the unit is the heart of the fraction struggle, so let's make it explicit.
2. Choose contextual problems to which students can relate (for example, pieces of string, segments of a strand of licorice, and the like), but make sure the visual representations used don't reinforce students seeing *only* two quantities rather than a quantity and a size of unit. No partial shading of visual images! If these images are part of your curriculum, challenge students

to communicate using the terms *quantity* and *size of unit*. This language supports the development of fraction-as-measure conceptions.

3. Instead of drawing visual representations on the board, engage students in folding whole units into halves, fourths, eighths, and sixteenths (same folding schema) and thirds, sixths, and twelfths (slightly different folding schema). This engages them in the partitioning activity with the goal of their seeing that the sizes of unit are the same length and the relationship between the quantity and size of unit to create 1 whole unit. That is, *n* copies of 1 *n*th are needed to create a length the same length as 1 whole unit. No need to discuss fifths, sevenths, and elevenths—try folding those! I can think of only one need for fifths—cheers!
4. Utilize the fractions (folding them to see only the unit fraction) and iterate this piece multiple times, placing the fraction strip on a number line as shown in figures 3.6 (page 54), 3.7 (page 55), and 3.8 (page 55). This will hopefully enable students to see that fractions with a denominator greater than 1 are merely copies of the unit fraction—for example, seeing that 3 eighths of the whole unit are formed from 3 copies of the unit fraction of 1 eighth.
5. Make every fraction task a comparison task. It's what we do with numbers—we compare them!
6. Related to the previous recommendation, avoid procedural strategies (for example, finding a common denominator or using the butterfly method) that limit students' opportunity to reason about fractions by coordinating their understanding of the number of copies, or quantity (numerator), and the size of the unit (denominator). Save these procedures until much later. They are fraction-comparison-reasoning stoppers!

Decimals as Fractions in Disguise

Did you know that decimals are fractions in disguise? Decimals are fractions in which the denominator, or size of the unit, is a power of ten—for example, 10, 100, 1,000, and so on or tenths, hundredths, thousandths, and so forth. This was introduced briefly in chapter 2 (page 31). Decimals should not be a big stretch because they still represent quantities of different sizes of units. For example, the decimal 0.7 is the fraction 7⁄10, or 7 tenths. Likewise, the decimal 0.75 is the fraction 75⁄100, or 75 hundredths. In each case, the same number is represented three different ways (that is, decimal notation, standard fraction notation, and numeral-unit-name notation).

In this section, I don't spend too much time discussing decimals because the ideas we discussed with fractions hold for decimals, and we already connected decimal place value ideas to whole-number ideas. It's no wonder that when students struggle understanding fractions, they struggle understanding decimals, especially if we don't connect these ideas to whole numbers. It's like playing the game of Jenga. Once some of the lower building blocks of mathematics are removed, it becomes more and more difficult for the student to make sense of new concepts (for example, decimals) that are connected to the old concepts (for example, fractions) with which they already struggle.

I do want to take a brief side trip into decimals to illuminate one distinction between comparing whole numbers (numbers to the left of the decimal place) and comparing decimals (numbers to the right of the decimal). In a study involving over 100 fifth and sixth graders, when asked to compare which decimal was greater, 0.274 or 0.83, most students chose 0.274 (as cited in Leinwand & Milou, 2021). Not surprising, really! Think about what's likely in the mind's eye of many students. Is the whole number 274 greater than 83? Of course it is! The number 274 represents 2 hundreds, 7 tens, and 4 ones, while the number 83 represents 8 tens and 3 ones. The largest unit is hundreds, and since the number 274 has 2 of that size of unit and the number 83 doesn't have any hundreds, the number 274 must be a greater quantity than 83.

What happens differently when comparing 0.274 and 0.83? As discussed in chapter 2 (page 31), many students see the decimal point as a demarcation line—incorrectly reasoning that numerals farther away from the decimal point are greater sizes of units. While this reasoning is true for numerals to the left of the decimal point, it's incorrect for numerals to the right of the decimal point. For example, consider the numbers 274 and 0.274. The numeral 2 in 274, *farthest* from the decimal point, is the greatest size of unit; however, the numeral 2 in 0.274, *closest* to the decimal point, is the greatest size of unit. As shown in figure 3.21, the greatest size of unit in the whole-number comparison of 274 and 83 is hundreds (**2**74 > **0**83), while the greatest size of unit in the comparison of 0.274 and 0.83 is tenths (0.**8**3 > 0.**2**74).

hundreds	tens	ones
2	7	4
	8	3

274 is greater than 83

tenths	hundredths	thousandths
2	7	4
8	3	

830 thousandths (83 hundredths) is greater than 274 thousandths.

Figure 3.21: Comparing decimals with sizes of units to the left of the decimal point and those same quantities representing sizes of units to the right of the decimal point.

Showing a size of unit flexibility, we can also utilize a free zero and an equal exchange of 83 hundredths to show that 830 thousandths is greater than 274 thousandths (0.**830** > 0.**274**). In other words, the whole-number analogous comparison problem to 0.83 and 0.274 was 830 and 274, not 274 and 83. All about knowing those units!

Key Points

Before proceeding, please take a moment to review the following takeaways from this chapter.

- One of the biggest mistakes we make in introducing fractions to students is not making the size of the unit explicit. It's more helpful to their development if the adult fraction notation $3/8$ is introduced after students have had experiences with a fraction notation in which the size of the unit is made explicit, 3 eighths. Doing so connects to what they have already done with whole numbers. Teachers often ask me when to introduce the standard fraction notation. My response is always "When you are convinced that *all* students see fractions as numbers." This involves their seeing a quantity and a size of unit evidenced by their ability to create unit fraction lengths (for example, 1 eighth of the whole unit) and placing those numbers on a bar-number line to make fraction comparisons (for example, 1 sixth and 1 eighth).

- The concept of a unit fraction as a measure is a superpower understanding because the unit fraction defines the size of the unit. Once the length of the unit fraction is established (for example, 1 eighth), all the other fractions involving the size of unit eighth are copies of this size of unit. For example, 2 eighths is 2 copies of 1 eighth, 3 eighths is 3 copies of 1 eighth, and so on.

- Equivalent fraction relationships and mixed numbers are easier to understand if the sizes of units involved are made explicit. They both represent equal exchanges. For example, 1 third is the same quantity as 2 sixths because the size of the unit is halved, but the quantity of those units is doubled. Similarly, the mixed number 2 $1/3$ consists of 2 whole units and 1 third. Each 1 whole unit consists of 3 thirds, so 2 whole units and 1 third is the same as 7 thirds.

- Despite our best efforts to prevent it, students will use faulty fraction comparison strategies. We can minimize the potential of these strategies taking root in their minds by using the unit name to denote the size of the unit when representing fractions.

- Decimals are fractions in disguise. For example, the decimal 0.7 is the fraction 7 tenths.

The key points in this chapter emphasize strategies and representations to help students "see" fractions in terms of lengths consisting of quantities of a unit fraction. A dynamic understanding of fractions begins with one "seeing" the size of the unit in relation to the whole unit. The application guide for this chapter provides suggestions as to how to provide experiences for your own students that will help them "see" fractions in terms of lengths representing quantities of the unit fraction length.

Chapter 3 Application Guide

Chapter Concepts	How Can I Incorporate This Into My Teaching Practice Moving Forward?
Fraction as a Measure/Number	1. Use the numeral-unit-name notation to write fractions. 2. Avoid using missing-piece area models.
Partitioning/Iterating	1. Provide opportunities for students to fold (partition) paper strips into different sizes of unit (for example, fourths, sixths, and eighths). 2. Create a number line that is the same length as the paper strip and iterate the unit fraction represented by the paper strip. Mark each iteration with the correct quantity and size of unit.
Equal Exchanges (or Not)	1. Use the fraction strips coupled with number lines to compare fractions. Make the language of an equal exchange explicit (for example, 2 thirds is an equal exchange for 4 sixths because as the quantity doubles, the size of the unit is halved). 2. Connect the concepts of equivalent fractions, mixed numbers, and improper fractions around this idea.
Unit Fraction	1. Make explicit once the length of the unit fraction is known (for example, 1 eighth) that other lengths with the same size of unit are copies of that unit. For example, the length of 3 eighths can be determined by iterating, or copying, 1 eighth three times.

Arithmetic is where
numbers fly like pigeons
in and out of your head.

—Carl Sandburg

CHAPTER 4

Addition

Much of mathematics is about performing actions on numbers and quantities. In elementary mathematics, those actions typically involve one of four operations: (1) addition, (2) subtraction, (3) multiplication, or (4) division. Each operation signifies a different type of action on the numbers involved. Up to this point in the book, we've conceptualized numbers in terms of quantities and sizes of units. This conception enables us to navigate the operations of addition and subtraction. However, multiplication and division require some new conceptions, especially with numbers represented as fractions. Beginning with an in-depth exploration of addition in this chapter, we discuss the concepts underpinning each of the four operations, along with examples that illuminate important features of these concepts. The hope is that after reading each chapter, you'll see how what seemed like disjointed concepts within each operation are connected. You'll also develop new understandings that you can leverage to give your own students a more powerful understanding of these operations.

Now, let's start with addition—a combining action. The action of adding involves our combining quantities of the same size of unit. The number representing the combination of two or more parts is called the whole. This action results in the same amount. The understanding that underpins the addition of any type of number is that you can only combine quantities when the size of the unit is the same. This one idea connects *every* addition concept in this chapter. (So much for waiting for the big finish!) With that in mind, we ease into our discussion by focusing on the addition of single-digit whole numbers, then transition into multidigit addition. From there, we examine the power of part-part-whole relationships within this operation before zeroing in on the addition of fractions and decimals. Finally, we reflect on the properties of addition and connect the dots between addition in arithmetic and algebra.

Adding Single-Digit Whole Numbers

As we've discussed throughout the book, because the number system that we use is base 10, the only digits available to us are 0–9. Accordingly, each place value is a power of ten (hundreds, tens, ones, tenths, hundredths, and so on). This also means that recomposing, or regrouping, happens anytime we have 10 or more of a size of unit. The idea of recomposing is an example of equal exchanges—one of our superpower understandings. Let's take a look at how all these ideas play out with addition by approaching this operation both without and with regrouping in the context of single-digit whole numbers.

ADDING WHOLE NUMBERS WITHOUT REGROUPING

As we've done before, I'd like for us to first consider a couple of whole-number addition problems that will help us make sense of the concepts to come, beginning with the nonregrouping problem "Latisha has 4 oranges, and Sammy has 5 oranges. How many oranges total do they have?"—or the noncontextual problem 4 + 5.

Recall from our early number discussions in chapter 1 (page 21) that the numerals 4 and 5 signify a quantity and a size of unit, 4 *ones* and 5 *ones*, respectively. We often don't write the unit name *one* when describing single-digit numbers. Students first learning this idea may use different early number understandings to solve the problem. For example, they may subitize one of the parts (for example, "five") and count on (for example, "six, seven, eight, nine"). Other students, however, may subitize the entire set and simply say "nine," while others may need to count each object individually (that is, "one, two, three, four, five, six, seven, eight, nine"). The mental strategies that students use to solve these problems provide insight into the nature of how they see the sets of numbers. This provides insight into what students are ready to do next. It's important to note that students will *not* have to create a new composed unit to solve this problem because the result of combining 4 *ones* and 5 *ones* is only 9 *ones*, not 10 *ones*; we don't have enough of the quantity of *ones* (9) to create an equal exchange for 1 *ten*.

Now, it's time that I introduce you to another idea that I only alluded to toward the end of the previous chapter. It's one I'll use throughout the book to help you and your students make connections between ideas that may often seem unrelated. Suppose that instead of 4 oranges and 5 oranges, respectively, Latisha and Sammy had 40 oranges and 50 oranges—or, changing the *context*, 4 *tenths* of a whole candy bar (0.4) and 5 *tenths* (0.5) of a whole candy bar—and the question asked how much they had in total. In each instance, the action would be the same, combining quantities of 4 and 5. As shown in figure 4.1 (page 75), the only difference in solving these three problems is the size of the unit (that is, one, tens, and tenths) we're performing this action on.

	4 + 5 = 9	
	4	ones
+	5	ones
	9	**ones**

	40 + 50 = 90	
	4	tens
+	5	tens
	9	**tens**

	0.4 + 0.5 = 0.90	
	4	tenths
+	5	tenths
	9	**tenths**

Figure 4.1: Same quantities, but different size of unit.

These three problems are examples of *analogous problems*—problems that have the same structure that can be solved using a similar strategy. The ability to see and create analogous problems is another superpower understanding. Seeing and creating analogous problems plays a significant role in students' ability to make connections between ideas that may on the surface seem disjointed, so it's a critical aspect of a dynamic, flexible view of numbers and operations. In this instance, the quantities in each problem were the same, so the action to combine these quantities was the same (4 + 5 = 9). The only difference among the problems is the size of the unit.

ADDING WHOLE NUMBERS WITH REGROUPING

Now let's kick it up a notch by solving a slightly different problem: "Latisha has 5 oranges, and Sammy has 9 oranges. How many oranges total do they have?"

What's different about combining 5 oranges and 9 oranges compared to combining 5 oranges and 4 oranges? Because we're working in the base 10 system and the result of combining 5 oranges and 9 oranges is more than a quantity of 10, we now must create a new composed unit: *tens*. As we discussed at the outset of the book, most of us educators are familiar with phrases such as "bring down the four and carry the one" when we approach such a problem. Remember, though, that our goal is no longer to simply help students get correct answers but to facilitate students' understanding of why those answers make sense. Hidden behind the action of "bringing down the four and carrying the one" is the creation of a new composed unit, *ten*.

Let's take a few moments to unpack what's hidden and adjust the language to activate our superpower understandings. This problem is modeled three different ways in figure 4.2 (page 76), pictorially using connectable blocks, using the numeral-unit-name representation, and using the traditional notation.

The action we often call "carrying the one" is an equal exchange. That is, the 10 units of *one* whole orange are recomposed into 1 *ten*-pack of whole oranges. As shown in figure 4.2, writing the small 1 to the left of the 5 signifies that action. "Bringing down the four" signifies that the size of the unit didn't change for that quantity, 4 *ones*. The result of this combining action is 1 ten-pack of oranges and 4 single whole oranges. The numeral 14 signifies this relationship—1 *ten*-pack of oranges and 4 individual oranges (that is, 4 *ones*).

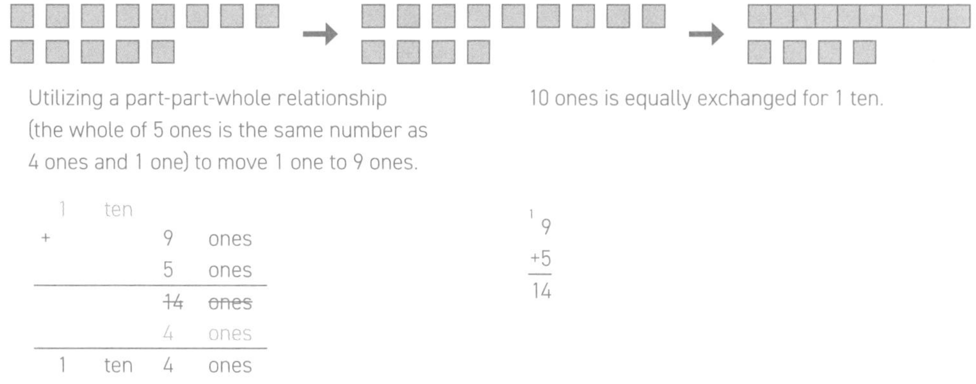

Utilizing a part-part-whole relationship (the whole of 5 ones is the same number as 4 ones and 1 one) to move 1 one to 9 ones.
10 ones is equally exchanged for 1 ten.
1 ten
+ 9 ones
5 ones
14 ones
4 ones
1 ten 4 ones
1
9
+5
14

Figure 4.2: Using multiple representations to connect the big ideas of addition.

Here we need to keep in mind our see it–say it–symbolize it approach. The *see it* element is about illuminating the critical concepts so that students have the best chance of understanding them. The concepts for single-digit addition involve utilizing part-part-whole relationships to make a ten and recognizing the composite unit of 1 *ten* formed by an equal exchange of 10 *ones*. How we represent or record problems plays a role in what students see. To illustrate, consider the solution to the Latisha and Sammy problem represented three different ways using number lines as shown in figure 4.3.

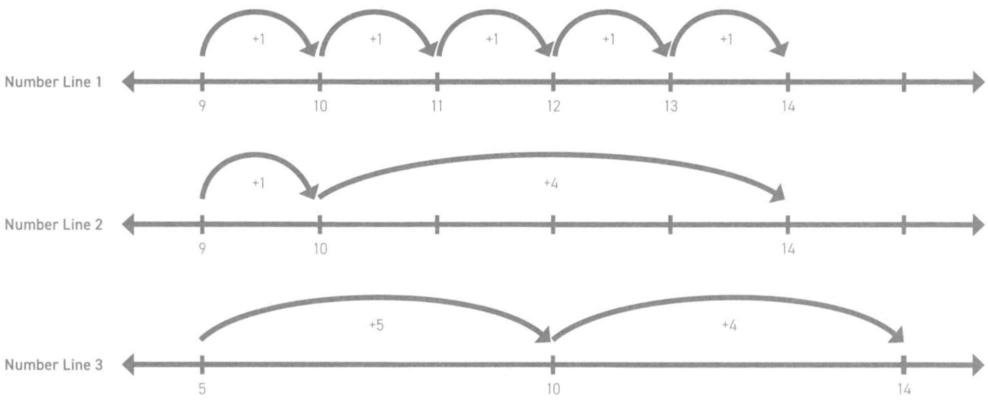

Figure 4.3: Using number lines to represent the solution to 9 + 5.

Often number lines are presented to students as *closed*, such as number line 1 in figure 4.3. That is, the numbers on the line are already provided, and all that's required of students is that they perform a counting exercise, starting with the larger number (9) and counting on 5 more numbers (that is, "ten, eleven, twelve, thirteen, fourteen"). This type of number line doesn't illuminate the new composed unit (1 ten) or the part-part-whole relationship needed to create that new unit. *Open number lines*, on the other hand, such as number lines 2 and 3 in figure 4.3, have the potential to illuminate these ideas. An *open number line* is a blank number line in which students must record how they're making sense of the addition problem while also creating unit lengths that reflect somewhat the relationship between the numbers. The work shown in number lines 2 and 3 in figure 4.3 represents two examples of student work that make explicit the part-whole relationship utilized to make a ten.

Ask your students to solve a single-digit addition problem that involves regrouping like the Latisha and Sammy problem (that is, "Latisha has 5 oranges, and Sammy has 9 oranges. How many oranges total do they have?"). Observe the strategies they use to solve the problem and the language they use to communicate their understanding.

Are you open to introducing your students to open number lines? (Pun intended!) If so, how will you introduce these to your students? Based on what we've discussed so far in this chapter, what language will you hold them accountable to using?

____

____

____

____

____

____

____

____

____

Moving Toward Multidigit Addition

Multidigit addition involves repeatedly combining quantities of the same unit and recomposing quantities of 10 of a unit into 1 of the next greater size of unit. See figure 4.4.

1	1 ten	
27	2 tens	7 ones
+ 0.69	6 tens	9 ones
0.96	~~8 tens~~	~~16 ones~~
	9 tens	6 ones

1	1 tenth	
0.27	2 tenths	7 hundredths
+ 0.69	6 tenths	9 hundredths
0.96	~~8 tenths~~	~~16 hundredths~~
	9 tenths	6 hundredths

	1 thousand			
2700	2 thousands	7 hundreds	0 tens	0 ones
+ 6900	6 thousands	9 hundreds	0 tens	0 ones
9600	~~8 thousands~~	~~16 hundreds~~		
	9 thousands	6 hundreds		

Figure 4.4: Three analogous addition problems.

PAUSE AND PONDER

Think about how you would have solved the addition problem 379 + 245 before reading up to this point in the book. Take note of the language you would have mentally used as you worked through the problem.

Now use the ideas we have discussed in this book to solve the same problem, 379 + 245.

What ideas have been most challenging to wrap your head around? How will you utilize what you've learned about whole-number addition in your own classroom?

Let's look at one more whole-number addition problem—the one you just solved in the Pause and Ponder: 379 + 245. Think about the way most of us learned to solve three-digit addition problems. Did you know that you could think about a problem like this as a series of single-digit addition problems? All you need to do is keep track of corresponding sizes of units and perform the necessary equal exchanges. This work and accompanying equal exchanges are shown in figure 4.5.

Partial Sum Algorithm

2 hundreds	4 tens	5 ones
3 hundreds	7 tens	9 ones
5 hundreds	**11 tens**	**14 ones**

	h	t	o
	2	4	5
+	3	7	9
		1	4
	1	**1**	**0**
	5	0	0
	6	2	4

Traditional Algorithm

1 hundred	1 ten	
2 hundreds	4 tens	5 ones
3 hundreds	7 tens	9 ones
~~5 hundreds~~	~~11 tens~~[2]	~~14 ones~~[1]
6 hundreds	~~12 tens~~	4 ones
	2 tens	

[1] 10 ones are equally exchanged for 1 ten.
[2] 10 tens are equally exchanged for 1 hundred.

	h	t	o
	1	1	
	2	4	5
+	3	7	9
			4
		2	0
	6	0	0
	6	2	4

Figure 4.5: Comparing partial sum algorithm and traditional algorithm.

While a number represented as 5 *hundreds*, 11 *tens*, and 14 *ones* may seem a little odd (is it an improper number?), it's the same as 6 *hundreds*, 2 *tens*, and 4 *ones*. This is an example of what is known as the *partial sum algorithm*.

Take a moment to consider the traditional algorithm that you've used to solve addition problems and compare it to the partial sum algorithm. Both are shown in figure 4.5. As we have previously discussed, the "carry the one" is about creating equal exchanges. In both algorithms, it can be seen, but in different ways, that 10 *ones* are exchanged for 1 *ten* and 10 *tens* are exchanged for 1 *hundred*. In the traditional algorithm, the small 1 signifies these two actions. However, in the partial sum algorithm, there is no "carrying the one." Each numeral is recorded in its corresponding size of unit. For example, as shown in figure 4.5, the combining of the 4 tens and 7 tens is recorded as 11 tens, with the rightmost 1 recorded in the tens place and the leftmost 1 recorded in the hundreds place (that is, 110). This signifies the equal exchange of 4 tens and 7 tens for 1 hundred and 1 ten. Likewise, in the traditional method, the "bringing down the zero" is about ensuring that the recording of the appropriate quantity is placed with the corresponding size of unit. For example, the quantity of tens is 12, so the 2 signifies the quantity of tens (that is, 20) and the 1 is carried to the quantity of hundreds.

Realizing the Power of Part-Part-Whole Relationships

As mentioned earlier, equal exchanges and part-part-whole relationships support the development of a dynamic and flexible view of adding numbers. Take a moment and think about how you would mentally solve the addition problem 69 + 27. Don't solve it on paper; just solve it in your head.

The most obvious part-part-whole relationship is the one formed by the place value of the numerals. For example, the whole of 69 is composed of two parts, 6 tens (60) and 9 ones (9). There are other part-part-whole relationships that support mental arithmetic strategies. For example, consider the numbers 69 (part 1) and 27 (part 2) as two parts combined to create a whole, but those two parts also consist of parts. Suppose we moved 1 one from part 2 (27 − 1 = 26) to part 1 (69 + 1 = 70). Now the two numbers to be combined are 70 and 26. Which is easier to mentally combine, 69 and 27 or 70 and 26? The whole, or total, as shown in figure 4.6 is still the same, but what has changed is the parts.

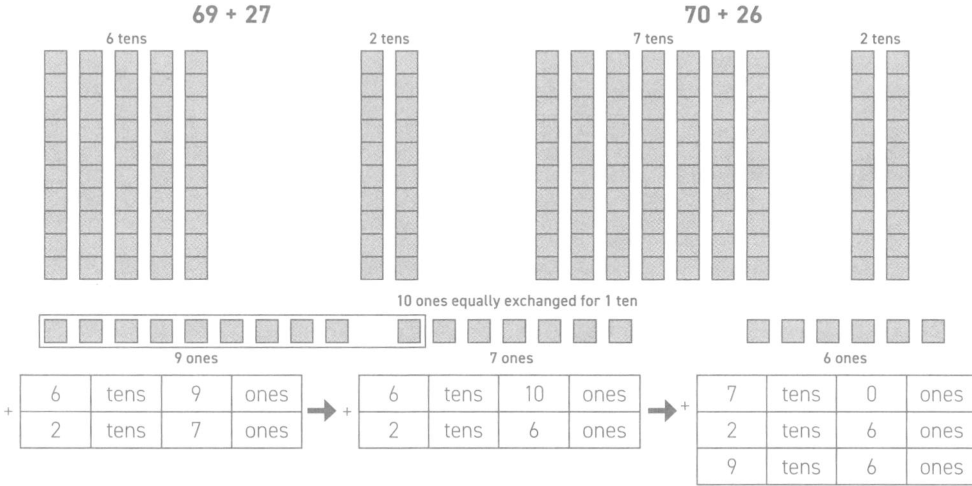

Figure 4.6: Using part-part-whole relationships to create a mentally easier problem.

Take a moment to think about how you could use this same idea to mentally solve the problem 68 + 24 or 99 + 37.

Identify three other two-digit addition problems in which this strategy would be helpful to mentally solve the problem.

It seems important to note once students begin solving addition problems that involve more than one size of unit you can begin developing their estimation reasoning powers. Before introducing a strategy to obtain an exact answer, ask them to estimate an answer. For example, consider the earlier problem 69 + 27. You could ask them to estimate the quantities of *ten* that the answer to this problem is going to lie between. Is the answer going to be more than 70? 80? 90? 100?

Adding Fractions

Here we are again—dreaded fractions. But good news! There's not much new to learn. Recall the connector understanding of addition—adding involves combining quantities of the same size of unit. No need to talk about "finding common denominators" or "lining up decimals." The conceptually consistent idea that underpins both actions is the need for the same size of unit. The only difference between adding whole numbers and adding fractions is the nature of the equal exchange. To illuminate this difference, I want to compare the nature of the equal exchanges to solve three problems, one whole-number problem and two problems that involve fractions.

- 15 + 38
- ¾ + ⅔
- 4 ⅞ + 5 ½

I'm going to write these problems again, but this time using the unit name to make the size of the units explicit.

- 1 ten and 5 ones + 3 tens and 8 ones
- 3 fourths + 2 thirds
- 4 wholes (or ones) and 7 eighths + 5 wholes (or ones) and 1 half

We've already discussed solving problems like 15 + 38, so we're familiar with the nature of decimal equal exchanges. In this instance, 10 ones are equally exchanged for 1 ten. But what happens when the two parts (3 fourths and 2 thirds) of an additional problem are not decimal numbers but fractions? Neither *thirds* nor *fourths* is a size of unit in base 10. Nondecimal fractions are treated differently. As discussed in chapter 3 (page 47), we can still create an equal exchange so that both 2 thirds and 3 fourths have the same size of unit. As shown in figure 4.7, 2 *thirds* can be equally exchanged for 8 *twelfths*, and 3 *fourths* can be equally exchanged for 9 *twelfths*. Combining these two parts results in a whole of 17 *twelfths*. This is where we need a new type of equal exchange—one that depends on the size of the unit represented by the fraction. In this case, the size of the unit is *twelfths*. We also know from chapter 3 that 12 *twelfths* are required to make 1 whole unit (1 one). In this instance, the 17 *twelfths*, an "improper" fraction, can be described, using this equal exchange, as a mixed number, 1 whole unit and 5 *twelfths* (1 5⁄12). These steps are shown pictorially using a bar–number line model and using a numeral-unit-name chart in figure 4.7.

Now let's consider the third problem involving the fractions, combining 4 wholes and 7 eighths and 5 wholes and 1 half. This problem involves a multitude of equal exchanges.

We can combine the quantity of whole units (4 *ones* + 5 *ones* = 9 *ones*). The fractions 7 *eighths* and 1 *half* cannot be combined because the size of the units is not the same. However, 1 *half* can be equally exchanged for 4 *eighths*. Since the size of the unit is different from that of the last problem, *eighths* compared to *twelfths*, the quantity of the unit needed to create a whole unit is different, which changes the nature of the equal exchange.

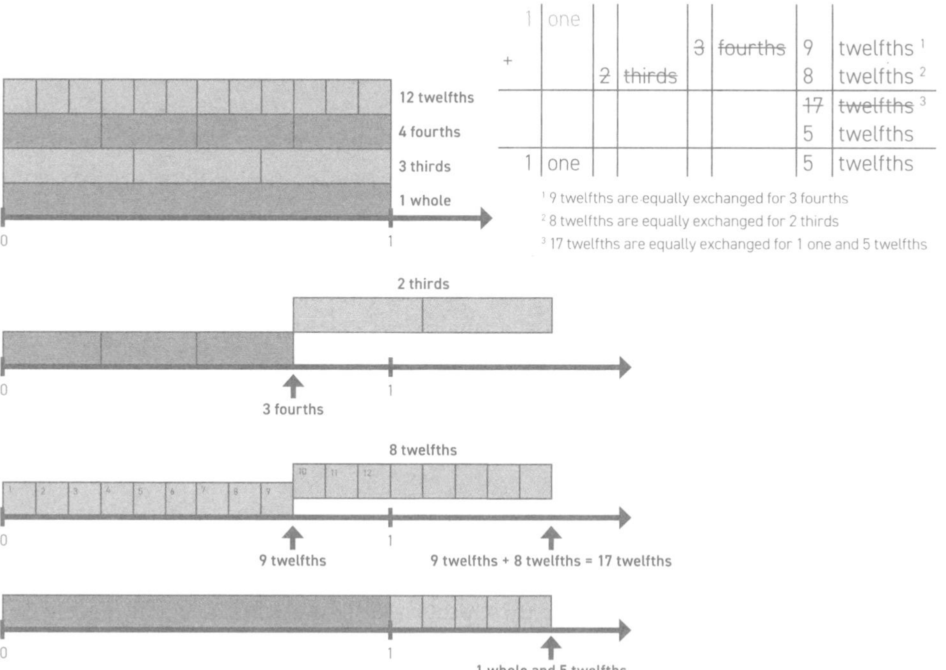

Figure 4.7: Utilizing different types of equal exchanges to combine 3 fourths and 2 thirds.

In this instance, 8 *eighths*—not 12, as in the previous problem—are needed to create an equal exchange of 1 whole unit (that is, 1 *one*). Combining 7 *eighths* and 4 *eighths* yields 11 *eighths*, or 1 *one* and 3 *eighths*. Recall that we already have 9 *ones*, so adding 1 more one yields 10 *ones*, which creates another equal exchange, 1 *ten*. This means that combining 4 *ones* and 7 *eighths* and 5 *ones* and 1 *half* results in 1 *ten* and 3 *eighths*. This work using a numeral-unit-name chart and an open number line is shown in figure 4.8.

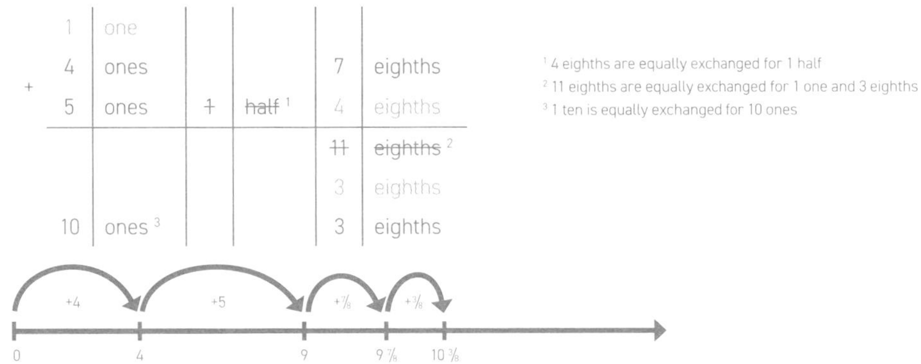

Figure 4.8: Using a numeral-unit-name chart and an open number line to model solving $4\frac{7}{8} + 5\frac{1}{2}$.

The purpose of sharing these three different addition problems is to show that with fractions, the quantity needed to make an equal exchange from a nondecimal fractional size of unit (for example, eighths and twelfths) depends on the size of the unit. This is unlike decimal size of units, in which the equal exchange *always* happens at a quantity of 10 of the size of the unit.

Using numeral-unit-name notation and fraction-as-measure bars (see figure 4.7, page 82), show and explain, taking note of equal exchanges, the process to solve the problem $\frac{5}{8} + \frac{1}{2}$.

What is the whole-number addition problem that is analogous to this problem?

Using numeral-unit-name notation and an open number line, show and explain, taking note of equal exchanges, the process to solve the problem 3 ⅔ + 4 ⅚.

Adding Decimals

As mentioned in chapter 3 (page 47), decimals are fractions in disguise. The connector understanding for addition still applies. Consider the problem 0.45 + 0.783—one that could also be represented as fractions, 45⁄100 + 783⁄1000, or, emphasizing the size of the unit, 45 *hundredths* + 783 *thousands*. We adult educators were taught a trick, "line up the decimals," without maybe ever being told why. What's funny is that the why is the same as it is for adding whole numbers and fractions. That is, the action of "lining up the decimals," like "getting a common denominator," is about ensuring that the quantities being combined have the same size of unit. The process of adding decimals is the same as adding whole numbers. Technically speaking, whole numbers are decimals, a point (pun intended!) that was discussed in chapter 2 (page 31). The only difference is that with decimals, the size of the units, those to the right of the decimal place, are less than one. For example, units in the decimal addition problem 0.45 + 0.783 are tenths, hundredths, and thousandths. The work to solve the decimal problem 0.45 + 0.783 is shown in figure 4.9.

	1	one	1	tenth				
+			4	tenths	5	hundredths		
			7	tenths	8	hundredths	3	thousandths
			~~12~~	~~tenths~~	~~13~~	~~hundredths~~		
	1	one	2	tenths	3	hundredths	3	thousandths

Figure 4.9: Using a numeral-unit-name chart to solve 0.45 + 0.783.

Leveraging the Properties of Addition

Remember how we need to be mindful about the language we choose to communicate mathematics concepts to the students first learning them? It's because of the distinction between our adult language and the language most appropriate and meaningful for students that I deliberately hold off on using formal mathematical terms, such as *commutativity* and *associativity*, to describe properties of addition. These ideas are better understood, at least initially, when students are given the opportunity to make sense of what these properties afford using language that clearly communicates this. In the case of these two properties, that language is *reordering* (commutativity) and *regrouping* (associativity). Let's briefly discuss each of these properties in the context of earlier problems. Is there any difference between combining 6 tens and 9 ones and 2 tens and 6 ones (69 + 26) and combining 2 tens and 6 ones and 6 tens and 9 ones (26 + 69)? If you answered no, you are correct. We are merely *reordering* parts while maintaining the same whole (**26 + 69** = 95 and **69 + 26** = 95). That's an example of the *commutative property of addition*. Let's continue to focus on that same problem, 69 (part 1) + 26 (part 2), but using a slightly different strategy. We can break up part 2, 26, into two subparts, 1 and 25. Then, using parentheses to denote, we can *regroup* the 1 with the 69 to create a "new" part 1 (70). This regrouping results in two parts, 70 and 25, that are much easier to mentally combine. These actions are shown symbolically as 69 + 26 = 69 + (1 + 25) = (69 + 1) + 25 = 70 + 25 = 95. This is an example of the application of the *associative property of addition*. While those more formal terms can wait until algebra, we can still help students "see" and "say" these properties in meaningful ways in elementary mathematics.

Making the Connection: Addition in Arithmetic and Algebra

I am not going to spend time in each chapter making connections between arithmetic and algebra concepts, which is beyond the scope of this book, but I want to do it once to show you how the ideas in this chapter bind together in a way that supports students' future algebraic thinking. A conceptually consistent approach involves introducing ideas in a way that doesn't lose value as students move from arithmetic to algebra. For example, the understanding that underpins addition of numbers—only quantities of the same size of unit can be combined—also applies to algebraic expressions. That is why 7 of some unit and 5 of the same unit is equal to 12 of that same unit regardless of whether the unit is a physical object, a unit fraction, or an algebraic expression. This idea is exemplified in the following range of addition problems that involve combining a quantity of 7 and 5 of various numerical and algebraic units.

7 oranges + 5 oranges = 12 oranges

$\frac{7}{3} + \frac{5}{3}$ = 7 thirds + 5 thirds = 12 thirds

0.7 + 0.5 = 7 tenths + 5 tenths = 12 tenths

$7x + 5x = 12x$

$7(\frac{1}{x}) + 5(\frac{1}{x}) = 12(\frac{1}{x})$

Figure 4.10: Range of addition problems.

Walking into the first day of college mathematics classes, many of my students are unsure whether the algebraic expression $x + x$ is an equal exchange for x^2 or $2x$. Let x represent an unknown length, or a size of unit. Combining 1 unit of x and 1 unit of x results in 2 units of x. Likewise, the algebraic quantities $2x^2$ and $3x^2$ can be combined to form $5x^2$ because 2 units of x^2 and 3 units of x^2 are 5 units of x^2 or $5x^2$. The algebraic expressions $2x^2$ and $3x$, however, cannot be combined because 2 units of x^2 and 3 units of x do not involve quantities of the same unit. Unlike numerical quantities, units of algebraic quantities cannot be transformed using equal exchanges to create units that enable the quantities to be combined. That's enough algebra!

PAUSE AND PONDER

Take a moment to reflect on what you've learned in this chapter about addition.

As a result of reading this chapter, what changes or modifications to your instructional practices related to teaching addition will you make?

A parent or administrator wants to know why you're using the numeral-unit-name notation as part of your instructional practices. What are the key points that will best communicate your position?

Key Points

Before proceeding, please take a moment to review the following takeaways from this chapter.

- The understanding that underpins all addition is that quantities of sizes of units can only be combined when the size of the units is the same. This holds from whole-number numerical expressions through different types of algebraic expressions.
- Equal exchanges are a superpower understanding that is utilized throughout addition. There are two different types that occur depending on whether the number has decimal sizes of units. With decimal sizes of units, the equal exchange occurs with 10 of a particular size of a unit. For example, combining 9 tens and 5 tens results in 14 tens. The 14 tens can be recomposed into 1 hundred and 4 tens by equally exchanging 10 tens for 1 hundred. This idea is slightly different with fractions (except for tenths). The recomposing action depends on the size of the unit represented in the fraction. For example, if the size of the unit is thirds, then the recomposing action into 1 whole unit happens at 3 thirds. In other words, 3 thirds are equally exchanged for 1 whole. If the size of the unit is fourths, then the recomposing action happens at 4 fourths. If it is eighths, then recomposing action happens at 8 eighths.
- The why behind actions we commonly associate with adding fractions, "getting a common denominator," and decimals, "lining up the decimals," is underpinned by the connector understanding of addition.
- The ability to see and create analogous problems is a superpower understanding. Analogous problems are those that involve the same actions to solve, but on different sizes of units. For example, 69 + 27 is an analogous problem to 690 + 270 and 0.69 + 0.27 and 0.069 + 0.027. In each problem, the combined quantities are the same: (6 + 2 = 8) and (9 + 7 = 16). The only difference is the size of the unit that these quantities (8 and 16) represent.

The key points of Chapter 4 focus attention on giving students an efficient and transferable way to communicate the actions involved in adding different types of numbers. They also focus students' attention on "seeing" connections between problems with the same quantities, but different sizes of units. The suggestions in the application guide are provided to help you reflect on how you can incorporate these ideas into your own classroom.

Chapter 4 Application Guide

Chapter Concepts	How Can I Incorporate This Into My Teaching Practice Moving Forward?
Numeral-Unit-Name Notation	Write addition problems using this notation to illuminate the size of the unit and connect solving whole-number, decimal, and fraction addition problems.
Analogous Problems	Provide students with sets of analogous addition problems so they see the same actions on the same quantities, but on different sizes of units. Once students are familiar with the idea, have them generate these types of addition problems.
Part-Part-Whole Relationships	Provide students with opportunities to mentally decompose and compose parts to make addition problems mentally easier to solve. For example, the addition problem 98 + 37 can be transformed into 100 + 35 by moving 2 units of one from 37 (37 − 2 = 35) to 98 (98 + 2 = 100). This is a great opportunity to engage them in a number talk.

Your net worth to the world
is usually determined by
what remains after
your bad habits are subtracted
from your good ones.

—Benjamin Franklin

CHAPTER 5

Subtraction

In this chapter, we explore a conceptually consistent approach to understanding subtraction of whole numbers, fractions, and decimals. As with addition, those early number part-part-whole relationships will be helpful. The leap from chapter 4 (page 73) to chapter 5 should be short because we're utilizing many of the same ideas: As addition is a combining action, bringing together two or more parts to form a whole, subtraction is the counteraction, removing a known part from the whole to determine the remaining unknown part. That is, *subtraction* is the pulling apart or separating action of the whole into two parts, a part to remove from the whole and a remaining part. The overarching understanding that unifies subtraction of any type of number is similar to the one for addition, with one more caveat—*a quantity can only be removed from a quantity of the same size of unit*, and *there must be enough of the quantity of that unit in the whole to perform the removing action* (for example, 8 *tens* – 5 *tens* = 3 *tens*).

A major difference between the two operations is that with addition, we create equal exchanges to *recompose* 10 of a size of a unit into 1 of the next greater size of unit (for example, 1 *ten* for 10 *ones*). However, with subtraction, we create equal exchanges to *decompose* 1 of a size of unit into 10 of the next lesser size of unit (for example, 10 *ones* for *1 ten*). The difference in these actions is illustrated in figure 5.1 (page 92).

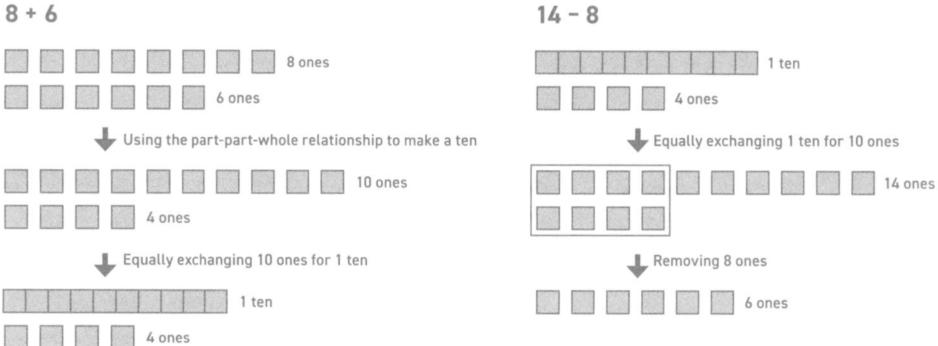

Figure 5.1: Recomposing a size of unit to add and decomposing a size of unit to subtract.

I know that among adult educators, who, like myself, began learning mathematics concepts many years ago, sometimes there's an internal struggle to buy into the employment of specific terms for these "recomposing" and "decomposing" actions, or to offer instruction that lingers on these matters. This is especially true with easier problems because the actions themselves are automatic in our minds. I can hear some saying, "There's no need for all of this! It is just 14 – 8, which is 6. There is no difference between 14 ones and 1 ten and 4 ones! You're making it harder on students by doing this."

I understand that response! I really do! But I've also witnessed firsthand the number of preservice teachers, developmental mathematics students, and middle school students who struggle to make meaningful sense of what we ask them to do. My hope is every student will develop a dynamic understanding of numbers and have great flexibility in reasoning about the problems we place before them. As a teacher, consider the possibilities of what might happen if you take your own students down the path of "you're just making it harder." First, I urge you to reflect with a growth mindset on the students in your own classroom and identify those students who might benefit the most from what I'm sharing. Which students do you see struggling to stay in the mathematics game? What if they just need a different way to tap into their mathematical superpowers?

Much of what we will discuss in this chapter will involve revisiting topics (that is equal exchanges and analogous problems), but with an "eye" toward subtraction. We will reflect upon the language that we commonly use to teach subtraction and learn alternative language that connects with what we have already discussed related to addition. We will also revisit the importance of making the size of the unit explicit and explore strategies that will help students mentally reason about subtraction problems.

Shifting the Language of Subtraction From Procedural to Conceptual

Let's begin by considering a two-digit subtraction problem, 53 – 38.

PAUSE AND PONDER

Take a moment to reflect on the language you would traditionally use to explain to someone else how to solve 53 – 38.

Now try to use the language of quantities and size of unit that we learned with addition to explain solving the same problem.

You might normally explain to someone else how to solve this problem by saying something like "Borrow 1 from the 5, change the 5 to a 4, subtract 8 from 13, bring down the 5, subtract 3 from 4, and bring down the 1, which gives an answer of 15."

Now let's think about the same problem in terms of quantities and sizes of unit. Recall that the action of addition involves combining two parts to create a whole. Subtraction, on the other hand, involves removing a known part from the whole to determine an unknown part. With addition we could only combine quantities of the same size of unit. Similarly, with subtraction we can only remove quantities of the same size of unit.

In the problem 53 – 38 the first number, 53, represents the whole, and the second number, 38, represents the known part, or the part to be removed from the whole. Solving a subtraction problem answers the question, What is the remaining part? There are other possible questions—for example, How much more is one number than the other number? or How much does the other part have to be to create the whole?—but for the sake of consistency, I'm going to focus on the question I posed.

The whole (53) consists of quantities of two different sizes of units, 5 *tens* and 3 *ones*, as does the part to be removed (38), 3 *tens* and 8 *ones*. Working from right (least-sized unit) to left (greatest-sized unit), a part of 8 *ones* is to be removed from the whole of 3 *ones*. The problem is that there aren't enough units of *one* in the whole (3) to remove the necessary quantity (8). However, there are 5 *tens* in the whole, which we can use to create enough units of *one* to perform the action of removing 8 units of one from the whole. Using an equal exchange, 1 of those 5 *tens* can be decomposed into 10 *ones*. This changes the whole from 5 *tens* and 3 *ones* to 4 *tens* and 13 *ones*. Now there are enough units of *one* in the whole to remove the required part (13 *ones* – 8 *ones* = 5 *ones*). Moving to the next size of unit, the whole now consists of 4 tens, and the required part to be removed is 3 tens. This action can be completed since there are enough units of *ten* in the whole (4 *tens* – 3 *ten* = 1 *ten*). These actions answer the implied question of a subtraction problem—the remaining part after removing 3 *tens* and 8 *ones* from a whole of 5 *tens* and 3 *ones* is 1 *ten* and 5 *ones* (53 – 38 = 15). This work is represented in figure 5.2 using both traditional and numeral-unit-name notations. The contrast between traditional-algorithm-focused language and size-of-unit-illuminating conceptual language is also shared.

	4	1
	~~5~~	3
–	3	8
	1	5

	4 tens	13 ones	
	~~5 tens~~	~~3 ones~~	1 ten decomposed into 10 ones
–	3 tens	8 ones	
	1 ten	5 ones	

	Traditional Language	Size-of-Unit-Illuminating Language
1	Borrow 1 from the 5	Decompose 1 ten into 10 ones (equal exchange)
2	Change the 5 to a 4	5 tens and 3 ones is now represented as 4 tens and 13 ones
3	Subtract 8 from 13	13 ones – 8 ones = 5 ones
4	Bring down the 5	Record 5 ones
5	Subtract 3 from 4	4 tens – 3 tens = 1 ten
6	Bring down the 1	Record 1 ten

Figure 5.2: Thinking of subtraction in terms of the quantity and size of unit.

Reflect on how you would communicate solving the problem 64 − 38 using the size-of-unit-illuminating language from the previous example.

Repeat this process for the problem 123 − 78.

If appropriate, ask your students to solve these same problems (note: you may choose to add context) communicating the why behind their actions. Reflect on the nature of their understandings and how they "see" and "say" subtraction.

It is important to re-emphasize a key point mentioned earlier. The way that subtraction is organized in curricula and taught often leads students to believe that there are *different rules* for subtracting whole numbers, fractions (that is, get a common denominator), and decimals (that is, line up the decimals), when in fact these rules are based on the same idea—the need for the same size of units!

To illustrate this point, let's consider a decimal subtraction problem that involves the same actions as solving 53 − 38, but with different sizes of units, 0.53 − 0.38. As shown in figure 5.3, the actions on quantities are the same. The only difference is the size of the units. These two problems exemplify analogous subtraction problems.

4	1	4 tens	13 ones	
~~5~~	3	~~5 tens~~	~~3 ones~~	1 ten decomposed into 10 ones
− 3	8	− 3 tens	8 ones	
1	5	1 ten	5 ones	

4	1	4 tenths	13 hundredths	
.~~5~~	3	~~5 tenths~~	~~3 hundredths~~	1 tenth decomposed into 10 hundredths
− .3	8	− 3 tenths	8 hundredths	
.1	5	1 tenth	5 hundredths	

Figure 5.3: Two analogous subtraction problems.

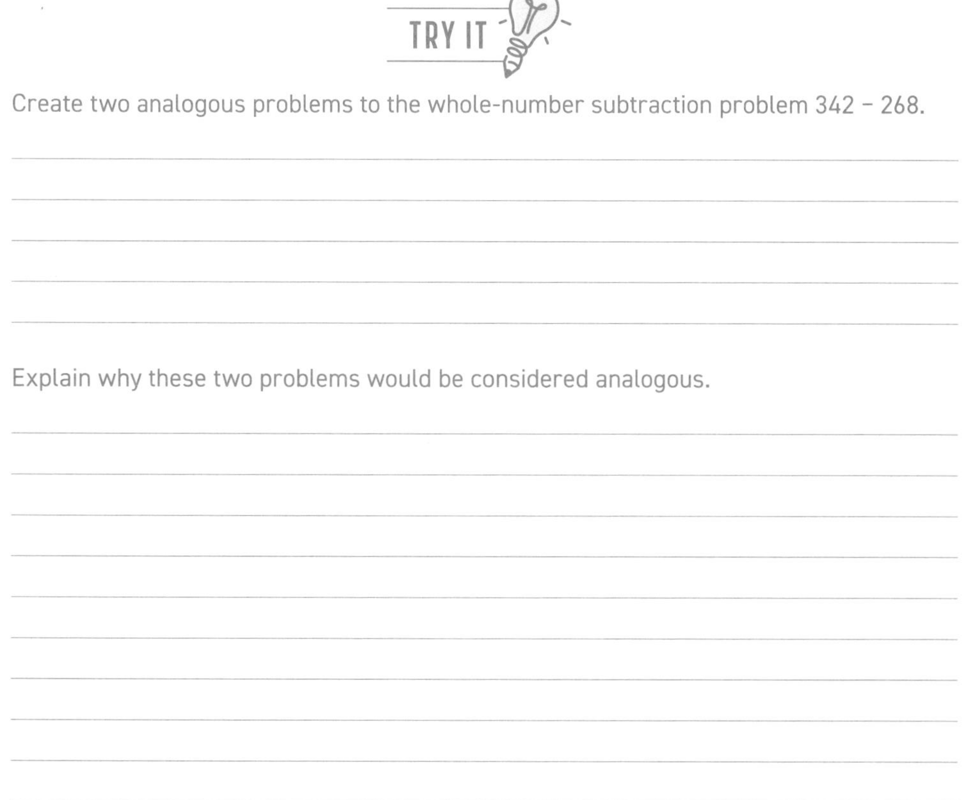

TRY IT
Create two analogous problems to the whole-number subtraction problem 342 − 268.
Explain why these two problems would be considered analogous.

Subtracting whole numbers, fractions, and decimals involves the same idea—*removing quantities of the same unit (part to be removed) from the whole to determine a remaining part.* All we need to do is make sure the sizes of the units are the same and remove quantities of the same sizes of units from the whole. To further illuminate this idea, consider two subtraction problems involving fractions: (1) $\frac{7}{8} - \frac{3}{8}$ and (2) $\frac{7}{8} - \frac{1}{4}$. Take a moment to reflect on the language you would use to explain to someone else how to solve each problem.

As shown in figure 5.4, in the first problem, $\frac{7}{8} - \frac{3}{8}$, the whole and the part to be removed have the same size of unit, *eighths*, and there are enough of the quantity in the whole (7) to remove the part (3).

$\frac{7}{8} - \frac{3}{8}$

	7	eighths
−	3	eighths
	4	eighths

$\frac{7}{8} - \frac{1}{4}$

	7	eighths		
−	2	eighths	+	~~fourth~~
	5	eighths		

Figure 5.4: Using numeral-unit-name chart to subtract fractions.

The remaining part is 4 *eighths*. The actions to solve $\frac{7}{8} - \frac{3}{8}$ are the same as the actions to solve the problems 7 − 3, 0.7 − 0.3, and $\frac{7}{4} - \frac{3}{4}$. In each instance, you're removing a quantity from the whole (3) that has the same unit as the whole. The only difference is the size of the unit (that is, *ones*, *tenths*, and *fourths*), which doesn't impact the action on the quantities. Once again, we have analogous subtraction problems.

In the second problem, $\frac{7}{8} - \frac{1}{4}$, the whole and the part to be removed don't have the same size of unit. Once again, as has been the case many times before, equal exchanges to the rescue! The part to be removed, 1 *fourth*, can be equally exchanged for 2 *eighths*. Now the whole and the part to be removed have the same size of unit. The original problem 7 *eighths* − 1 *fourth* is now 7 *eighths* − 2 *eighths*. The subtracting action can now be performed.

The same idea holds when you're subtracting a fraction from a mixed number. Figure 5.5 shows an example of solving this type of problem, $1\frac{1}{4} - \frac{1}{3}$, using a numeral-unit-name chart and a bar–number line. It's all about obtaining same-size units.

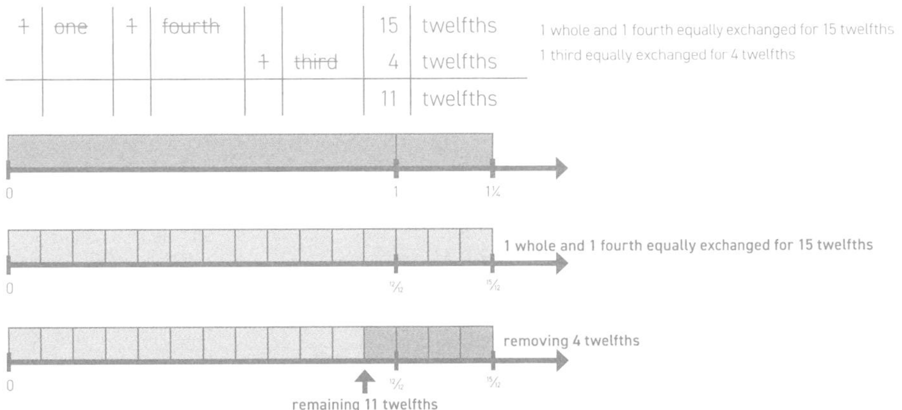

Figure 5.5: Modeling the solution to problem $1\frac{1}{4} - \frac{1}{3}$.

The actions involved in solving subtraction problems involving decimals are like those involving fractions. They both involve the use of our equal exchange superpowers.

PAUSE AND PONDER

Use what you've learned to reflect on what you would say to solve the problem 3 − 1.473, making sure the quantities and sizes of units are explicit.

Solving this problem involves three equal exchanges. What are they?

As shown in figure 5.6, solving 3 − 1.473 requires multiple equal exchanges. In this problem, three of them can be shown individually or all at once.

					9	hundredths	10	thousandths
			9	tenths	~~10~~	~~hundredths~~		
	2	ones	~~10~~	~~tenths~~				
	~~3~~	~~ones~~						
−	1	one	4	tenths	7	hundredths	3	thousandths
	1	one	5	tenths	2	hundredths	7	thousandths

10 thousandths are exchanged for 1 hundredth
10 hundredths are exchanged for 1 tenth
10 tenths are exchanged for 1 one

Figure 5.6: Using equal exchanges to solve 3 − 1.473.

PAUSE AND PONDER

After reading this part of the chapter, what is one idea that you're excited to implement in your classroom?

What would you say to administrators or parents as to why you're implementing this idea?

What is the language that you'll need to introduce to students to help them make sense of this instructional shift?

As I mentioned in chapter 4 (page 73), estimation is a powerful tool to develop in the minds of students before introducing strategies that obtain an exact answer. For example, simply asking students whether the answer to the whole-number subtraction problem 123 – 78 will be less than 50 or greater than 50 or whether the fraction subtraction problem 1 ¼ – ⅞ will have an answer less than or greater than 6/8 will begin to help them "see" relationships between numbers in ways that they may have never considered. We have the technology that will quickly give us answers. What we want to develop is their ability to reason about the relationship between numbers. Asking students to estimate an answer is a great way to engage them in this type of reasoning.

Developing a Dynamic Understanding of Subtraction

A dynamic understanding of subtraction involves more than obtaining correct answers. It's about seeing possibilities for how problems can be adjusted to be more easily computed mentally. Seeing possibilities with subtraction problems requires students to have proficiency using three lenses: (1) transforming given problems into other problems that can more easily be mentally solved, (2) leveraging what is already known about the related operation of addition, and (3) decomposing actions involving equal exchanges. We'll spend some time examining how each of these lenses lends itself to the development of a dynamic view of subtraction that supports mental arithmetic superpowers.

USING THE COMPENSATION METHOD

With subtraction, adjusting a problem requires something different than it did with addition. Remember with addition we could move a quantity of a unit from one part to another part while keeping the whole the same (for example, 69 + 27 = (69 **+ 1**) + (27 – **1**) = 70 + 26 = 96). With subtraction, we need a strategy that keeps the remaining part the same. The strategy that keeps the remaining part, or unknown part, the same while adjusting the whole and part to be removed is called *compensation*. Let's think about this strategy using a problem we discussed earlier, 53 – 38. The whole is 53, and the part to be removed is 38. Adding 2 units of one to both the whole and the part to be removed results in a new whole (55) and a new part to be removed (40), which yields the same remaining part (15). In other words, the subtraction problems 53 – 38 and 55 – 40 have the same answer. Why does the compensation strategy work? As shown in figure 5.7, using a number line, the why is that the difference between the whole and the remaining part remains the same.

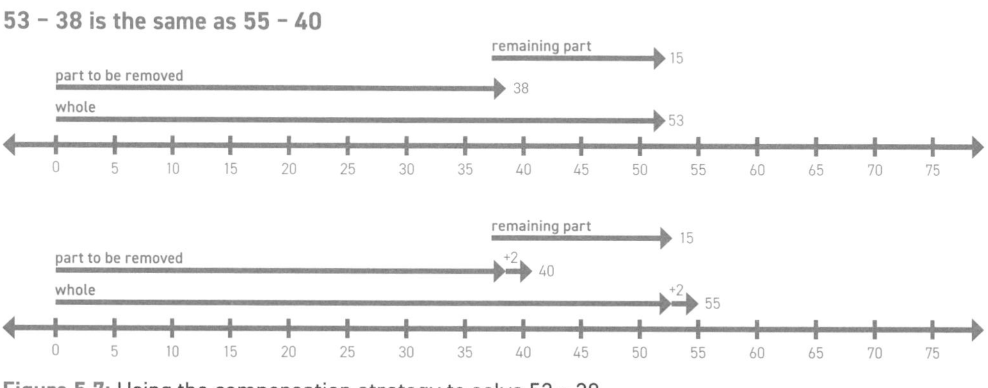

Figure 5.7: Using the compensation strategy to solve 53 – 38.

Take a moment to think about how you would use the compensation strategy to mentally compute 62 − 19 and 62 − 24. How about 201 − 99?

Create three subtraction problems in which the compensation strategy would be a great strategy for solving the problem mentally.

LEVERAGING ADDITION

Another mental subtraction strategy that leverages our understanding of addition to solve a subtraction problem is *counting up*. Remember that addition is about combining parts to create a whole while subtraction is about removing a known part from the whole to determine the other unknown part. Consider the subtraction problem 53 – 38 once again. We have a known part (38) and a whole (53), so we can *count up* from the known part (38) to determine the unknown part to reach the whole (53). For example, as shown in figure 5.8, starting with the known part 38, 2 more would be 40, 10 more would be 50, and 3 more would be 53. This means the unknown part is 2 + 10 + 3, or 15.

Figure 5.8: Using the compensation method to solve 53 − 38.

A moment ago, you thought about how you'd use the compensation strategy to mentally compute 62 − 19 and 62 − 24, then 201 − 99.

Now take a moment to think about how you would use the counting-up strategy to solve those problems.

Create three subtraction problems in which counting up would be a great strategy for solving the problem mentally.

One more thing about the counting-up strategy. We use it all the time when we count back change! What's funny is that when I talk to adults about the mathematics students are learning, they often bring up that "kids these days can't count back change!" It's a persistent generational argument. But aside from the fact that most people use credit or debit cards, and some establishments no longer accept cash, there is one fundamental reason why many young adults can't count back change. Ready for this? The strategy to count back change isn't the strategy students are shown in school to perform subtraction. Most of us learned the "take away" strategy, removing a part from the whole to find the remaining part, to perform subtraction. Counting back change often requires a counting-up strategy—that is, starting with the known part and counting up to determine the unknown part to reach the whole.

Hear me out! Suppose that you're working at a store and someone hands you a $10 bill for an item that costs $9.32. How are you going to determine how much change to give? Before reading on, take a moment and reflect on how you would do this. Take another moment to record your mental work.

I could see some people doing something similar to what is shown in figure 5.9—adding 3 cents to $9.32 ($9.35), maybe adding another 5 cents ($9.40), another 10 cents ($9.50), another 25 cents ($9.75), and another 25 cents ($10.00) and handing the person 3 pennies, a nickel, a dime, and two quarters (that is, 68 cents). As you can see, recording the counting-up strategy requires more physical space than the standard subtraction algorithm, but it's much easier to see, and it's what we often use in real-life situations.

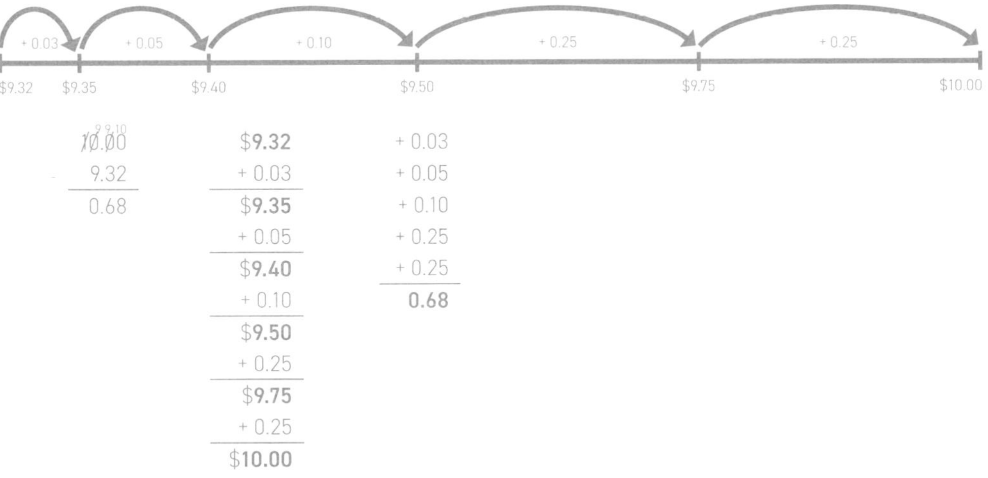

Figure 5.9: Using the counting-up strategy to count back change.

I'm certain that you did not, when counting back change, use the standard subtraction algorithm shown on the left side of figure 5.9—crossing out the 10 units, subtracting, crossing out the 0, making it a 9, subtracting, crossing out the 0, and making it a 10. But that's the subtraction procedure many students will learn! This strategy doesn't align with what we do when we count back change. Why not give our students a mental subtraction superpower that does and will end the discussion around students and young adults not being able to count back change?

Yes, the written record of the mental work is longer than the traditional strategy, but it's consistent with what's done when counting back change. In this strategy, we started with the part to be removed ($9.32) and added up to the whole ($10.00) to find the remaining part ($0.68). See! Now that's a real-world problem that can be solved quickly and efficiently!

Introducing subtraction as a relationship between the whole and parts is conceptually connected to addition because, in addition, the two parts are known and the goal is to find the whole. Meanwhile, in subtraction, the whole and a part are given, and the goal is to find the other part. As the counting change example illustrates, sometimes it is easier to think about subtraction in terms of addition. Often, by using our adult brains to teach, instead of thinking of our students' brains to learn, this connection may not be made explicit. It is important that we give students opportunities to think about subtraction in the ways that they might use these ideas in the real world.

SEEING FLEXIBILITY WITH EQUAL EXCHANGES

To see how flexibility with equal exchanges is a powerful tool for unleashing students' mental arithmetic superpowers, let's consider the subtraction problem 2,003 – 197. This problem could just as easily be solved with either of the two strategies we have already discussed, compensation (that is, [2,003 + **3**] – [197 + **3**] = 2,006 – 200 = **1,806**) or counting up (that is, 197 + **3** = 200; 200 + **1,800** = 2,000; 2,000 + **3** = 2,003). There is, however, a third option. As shown in figure 5.10, instead of creating multiple equal exchanges to solve the problem, we can strategically create one equal exchange that enables us to perform all the subtracting of quantities in one step.

1	thousand	9	hundreds	9	tens	13	ones
~~2~~	~~thousands~~	~~0~~	~~hundreds~~	~~0~~	~~tens~~	~~3~~	~~ones~~
		1	hundred	9	tens	7	ones
1	**thousand**	**8**	**hundreds**	**0**	**tens**	**6**	**ones**

1 thousand is equally exchanged for 9 hundreds, 9 tens, and 10 ones.

Figure 5.10: Strategically using an equal exchange to solve 2,003 – 197.

In this instance, 1 *thousand* is equally exchanged for 9 *hundreds*, 9 *tens*, and 10 *ones*. We have essentially decomposed the whole of 2,003 into two parts, 1,990 and 13. Seeing the parts to be removed as 190 and 7, we can mentally remove the necessary quantities, 1,990 – 190 = 1,800 and 13 – 7 = 6, to determine the remaining part, 1,800 + 6 = 1,806. Oh, the power students have when they can do this type of thinking!

Take a moment to think about how you would use the three different lenses to mentally compute the subtraction problem 3,008 − 296.

Create two subtraction problems that lend themselves to using one or more of these strategies to mentally solve.

Choose one of these problems to engage your students in a number talk. This should shed light on what students are seeing in relationship to subtraction.

Throughout this chapter, the goal has been to share a conceptually consistent approach to subtraction. Seeing this conceptually consistent approach has involved some of the same superpower understandings as addition. These include seeing numbers in terms of quantities of sizes of units and equal exchanges and making connections between actions on analogous problems.

PAUSE AND PONDER

What are one or two ideas from this chapter that resonated with you? Reflect on why.

After reading this chapter, what are one or two instructional shifts that you are planning to make in how you teach subtraction?

Key Points

Before proceeding, please take a moment to review the following takeaways from this chapter.

- One way to interpret a subtraction problem is in terms of a whole, a part to be removed, and a remaining part. For example, in the problem 53 - 39, the number 53 represents the whole, and the number 39 represents the part to be removed from the whole. The implied question in a subtraction problem is, What is the remaining part?
- The connector understanding of subtraction is the same as addition. To perform the action of subtraction, the quantities must have the same size of unit.
- Subtracting, like adding, some quantities of units may require an equal exchange before the action can occur. Unlike addition, which involves recomposing, subtraction involves decomposing 1 of a greater size of unit into 10 of the next lesser size of unit. For example, to solve the problem 53 - 39, 1 ten in the whole (5 tens and 3 ones) is decomposed into 10 ones (4 tens and 13 ones) so that the necessary quantities of each size of unit in the part (3 tens and 9 ones) can be removed. That is, 9 ones can be removed from 13 ones (13 - 9 = 4) and 3 tens can be removed from 4 tens (4 - 3 = 1), which results in a remaining part of 1 ten and 4 ones (14).
- Compensation and counting on are mental arithmetic strategies that can be used to solve subtraction problems. For example, the compensation strategy involves changing the whole and part to be removed by the same quantity. For example, consider the problem 66 - 38. By adding 2 to both the whole (66 + 2 = 68) and the part to be removed (38 + 2 = 40), a mentally easier problem to solve is created, 68 - 40, that has the same remaining part. On a number line, this is represented by the distances between the part to be removed and the whole remaining the same.

The key points in chapter 5 emphasize the ideas necessary for students to "see" subtraction in terms of quantities of units and "say" subtraction using conceptual, not procedural, language. Several strategies are also shared that help students develop a flexible and dynamic understanding of subtraction. The application guide provides you with ideas to support you in engaging your students in the reasoning necessary to develop these understandings.

Chapter 5 Application Guide

Chapter Concepts	How Can I Incorporate This Into My Teaching Practice Moving Forward?
Language of Subtraction	Model the use of conceptual language (that is, "whole," "part to be removed," "remaining part") to interpret a subtraction problem and the actions involved in seeing a problem. Continue to use numeral-unit-name notation and emphasize the derivation of our understanding that we can only break apart quantities of the same size of unit from the whole.
Equal Exchanges	Make the instances in which an equal exchange is needed explicit, and press students to state the nature of the equal exchange they used to solve the problem. Physically demonstrate these actions with base 10 blocks and have them record the problem using unit-number-name notation.
Analogous Problems	Once students are familiar with what makes a subtraction problem analogous to another problem, ask them to generate their own problems.
Compensation and Counting Up	Introduce these strategies to students and focus their attention on seeing when they are appropriate strategies to mentally compute subtraction problems.

There comes a point
where we need to stop
just pulling people out of the river.
We need to go upstream
and find out why they are falling in.

—Bishop Desmond Tutu

CHAPTER 6

Multiplication

As you may have gathered from the book's introduction (page 1), there is no topic more personal to me than multiplication. Despite my automaticity with single-digit multiplication facts, I struggled mightily with two-digit multiplication. Remember from chapter 3 (page 47) the statement I like to ask adult learners to complete: "I stopped liking mathematics when . . . ." While the majority convey that fractions did them in, many others convey their experience with mathematics changed when they encountered challenges in learning their multiplication facts. "I just could never learn them!" is a refrain I often hear from my college students.

Though I primarily teach adult learners, I have frequently had the opportunity to work with a few fourth- and fifth-grade students who were struggling with their multiplication facts. All their parents indicated that they had been taught predominantly with flash cards without pictorial representations and sets of multiplication fact sheets. There were two moments in these interactions that shed light on the challenges many students face learning their multiplication facts. The first moment was when I wrote the multiplication problem 3×9 on paper and asked a student how they thought about solving the problem. They indicated they knew that "two times nine was eighteen," and then I watched as they counted on by ones to determine the answer, "nineteen, twenty, twenty-one . . . twenty-six, twenty-seven." The second moment was when I asked another student to compute 6×20

after they had already told me that the answer to 6×2 was "twelve" because "six plus six is twelve." This student had already told me she had a "trick for multiplying by eleven" so she wrote $6 \times 11 = 66$ on paper and started to count on by ones, while keeping track of groups of six, but stopped because "it was going to take a long time." These interactions speak to the complexity of the challenges that students face in learning multiplication. I will return to these interactions later in the chapter to illuminate important aspects of developing a dynamic understanding of multiplication.

In this chapter, we'll take a deep dive into multiplication. As with the earlier operations, I intend to share ideas and tools that will help you develop a dynamic understanding of multiplication in your students. Along the way, I'll share a rationale for the choice of representations and how each supports specific understandings of multiplication. When I think about teaching multiplication, I reflect on two specific questions: (1) "What can I do to get the biggest bang for the use of that time?" and (2) "What meaningful connections do I want students to make along the way?" Addressing these questions involves providing opportunities for students to "see" and say important multiplicative ideas (factors and multiples) while also leveraging the power of properties of multiplication (associativity, commutativity, and distributivity) before the students are formally introduced to them in algebra. We'll begin this chapter with single-digit multiplication and the concept of unit coordination before discussing multiplication facts, multiplication beyond a single digit, and analogous problems in multiplication. Then, we'll dive into more complex multidigit multiplication, the utility of halving and doubling, multiplication involving fractions, more analogous problems, multiplication involving decimals, and some final thoughts to consider as we move forward.

Entering Into Single-Digit Multiplication

Let's start by taking a moment to reflect on our own experience learning multiplication facts. Suppose that the flash card shown in figure 6.1 is placed before you.

Figure 6.1: The mathematics problem.

Write down what you see as well as the language associated with what you are seeing.

PAUSE AND PONDER

Think about what a student might see the first time they are shown a multiplication fact written in this form.

Think about how they must see the numerals 6 and 8 to understand multiplication and compare how this is different from how they saw the same numerals to understand addition (6 + 8).

Understanding multiplication dynamically requires a significant conceptual leap for a multitude of reasons that we will explore. Whether students learn multiplication by memorizing flash cards or other means, they're still trying to make sense as to why 6 × 8 equals 48. As we know from brain research, students are more likely to retain what they learn if it makes sense, has meaning, and is connected to other ideas (Sousa, 2016). With this goal in mind, as we've done in previous chapters, we're going to look at multiplication while ensuring that we attend to the elements of our see it–say it–symbolize it approach. Research shows that visual representations (for example, arrays) have been an effective tool in helping students master their multiplication facts while also developing a dynamic understanding of multiplication (Barmby, Harries, Higgins, & Suggate, 2009; Dubé & Robinson, 2018; Milton, Flores, Moore, Taylor, & Burton, 2019; Pape & Tchoshanov, 2001) The key to using any representation is ensuring that the understandings that underpin this dynamic understanding are made explicit. One of those understandings is unit coordination.

Connecting the Dots With Unit Coordination

Throughout this book, I've stressed the importance of seeing numbers in terms of quantities and sizes of units—the very first superpower understanding we covered. Using the unit name to represent the size of the unit is a conscious decision to help students understand the concept of equal exchanges (for example, 1 ten is the same as 10 ones) and the importance of part-part-whole relationships (for example, 6 ones and 4 ones is 10 ones). These understandings are part of a construct called *unit coordination*—the ability to create units and maintain their relationship with other units that they contain or constitute (Hackenberg et al., 2016; Steffe, 1994). Unit coordination is about how students construct, organize, and utilize units as they reason about problems (Hackenberg & Sevinc, 2024). In order for students to engage in unit coordination, they must be able to see units. In the context of multiplication, unit coordination involves not just knowing the multiplication fact (for example, 6 × 2 = 12) but recognizing that there are units embedded in this fact and that the fact itself can become a unit. Before digging further into unit coordination in multiplication, I want to take a moment to illustrate the advancement in unit coordination activity that's required to move from addition to multiplication using two problems involving the same numerals.

ADDITION

Consider the unit coordination needed to solve the problem 6 + 8. The unit in the problem is *one* (that is, 6 *ones* and 8 *ones*). As shown in figure 6.2, solving concretely using connectable blocks involves separating 6 *ones* into 2 *ones* and 4 *ones* (part-part-whole relationship) and recomposing 10 *ones* into 1 *ten* (equal exchange). There is a duality of meaning that students develop as they see 10 objects as separate individual units, 10 *ones*, or a different composed unit, 1 *ten*.

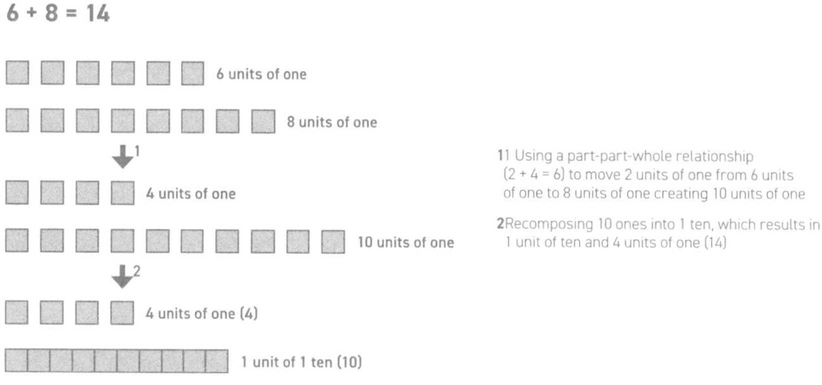
6 + 8 = 14
6 units of one
8 units of one
1
4 units of one
10 units of one
2
4 units of one (4)
1 unit of 1 ten (10)
1 Using a part-part-whole relationship (2 + 4 = 6) to move 2 units of one from 6 units of one to 8 units of one creating 10 units of one
2 Recomposing 10 ones into 1 ten, which results in 1 unit of ten and 4 units of one (14)

Figure 6.2: Contrasting unit coordination in addition and multiplication.

MULTIPLICATION

Before I discuss the unit coordination involved in multiplication, it's important to have a shared, student-friendly, conceptual language to discuss abstract multiplication problems like 6 × 8. For consistency throughout the book, the first numeral in a multiplication problem is the *multiplier*, and the second numeral is the *multiplicative unit* (Lannin, Chval, & Jones, 2013). The multiplier refers to the number of groups or scale factor, and the multiplicative unit refers to the size of the group. I'm also going to use the term *groups of* instead of the commonly used term *times*. For example, the multiplication problem 6 × 8 is interpreted as 6 groups of 8 *ones* or 6 groups of 1 *eight*. The numeral 6 represents the number of groups (multiplier), and the numeral 8 represents the size of the group (multiplicative unit). As I have done throughout the book, at least initially, I'm going to use the italicized unit name to illuminate the size of the unit.

The multiplication problem 6 × 8 involves a composite unit, 1 *eight*, that can be easily decomposed into a quantity of a decimal unit, 8 *ones*. Both can be utilized to create quantities of other composite units. Additively, the composite unit, 1 *eight*, or 8 *ones*, can be decomposed, using additive part-part-whole relationships, into unequal groups of the same unit (for example, 8 *ones* is the same as 5 *ones* and 3 *ones*) or equal groups of different composite units (for example, 1 unit of *five* and 1 unit of *three*). This same composite unit, 1 *eight*, can also be interpreted multiplicatively. That is, it can be decomposed using a multiplicative relationship into equal groups that involve a different composite unit (2 groups of *four*, 4 groups of *two*, or, as seen earlier, 8 groups of *one*), which themselves represent multiplicative relationships (2 × 4, 4 × 2, or 8 × 1, respectively). The distinction between seeing a set of objects in terms of an additive relationship and a multiplicative relationship is shown in figure 6.3.

Figure 6.3: Seeing an additive relationship versus seeing a multiplicative relationship.

Let's now explore from a unit coordination perspective what a student must navigate to make sense of the multiplication problem 6 × 8. Connectable physical blocks make this perspective most explicit. As stated previously, the multiplication problem 6 × 8 represents 6 groups of 1 *eight*. Moving forward I am going to use the unit name (for example, *eight*) to signify a quantity of 1 of that unit. The answers to whole-number multiplication problems are expressed in terms of decimal units (*tens* and *ones*), so to determine the whole, a transformation into decimal units is required. The only exception is when the composite unit is a decimal unit (for example, 5 × 10 is interpreted as 5 groups of *ten* or 5 *tens*). As shown in figure 6.4, to model solving the problem 6 groups of *eight*, 1 group of *eight* is strategically decomposed into 4 groups of *two*. The 4 groups of *two* are recomposed with 4 groups of *eight* to create the desired decimal composite unit, 4 groups of *ten*. The result is 4 groups of *ten* and 8 groups of *one* (utilizing the dual meaning of 1 group of *eight*). In summary, to determine the whole of 6 groups of *eight* (6 × 8) requires that 6 groups of the composite unit *eight* be transformed into two different decimal composite units, 4 groups of *ten* and 8 groups of *one* (48).

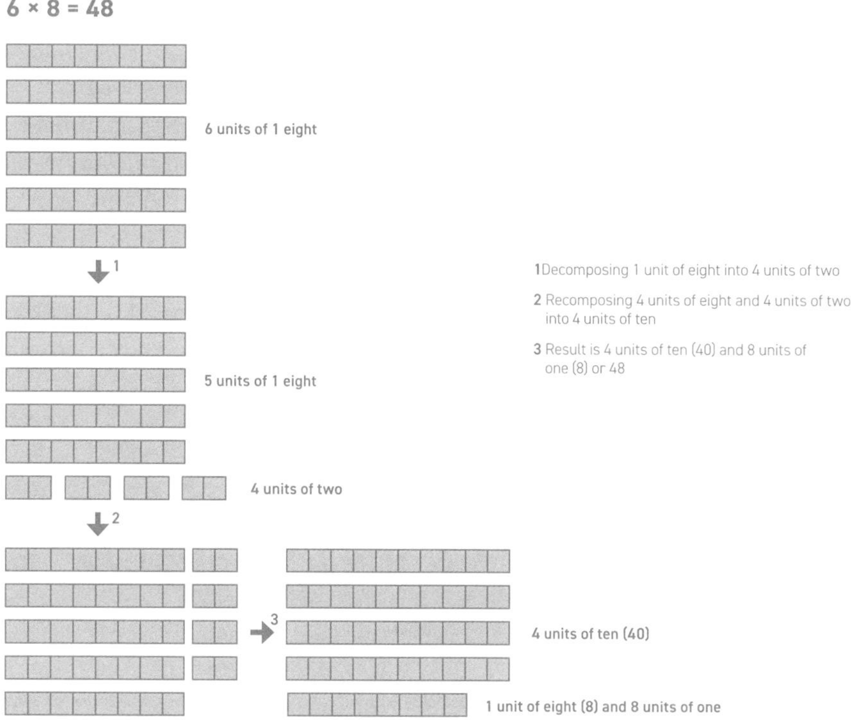

Figure 6.4: Seeing multiplication in terms of unit coordination.

Depending on our students' life experiences, they may come to us seeing multiple groups of a composed unit. For example, consider a game like Yahtzee®, which involves rolling multiple dice, as shown in figure 6.5.

Figure 6.5: Seeing multiplication in terms of addition of the same-size groups.

How a student determines the total number of dots on multiple dice will shed light on their readiness for seeing multiplicative relationships. This requires that they can subitize sets of objects. For example, in determining the whole of 2 groups of 6, do they see six and then count on (that is, "seven, eight, nine, ten, eleven, twelve")? Or are they able to repeatedly subitize and use known addition facts (for example, "six and six is ten-two") or part-whole relationships (for example, "six and four more is ten, and two more is 1 ten-two")? Without the ability to subitize 1 group of a set of objects, students will struggle with aspects of multiplication. Recall the student from the beginning of the chapter who knew that 2 × 9 was 18 but then counted on by ones to determine 3 × 9. The first step that I took to move this student's thinking forward was for them to see a concrete representation of 3 × 9, 3 groups of a unit of *nine*. As shown in figure 6.6, I then had them decompose, using a part-part-whole relationship, a unit of *nine* into 2 units of *one* and 7 units of *one* to create as many units of *ten* as possible so they could physically see 2 units of *ten* and 7 units of *one* (27).

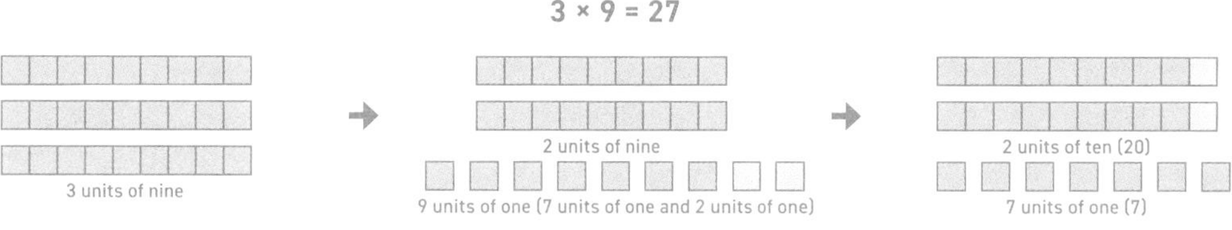

Figure 6.6: Decomposing 3 units of nine to decimal units.

The choice of representation used to introduce students to multiplication is important. A significant part of helping students develop a conceptually consistent and dynamic understanding of multiplication is that they see what we want them to see through the representations that we use. For example, as illustrated in the previous example, the use of individual concrete blocks that can be joined together to form composite units is purposeful—it provides opportunities for students to physically experience, as shown in figure 6.6, the actions of decomposing and recomposing composite units. While illuminating the composite unit and decomposing and recomposing actions, this representation also illuminates part-part-whole relationships that are part of additive thinking. For example, as shown in the previously discussed problem (that is, 3 × 9) in figure 6.6, one of the units of nine (whole) was decomposed into 2 units of *one* (part) and 7 units of *one* (part). The 2 units of *one* were recomposed with the 2 units of *nine* to form 2 units of *ten*.

Transitioning students to multiplicative thinking involves them seeing multiple groups of composite units. A discrete rectangular array is a representation that can be used to make this happen. There are several advantages to using discrete rectangular array models to develop students' concept image of multiplication. The first is that all three aspects of a multiplicative situation can be observed at the same time (Siemon et al., 2020). For example, consider the discrete rectangular array shown in figure 6.7.

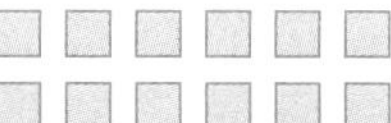

Figure 6.7: A discrete rectangular array representing a multiplication fact.

What is most visible to a student without much experience with multiplication is that the whole consists of 12 squares. At this point, their concept image of a discrete rectangular array should involve the number of objects in the array and recomposing units of *one* into units of *ten* and *one*. Seeing multiplication within a rectangular array requires a shift in students' concept image—a shift that involves multiplicative structures. These structures include seeing the multiplicative unit (size of groups) and repetitions of that multiplicative unit (number of equal groups). A scaffolded prompt to engage students in making sense of these structures is "Create as many equal-size groups as possible using only one direction of partitioning (vertical or horizontal) of the array." As shown in figure 6.8, a horizontal partitioning of the array into equally sized groups creates 2 units of *six* (2 × 6), and a vertical partitioning of the array into equally sized groups creates 6 units of *two* (6 × 2).

Figure 6.8: Seeing equally sized groups in a rectangular array of 12 objects.

Another benefit of using rectangular arrays to model multiplication is that students are able to see the *commutative property of multiplication* (Siemon et al., 2020), or, as I like to call it using student-friendly language, the *switcheroo*. In other words, rotating the array ninety degrees (students have been surprised when I place objects on an individual whiteboard and do this!), as shown in figure 6.9, preserves the whole while "switching" or "reversing" the multiplier (number of groups) and multiplicative unit (size of groups) or visually the number of rows and columns.

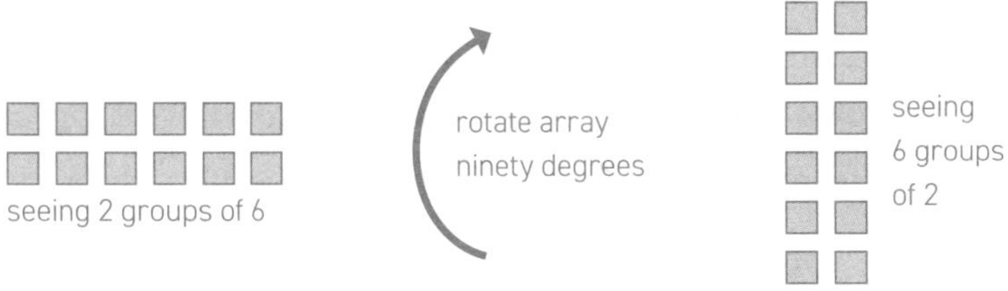

Figure 6.9: Seeing the commutative property of multiplication.

Students who see the switcheroo have cut the multiplication facts that they need to learn in half! There is a lot of power in a ninety-degree turn of a discrete rectangular array! It's also important to note that giving students opportunities to rearrange physical blocks into other possible rectangular arrays with the same whole provides opportunities for them to see another important mathematical idea. Take a moment to consider all of the different rectangles you could create using 12 blocks. These possibilities are illustrated in figure 6.10. The number of groups (rows) and size of groups (columns) of these different arrays represent the *factors* of 12.

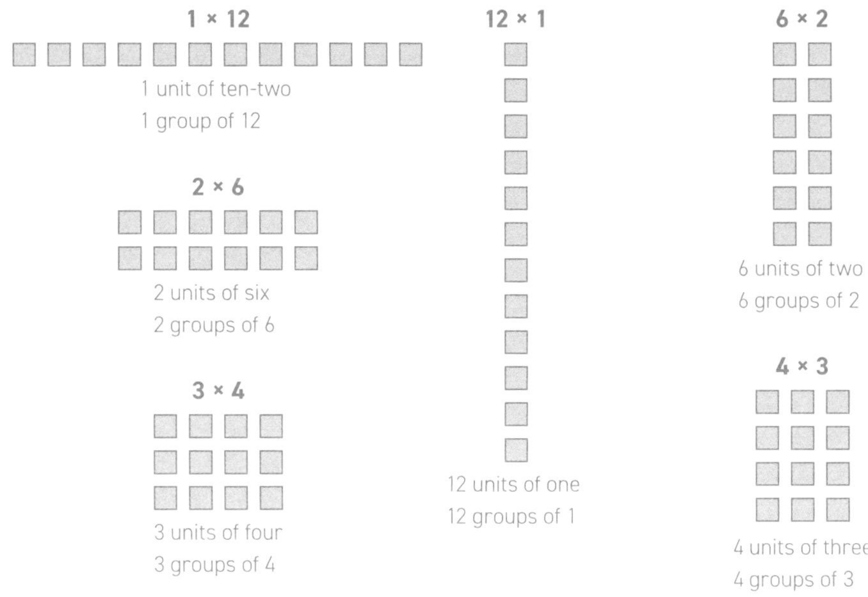

Figure 6.10: Seeing the factors of 12.

The third advantage of utilizing an array model for multiplication is that they afford the opportunity for students to see the *distributive property of multiplication over addition* (Barmby et al., 2009). Seeing this property involves a strategic partitioning of the array. Suppose that a student knows their multiplication facts up to 5 (for example, 3 × 4 = 12 and 5 × 5 = 25). Seeing the distributive property enables them to begin to reason about multiplication facts beyond 5. For example, as shown in figure 6.11, a student reasoning about the problem 6 × 2 partitioned a row to create 5 groups of 2 and 1 group of 2. The student knew the whole of both facts (5 × 2 = 10 and 1 × 2 = 2) and simply combined them to determine that 6 × 2 = 10 + 2 = 12. Two additional problems that students solved in a similar manner are also shown in figure 6.11.

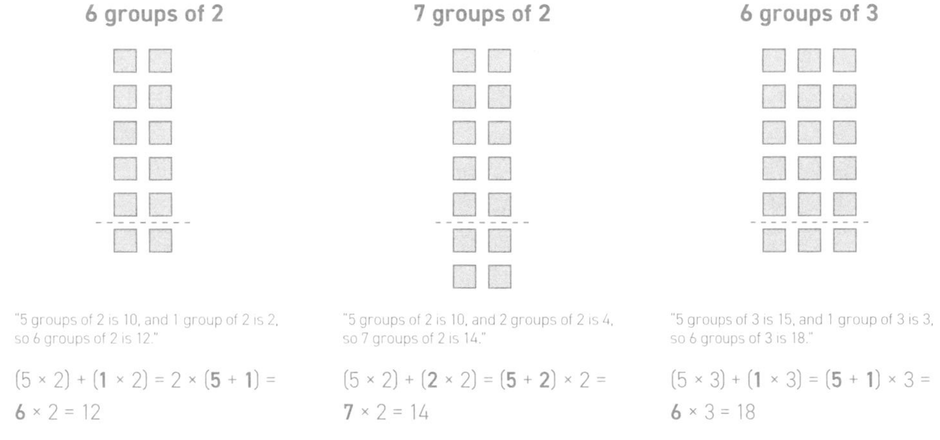

Figure 6.11: Seeing, saying, and symbolizing the distributive property.

Let's suppose that a hypothetical student has automaticity with their multiplication facts up to 5 as well as all the facts of a unit of 1 or 10. The darkest shading in figure 6.11 represents these multiplication facts. Now let's suppose this student sees the distributive property in arrays, so they can use known facts to make sense of other multiplication problems. For example, the student sees 9 × 3 as 5 groups of 3 (15) and 4 groups of 3 (12), and 8 × 4 as 5 groups of 4 (20) and 3 groups of 4 (12). The facts known by using the distributive property, coupled with known facts, while changing either the number of groups or size of the group but *not* both, are represented by the lighter shading in figure 6.12. This leaves 16 remaining facts of the 100 to master. This student is 84 percent of the way there!

×	1	2	3	4	5	6	7	8	9	10
1	1	2	3	4	5	6	7	8	9	10
2	2	4	6	8	10	12	14	16	18	20
3	3	6	9	12	15	18	21	24	27	30
4	4	8	12	16	20	24	28	32	36	40
5	5	10	15	20	25	30	35	40	45	50
6	6	12	18	24	30	36	42	48	54	60
7	7	14	21	28	35	42	49	56	63	70
8	8	16	24	32	40	48	56	64	72	80
9	9	18	27	36	45	54	63	72	81	90
10	10	20	30	40	50	60	70	80	90	100

Figure 6.12: The remaining multiplication facts that a hypothetical student needs strategies to see.

This is challenging, but this is a place in which the dynamic understandings of multiplication that a student has developed can support them in seeing more complex relationships. The challenge lies in the fact that for students to engage in this more complex seeing, they must see a multiplication problem in terms of two different sets of composed units. For example, a student must see 2 × 6 as 2 groups of *six* while also seeing that the whole is 1 *ten* and 2 *ones* (12). If they can, then it's possible for them to see either additively or multiplicatively a relationship between the whole of 6 groups of 2 and the wholes of 6 groups of 6 and 8 groups of 6.

PAUSE AND PONDER

Take a moment to think about how a student who knows that 2 groups of 6 is 12 might additively reason to determine 6 groups of 6 and 8 groups of 6.

What if they reasoned multiplicatively?

Let's consider how a student who has a dynamic understanding that utilizes the multiplication fact $2 \times 6 = 12$ and who sees both 2 groups of *six* and 1 *ten* and 2 *ones* could reason about 6 groups of 6. For example, reasoning multiplicatively, the student could conclude that 6 groups of 6 is 3 times the number of groups as 2 groups of 6, so the whole would be 3 times as much, or 3 times 1 *ten* and 2 *ones*, which is 3 *tens* and 6 *ones* (36). This thinking is shown in figure 6.13 (page 122).

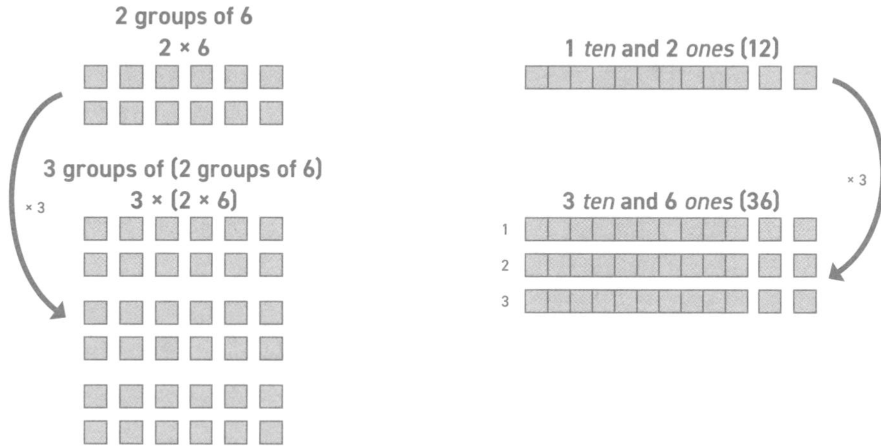

Figure 6.13: Seeing 6 groups of 6 as 3 groups of 2 groups of 6.

A student could use additive reasoning as well. That is, 6 groups of 6 is 2 groups of 6 added together 3 times. That is, 2 groups of 6 and 2 groups of 6 and 2 groups of 6 is 6 groups of 6 (12 + 12 + 12 = 36). Potential additive and multiplicative reasoning strategies that a student might leverage to solve 6 × 6 and 8 × 6 using what they know about 2 × 6 are shown in figure 6.14. A student thinking about multiplication in this way is utilizing the regrouping property of multiplication, *the associative property of multiplication*.

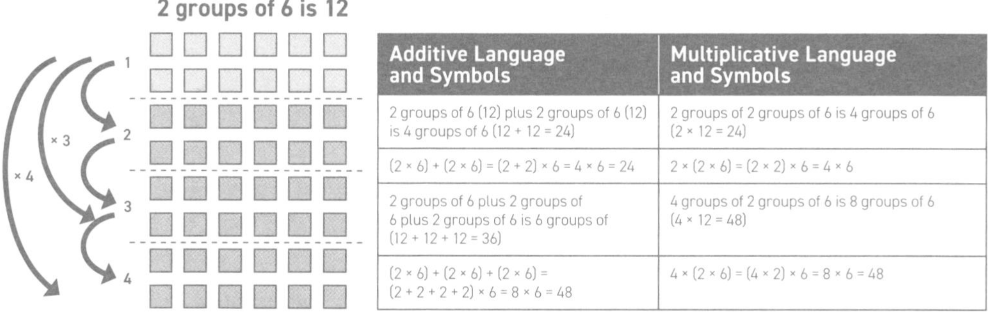

Additive Language and Symbols	Multiplicative Language and Symbols
2 groups of 6 (12) plus 2 groups of 6 (12) is 4 groups of 6 (12 + 12 = 24)	2 groups of 2 groups of 6 is 4 groups of 6 (2 × 12 = 24)
(2 × 6) + (2 × 6) = (2 + 2) × 6 = 4 × 6 = 24	2 × (2 × 6) = (2 × 2) × 6 = 4 × 6
2 groups of 6 plus 2 groups of 6 plus 2 groups of 6 is 6 groups of (12 + 12 + 12 = 36)	4 groups of 2 groups of 6 is 8 groups of 6 (4 × 12 = 48)
(2 × 6) + (2 × 6) + (2 × 6) = (2 + 2 + 2 + 2) × 6 = 8 × 6 = 48	4 × (2 × 6) = (4 × 2) × 6 = 8 × 6 = 48

Figure 6.14: Seeing, saying, and symbolizing the associative property of multiplication.

This reasoning can be used without having to regroup quantities of units (for example, 3 groups of 1 *ten* and 2 *ones* is 3 *tens* and 6 *ones*) with known number facts to make sense of several more multiplication facts. For example, 9 × 7 is 3 groups of 3 × 7 (21), or 3 groups of [2 *tens* and 1 *one*], or 6 *tens* and 3 *ones* (63). Likewise, 8 × 8 is 2 groups of 4 × 8 (32), or 2 groups of [3 *tens* and 2 *ones*], or 6 *tens* and 4 *ones* (64). The additional known multiplication facts using this strategy are shown lightly shaded in figure 6.15. It is important to note that 8 × 8 could also be seen applying the distributive property as 5 groups of 8 (40) and 3 groups of 8 (24), 40 + 24 = 64.

×	1	2	3	4	5	6	7	8	9	10
1	1	2	3	4	5	6	7	8	9	10
2	2	4	6	8	10	12	14	16	18	20
3	3	6	9	12	15	18	21	24	27	30
4	4	8	12	16	20	24	28	32	36	40
5	5	10	15	20	25	30	35	40	45	50
6	6	12	18	24	30	36	42	48	54	60
7	7	14	21	28	35	42	49	56	63	70
8	8	16	24	32	40	48	56	64	72	80
9	9	18	27	36	45	54	63	72	81	90
10	10	20	30	40	50	60	70	80	90	100

Figure 6.15: The remaining multiplication facts that a hypothetical student needs strategies to see.

At this point, our hypothetical student has strategies to make sense of over 90 percent of their multiplication facts. All that's left is 7 × 7, 7 × 8, 9 × 6, 9 × 8, and 9 × 9. The other remaining facts (6 × 9 and 8 × 7) are known, applying the commutative property of multiplication, once 9 × 6 and 7 × 8 are known. Possible strategies leveraging known multiplication facts and the language of multiplication that the student could use are shown in figure 6.16.

Problem	Possible Reasoning
7 × 7	5 groups of 7 is 35 and 2 groups of 7 is 14 so 7 groups of 7 is 35 + 14 or **49**
7 × 8	5 groups of 8 is 40 and 2 groups of 8 is 16 so 7 groups of 8 is 40 + 16 or **56**
9 × 6	5 groups of 6 is 30 and 4 groups of 6 is 24 so 9 groups of 6 is 30 + 24 = **54**
9 × 8	5 groups of 8 is 40 and 4 groups of 8 is 32 so 9 groups of 8 is **72**
9 × 9	10 groups of 9 is 90 so 1 group of 9 less is 90 − 9 or **81**

Figure 6.16: Potential strategies to make sense of the remaining multiplication facts.

The reasoning for the first four problems involves applying the distributive property while also trying to limit the cognitive load by keeping the size of the unit (size of groups) of the known fact the same and not having to regroup units. For example, as shown in figure 6.15, 5 × **7** = 35 and 2 × **7** = 14 are known facts that involve the same unit (7) and, when combined using the distributive property [(5 × 7) + (2 × 7) = (5 + 2) × 7], yield the same whole as 7 × 7. Combining the result of these two partial sums doesn't involve regrouping. That is, 3 tens and 1 ten (30 + 10 = 40) and 5 ones and 4 ones (5 + 4 = 9) are combined without regrouping as 4 tens and 9 ones, or 49. The last problem (9 × 9) involves removing 1 group of a unit of 9 from 10 groups of a unit of 9 [(10 × 9) – (1 × 9) = (10 – 1) × 9]. Ironically, this strategy also involves the distributive property utilized in a slightly different way than the first four problems.

I've shared an in-depth hypothetical instance of how a student might utilize known facts because I wanted you to experience how a student might leverage seeing known facts in rectangular arrays to reason, using properties of multiplication and composed units, about other facts. This ability requires students to know the role of each number in a multiplication problem and be aware of possible transformations of those numbers that shed light on other multiplication problems. In other words, a known multiplication fact like 6 × 8 = 48 is seen not as a static fact but as one that can be put to work to understand other multiplication problems. Not only is 6 groups of 8 composed of 5 groups of 8 (40) and 1 group of 8 (8), or 3 groups of 8 (24) and 3 groups of 8 (24), but it can be used to think about other multiplication facts. For example, think about the power a student has if, as part of their concept image of the multiplication fact 6 × 8, they see 6 × 0.8 and 6 × 800 as analogous problems, or they can utilize the distributive property to reason about 6 × 9, or they know that 3 × 16 will have the same answer as 6 × 8 (more on that in a bit!). It gets me pumped just thinking about it!

Using ideas from this section, think about three ways that you could mentally reason about the problem 9 × 6.

If appropriate, give this problem to your students and ask them to do the same. It may help to have a rectangular array on the board and ask them think about how it can be "sliced" into two smaller rectangular arrays. Then, have them give the multiplication facts represented by these smaller arrays.

Practicing Multiplication Facts

A question teachers frequently ask me is "I want to develop a dynamic understanding of multiplication facts in my students, but what would practice look like?" Practice should reinforce the multiplication facts that students know and provide opportunities for them to flex their mental superpowers. It starts with an anchor multiplication fact that you're confident students know (for example, 6 × 2 = 12), and then they, or you, can create problem strings that challenge them to reason from there. The key is to have students communicate in a way that conveys to you what they're seeing mentally. Figure 6.17 represents two problem strings involving the anchor multiplication facts 6 × 2 = 12 and 7 × 3 = 21 and potential student reasoning using those facts. It is important to note that when possible, I try to keep the size of the group 5 or fewer because we have found in our research that students have difficulty subitizing a row of an array greater than 5.

Number Fact (6 × 2 = 12)	Reasoning	Number Fact (7 × 3 = 21)	Reasoning
7 × 2	6 groups of 2 is 12, so 1 more group of 2 is 14.	8 × 3	7 groups of 3 is 21. The number of groups increased by 1, so the answer is 3 more (24).
9 × 2	6 groups of 2 is 12, so 3 more groups of 2 is 18.	9 × 3	7 groups of 3 is 21. The number of groups is increased by 2, so the answer is 6 more (27).
6 × 4	The number of groups is the same, but the size of the group is doubled, so the answer will be 2 times greater (24).	7 × 6	The number of groups is the same, but the size of the groups is doubled, so the answer will be 2 times greater (42).
6 × 3	6 groups of 2 is 12, so 6 more groups of 1 is 18.	7 × 9	The number of groups is the same, but the size of the group is 3 times larger, so the answer will be 3 times more (63).

Figure 6.17: Two multiplication fact problem strings with potential student reasoning.

At least initially, it's important that students have the concrete rectangular array model in front of them so that they can physically partition existing groups or add groups or sizes of groups. Ideally, they would have two sets—one that models the original rectangular array and a second that models the array decomposed into decimal units. The key is to build connections among what they're physically seeing, the language to communicate what they're seeing, and the symbols to represent what they're seeing. At its foundation, mathematics is about exploring patterns and relationships. These problem strings give students opportunities to do this type of work while automatizing their multiplication facts.

Approaching Multiplication Beyond a Single Digit

Single-digit multiplication problems (for example, 6 × 8) involve a multiplier and multiplicative unit that is fewer than 10 or *ten*, respectively. Moving beyond single-digit multiplication involves the multiplier and/or the multiplicative unit being greater than 10. For example, consider the multiplication problem 6 × 14. In this instance, the multiplicative unit consists of two units, *tens* and *ones*. If students understand the units represented by each numeral in the problem and have a flexible understanding of unit, the jump to solve multiplication problems involving multiple units is not significant. They're utilizing the same single-digit multiplication facts. Five different strategies to think about solving 6 × 14 are shown in figure 6.18.

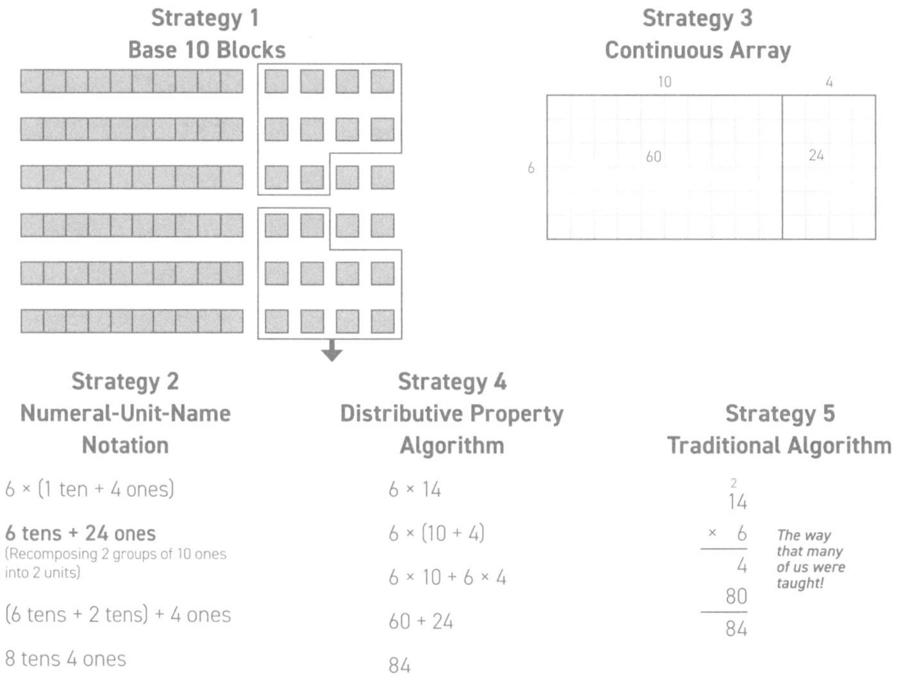

Figure 6.18: Multiple ways to see 6 × 14.

Strategy 1 involves using connectable blocks to illuminate the units (tens and ones) and the recomposing of units. This same idea represented by strategy 1 is shown symbolically in strategies 2 and 4 and, using a continuous rectangular array (for example, moving blocks together or graph paper), in strategy 3. All four of these strategies, some more visible than others, involve the distributive property of multiplication over addition. Strategy 5 is the traditional algorithm that most of us learned to use to perform multiplication.

As I mentioned in earlier chapters, asking students to estimate an answer before they have strategies to obtain an exact answer affords them opportunities to "see" structure by focusing their attention on the meaning of the numbers in the problem and what they might reveal. For example, you might ask students for a reasonable estimate of the answer to the multiplication problem 6 × 14. You would expect them to indicate that it is "greater than 60" and "fewer than 120" and, with a little more specificity, "fewer than 90."

Seeing Analogous Problems in Multiplication

One of our superpower understandings, analogous problems, can be utilized to help students make some powerful connections in multiplication. Recall the student from the beginning of the chapter who knew that 6 × 2 was 12 but struggled to make sense of 6 × 20. As with creating analogous problems in addition and subtraction, it's all about making the unit explicit. For example, 6 × 20 is also 6 × 2 *tens*, or 12 *tens*, or **12**0. The computation involves the same fact (6 × 2 = 12), but the unit is different (12 *tens* instead of 12 *ones*). Let's consider another multiplication problem, 6 × 8. Would you believe all the problems listed in figure 6.19 are analogous problems to 6 × 8? All involve the same multiplication fact, but with different units. Oh, the places you can go if you know your multiplication facts!

Multiplication Problem (with written units)	Multiplication Problem (without units)									Decimal Form
6 × 8 *thousands*	6 × 8000	4	8							**48**000
6 × 8 *hundreds*	6 × 800		4	8						**48**00
6 × 8 *tens*	6 × 80			4	8					**48**0
6 × 8 *ones*	6 × 8				4	8				**48**
6 × 8 *tenths*	6 × 0.8					4	8			0.**48**
6 × 8 *hundredths*	6 × 0.08						4	8		0.0**48**
6 × 8 *thousandths*	6 × 0.008							4	8	0.00**48**
		Ten-Thousands	Thousands	Hundreds	Tens	Ones	Tenths	Hundredths	Thousandths	

Figure 6.19: Analogous problems to 6 × 8.

Recall the multiplication problem that we recently explored, 6 × 14. Create three problems that are analogous to this problem. As shown in figure 6.19, attend to the size of the unit represented by each numeral.

Going Deeper Into Multidigit Multiplication

If you don't mind indulging me, write the multiplication problem 24 × 35 and take a moment to solve it using the strategy with which you're most comfortable.

As I shared in the book's introduction, this was the topic that almost took me out of the mathematics game! I vividly remember coming home crying because I didn't understand how to get the correct answers to two-digit multiplication problems. I felt inept! If it weren't for my grandmother sitting down with me and showing me a different method that made sense to me, I don't know that I would be writing this book today. This one topic truly took me from the lowest of lows to the highest of highs. What's wild is that I knew my multiplication facts well! I just didn't understand why we were "carrying," "bringing down the zero," and "doing all those multiplications."

More than likely, to solve 24 × 35, you used the algorithm that you learned—the one that is still widely used in many classrooms around the world. Typical language used to explain this algorithm is "carrying" and "bringing down." To illustrate all the actions involved in this process, I'm going to list out all of them using the procedural language, as shown in the left-hand column of table 6.1, and again making the units and recomposing actions underpinning the procedure explicit, as shown in the right-hand column of table 6.1.

Table 6.1: Steps to a Multiplication Algorithm

Steps of Traditional Algorithm	Units and Recomposing Made Explicit
1. Compute first product, 4 × 5 = 20	4 groups of 5 ones = 20 ones
2. Bring the 0 down (row 1)	0 ones
3. Carry the 2	2 tens
4. Compute second product, 4 × 3 = 12	4 groups of 3 tens = 12 tens
5. Compute sum of 2 and 12	2 tens + 12 tens = 14 tens
6. Cross out the 2	
7. Bring 14 down (row 1)	14 tens = 1 hundred and 4 tens (140)
8. Bring 0 down (row 2)	0 ones
9. Compute third product, 2 × 5 = 10	20 groups of 5 ones = 100 ones
10. Bring the 0 down (row 2)	0 tens
11. Carry the 1	1 hundred

12. Compute fourth product, 2 × 3 = 6	20 groups of 3 tens = 60 tens = 6 hundreds
13. Compute sum of 1 and 6	1 hundred + 6 hundred = 7 hundreds (700)
14. Bring 7 down (row 2)	7 hundreds
15. Compute sum of each column	8 hundreds = 7 hundreds + 1 hundred (840) 4 tens 0 ones

Amazing, isn't it? Fifteen steps! And many of us figured it out! Hidden in this method is the language that illuminates the units and the actions to recompose those units. The column on the right side of table 6.1 represents those same steps with the units and the recomposing actions made explicit. Which language do you believe would best support your own students' learning and development of two-digit multiplication?

Now let me show you what my grandmother showed me many years ago that put an end to my tears! I didn't know it at the time, but it's called the *partial product algorithm*, and it's underpinned by the distributive property of multiplication over addition. It's a little different from the standard algorithm that most of us learned. While my grandmother didn't make the units explicit using the unit name, she did share the language that has fueled my work to this day. Let me take you through this algorithm on the same problem you just did, 24 × 35, and the one that changed my life nearly fifty years ago!

At this point, it becomes a bit cumbersome to continue to use the unit name in text to illuminate the unit, so I'm going to stop using it unless it's needed to make a critical point. As shown in figure 6.20, the multiplication problem 24 × 35 can be expressed in terms of the unit represented by each numeral, (**20** + **4**) × (**30** + **5**). Applying the distributive property results in the expression **20** × (**30** + **5**) and **4** × (**30** + **5**), which can be applied again to determine the four partial products, **20** × **30** (600), **20** × **5** (100), **4** × **30** (120), and **4** × **5** (20). Adding together these four partial products yields the product of 24 × 35 (600 + 100 + 12 + 20 = **840**).

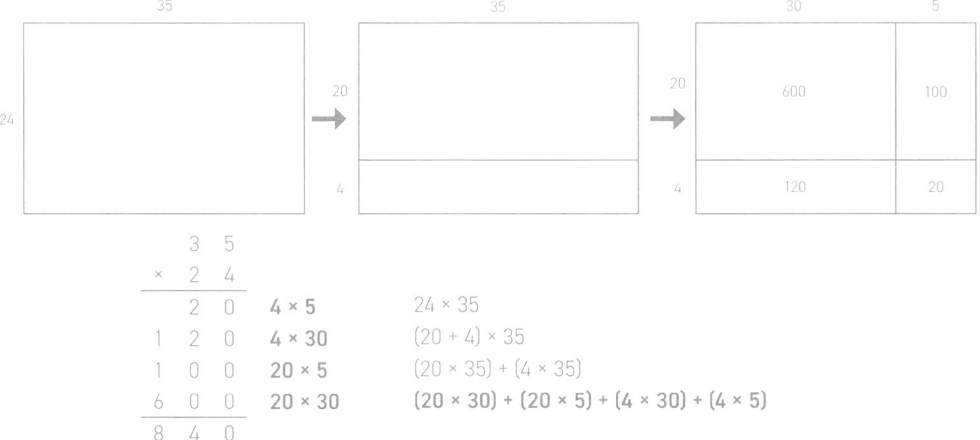

Figure 6.20: Using partial product algorithm to compute 24 × 35.

Just like the algorithm that many of us learned, there are four partial products involved in computing a two-digit by two-digit multiplication problem. The difference in using the partial product algorithm is that the units associated with those multiplications are made explicit, and there is no need to use phrases such as "carrying" and "bringing down the one." Figure 6.20 shows the computations of the partial product algorithm—the same algorithm my grandmother shared with me many years ago—to multiply 24 × 35 using an area model, vertical recording, and a horizontal recording. No "borrowing" or "carrying" is needed; simply an understanding of the distributive property of multiplication, the unit associated with each numeral, and single-digit multiplication facts enable a student to make sense of why 24 × 35 is 840. Remember I knew my multiplication facts, but I obviously didn't understand the unit associated with each numeral. If a student has the three understandings mentioned previously, they can handle more complex multiplication problem like 243 × 358 or even an analogous problem like 24.3 × 35.8.

Halving and Doubling

As students become more flexible in seeing multiplication problems using discrete and continuous rectangular arrays, there are transformations of these arrays that can further support students' mental arithmetic superpowers. Consider the multiplication problem 8 × 35, or 8 groups of 35. Imagine you had a rectangle in your hand with these dimensions. Now imagine using a pair of scissors to cut the length of the rectangle so that you had two rectangles in your hands that were 4 × 35. Move the one rectangle to the end of the other to create a transformed rectangle with a length of 4 and a length of 70 (35 + 35). Can you mentally compute 4 × 70? Of course you can! This second representation is an example of a strategy called *halving and doubling* because the number of groups is halved (from 8 to 4) and the size of the group is doubled (from 35 to 70) without changing the whole. These actions are shown in figure 6.21.

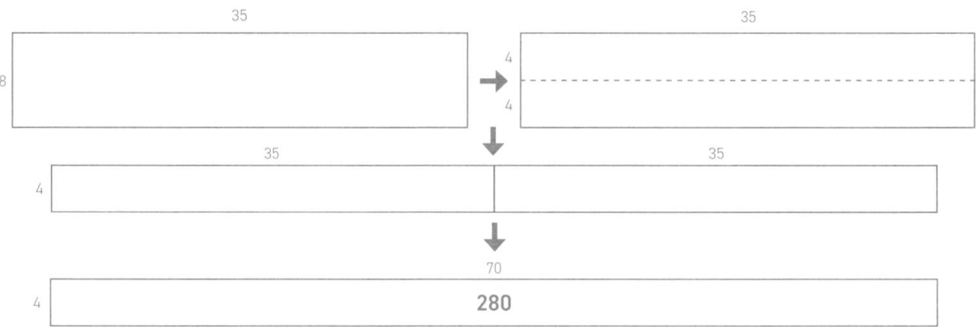

Figure 6.21: Using a halving and doubling strategy to mentally compute 8 × 35.

Use the halving and doubling mental arithmetic strategy to compute 8 × 45 and 18 × 35.

Generate three other multiplication problems to which you could apply this strategy to solve.

See if you can generate three multiplication problems that would warrant a thirding and tripling mental arithmetic strategy.

I introduce multiplication using discrete rectangular arrays because I want students to "see," using their early number subitizing abilities, multiple groups of the same size of unit (for example, 8 groups of 3). As the complexity of multiplication problems increases (for example, 8 × 13 or 28 × 13), it is important to shift to continuous rectangular arrays, not only to connect to a concept they will learn in the future (that is area), but also to turn their attention away from group sizes beyond their subitizing capacities (that is greater than groups of 5) toward the units represented by each numeral in the multiplication problem.

As we move to multiplication problems involving fractions, it is helpful to reintroduce a representational form that was introduced in chapter 3 (page 47), the *bar–number line* model. The use of the bar–number line model makes sense because fractions represent multiplicative relationships and this representation illuminates those structures. For example, the fraction ⅜ can be interpreted as 3 groups of a unit of ⅛ of a whole unit or 3 × ⅛. Recall that a number line illuminates the location of the number in relation to other numbers but hides that this location is a length that is dependent on the length of the whole unit. The bar is added to the number line to illuminate these lengths. This is a representation that I use to help students see multiplication involving fractions. Before we do this, I think it is important that you first experience how this representation illuminates other multiplicative structures with a problem involving whole numbers. Suppose that I gave you the location of 5 on a number line, as shown in figure 6.22, and I asked you to create a length that would be four times as long as that length. What would you do?

Figure 6.22: A length of a unit of *five*.

More than likely, you had no difficulty determining this length. As shown in figure 6.23, you most likely iterated the unit of 5 (*five*) multiple times to determine the length and the location of a number that corresponds with that length.

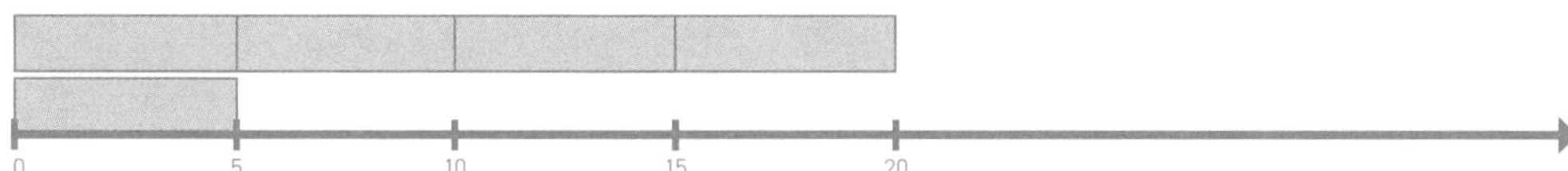

Figure 6.23: Iterating a unit of 5 to determine the location of 20.

The action of adding together multiple units of length 5 has an additive-thinking feel to it, but underlying these actions is a conception of multiplication that we have yet to discuss. Multiplication is a scalar process that involves a scaling factor (multiplier) that specifies how the operation resizes the multiplicative unit (Lannin et al., 2013, p. 11). In other words, the action in a multiplication problem is the first number, and that action is performed on the second number. Take a minute to reflect on the multiplication problem inherent in the prompt "Determine a length that's 4 times the length of 5." If you're thinking 4 × 5, you're on it! The first number, 4, is the scaling factor that represents the action on the second number, multiplicative unit 5. You can also see in figure 6.23 that the length of 20 is 4 times the length of 5. What does all of this have to do with multiplication involving fractions? I'm glad you asked!

Tackling Multiplication Involving Fractions

In this section, we will examine three different cases involving fractions in a multiplication problem. These three cases occur when the fraction in the multiplication problem is (1) the scaling factor, (2) the multiplicative unit, and (3) both.

PAUSE AND PONDER

Take a moment to think about how you would explain to a student how to solve the following multiplication problems involving fractions. Reflect on the language you would use.

- $6 \times \frac{8}{9}$
- $\frac{2}{3} \times 12$
- $\frac{2}{3} \times \frac{4}{5}$

Now, suppose the student replied, "OK, why do you do that?" What would be your response?

If you used the phrase "multiply straight across," don't feel bad. This is a common phrase that cues an action that results in correct answers. It's easy to follow, and students like it because it quickly obtains correct answers. Again, as I've indicated before, we live in a world in which all you have to do is consult Siri, Alexa, or Google, and *bam*—just like that you have an answer. By the way, I just asked Siri for the answer to "six times eight ninths," and she returned 5.3333. Siri still doesn't like fractions. More on that later!

Again, I think all of us want something more for our students because getting an answer is no longer the end goal. In some ways, it's the beginning. For example, why does an answer of 5.3333 to 6 × 8/9 make sense? Let's dig into the why. I will warn you, though. This might be one place in which you might say, "Can't we just multiply straight across and leave it at that?" You have come this far! Let's keep pushing!

The three multiplication problems that I had you think about exemplify the three different situations involving fractions in multiplication problems. In the first problem, 6 × 8/9, the fraction is the multiplicative unit (size of group). In the second problem, 2/3 × 12, the fraction is the scaling factor (multiplier or number of groups), and in the third problem, both the scaling factor and multiplicative unit are fractions. In multiplication problems, the fraction is interpreted differently depending on whether it's the scaling factor or the multiplicative unit. If the fraction is interpreted as a scale factor, or action, I will write it using standard fraction notation (for example, 2/3). If it represents a multiplicative unit, I will write it using number-unit-name notation (for example, 2 *thirds*) to make the unit explicit. These three problems are intended to illuminate how the fraction is interpreted differently and its role in each problem.

INTERPRETING A FRACTION AS A MULTIPLICATIVE UNIT

Let's start by revisiting the problem 6 × 8/9. Before we dig into this problem, can you tell me the answer to 6 × 1? Of course you can! This answer should shed some light on the answer to 6 × 8/9. The multiplicative unit of 8/9 is slightly less than 1, so the answer to the problem 6 × 8/9 must be a little less than 6. As I mentioned earlier in the chapter, asking students to estimate an answer focuses students' attention away from simply obtaining an answer and toward "seeing" the structure of the problem and what that structure might reveal about the answer. For example, in the previous problem, "seeing" that the multiplicative unit is less than 1 indicates that the answer will be less than 6.

Let's now think about obtaining an exact answer to 6 × 8/9. I am going to rewrite 6 × 8/9 making the unit of the multiplicative unit explicit: 6 × 8 *ninths*. Take a moment to reflect on what you see when I write the problem this way. Would you believe that any fraction multiplication problem in which the fraction is the multiplicative unit is analogous to a whole-number problem? In other words, 6 × 8 of *any size of unit* is analogous to 6 × 8 because the result will be 48 of *any size of unit*! Pretty cool, right?

In this instance, the answer to the problem 6 × 8 *ninths* is 48 ninths. The only challenge left is determining how many whole units (ones) are in 48 *ninths*. From our earlier work with fractions, we know that each whole has 9 *ninths*, so we must determine how many 9 *ninths* are in 48 *ninths*. Using a multiplication fact, **5** × 9 = 45, and our understanding of the relationship between whole units and the multiplicative unit of fractions, we know that 5 wholes is an equal exchange for 45 *ninths*, leaving 3 *ninths*. This means 48 *ninths* is an equal exchange for 5 wholes and 3 *ninths* (5 3/9) or, using another equal exchange of 1 *third* for 3 *ninths*, 5 wholes and 1 *third* (5 1/3). A pictorial representation of these actions is shown in figure 6.24. Recall that Siri gave an answer of 5.3333—an answer that is *not* technically the same as an actual answer of 5 1/3—bad Siri!

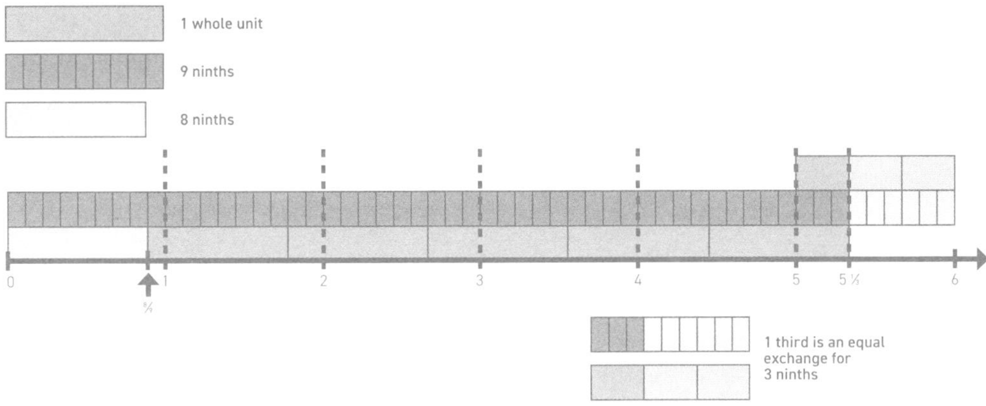

Figure 6.24: Seeing that 6 times a unit length of 8/9 is 5 1/3.

As I mentioned earlier, any problem of the form 6 × 8 of *any unit* is analogous to the whole-number multiplication problem 6 × 8. There is, however, one adjustment that needs to be made, and that adjustment depends on the unit. Earlier, when we discussed decimal problems that were analogous to 6 × 8, such as 6 × 0.8 and 6 × 80, there were no issues because the equal exchanges *always* occur when there are 10 of a particular unit (for example, 10 *tenths* = 1 *one* and 10 *hundredths* = 1 *tenth*). This is not true for nondecimal size of units (for example, *thirds*, *fifths*). The quantity of the unit to create an equal exchange of 1 whole unit depends on the unit itself. This is shown for a few examples of 6 × 8 of *any unit* in figure 6.25.

Problem	Unit Explicit	Improper Result	Whole-Unit Equal Exchange	Mixed Result
6 × 8/3	6 × 8 *thirds*	48 *thirds*	3 *thirds*	16 *ones* (16)
6 × 8/5	6 × 8 *fifths*	48 *fifths*	5 *fifths*	9 *ones* and 3 *fifths* (9 3/5)
6 × 8/12	6 × 8 *twelfths*	48 *twelfths*	12 *twelfths*	4 *ones* (4)
6 × 8/15	6 × 8 *fifteenths*	48 *fifteenths*	15 *fifteenths*	3 *ones* and 3 *fifteenths* (3 3/15) 3 *ones* and 1 *fifth* (3 1/5)

Figure 6.25: Analogous fraction multiplication problems.

INTERPRETING A FRACTION AS A SCALE FACTOR

Suppose that I gave you the length of a number bar as shown in figure 6.26. Take a moment to think about how you would determine 2/3 of the length of the whole bar.

Figure 6.26: Length of 1 whole bar.

Now suppose that I gave you the same bar, but I told you that the length, as shown in figure 6.27, of the bar is 12. What length of bar and number on the number line would correspond with ⅔ of that length?

Figure 6.27: Locating the endpoint of the length of a fraction bar that is ⅔ of the one given.

The thinking that you just engaged in exemplifies the thinking to solve the multiplication problem ⅔ × 12—an example of a problem in which the fraction is the scale factor. I like to call a fraction as a scale factor the action fraction because it cues what actions you are going to perform on the multiplicative unit. More than likely, to solve the problem, you partitioned the whole unit (12) into 3 equally sized lengths and determined the length of 2 of those equally sized lengths. These actions are shown in figure 6.28.

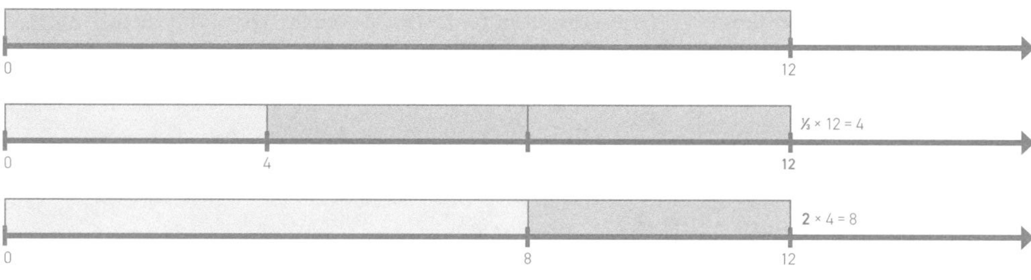

Figure 6.28: "Seeing" ⅔ × 12 = 2 × (⅓ × 12) = 2 × 4 = 8.

It is important to note that the multiplication problem we just solved, ⅔ × 12, can be rewritten to illuminate the order of our actions on the original composite unit. The fraction ⅔, 2 groups of ⅓, can be rewritten as a multiplication problem, 2 × ⅓, itself to create 2 × ⅓ × 12, and then we can use the associative property of multiplication to regroup, 2 × (⅓ × 12). Recall that, as shown in figure 6.28, our first action was to partition a unit length of 12 into 3 equally sized lengths, 2 × **(⅓ × 12)**, creating a new composite unit, 4, and the second action was doubling the length of the new unit, 2 × **(4)** = 8.

With this same idea in mind, we can apply the commutativity property of multiplication to model a different order of operations. Our first action could have been to double our original composite unit; instead of **2 × ⅓** × 12, we can think of the problem as **⅓ × 2** × 12 and regroup ⅓ × **(2 × 12)** to create a different composite unit, 24, and our second action is to partition this length, 24, into 3 equally sized lengths, ⅓ × **(24)** = 8. That is the beauty of commutativity—same result, different order of actions. Aligning the actions in a bar–number line model and the symbolic representation of those actions is part of building a conceptually consistent understanding of multiplication. The order of these actions is modeled in figure 6.29.

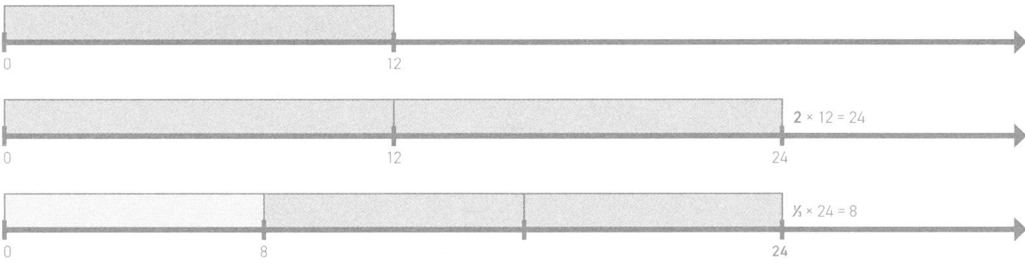

Figure 6.29: Modeling ⅓ × (2 × 12) = 8.

Now, I made it a little easier on you because the problem I gave you, ⅔ × 12, had a multiplicative unit that could be easily partitioned into 3 equal groups. Let's kick it up a notch by considering a problem that doesn't partition as easily: ⅔ × 14. As with some whole-number multiplication problems, this is a place in which the distributive property is helpful. Instead of ⅔ of a group of 14, we can think about this problem in terms of ⅔ of a group of 12 *and* ⅔ of a group of 2. We already know that ⅔ of a group of 12 is 8, so all we need to do is determine ⅔ of a group of 2. As shown in figure 6.30, partitioning a length of 2 into 3 equal lengths results in 3 lengths of ⅔. Two of those lengths is 2 × ⅔, or 4/3, or 1 ⅓. Combining the length of ⅔ × 12 (8) and the length of ⅔ × 2 (1 ⅓) results in a whole length of ⅔ × 14, or 9 ⅓.

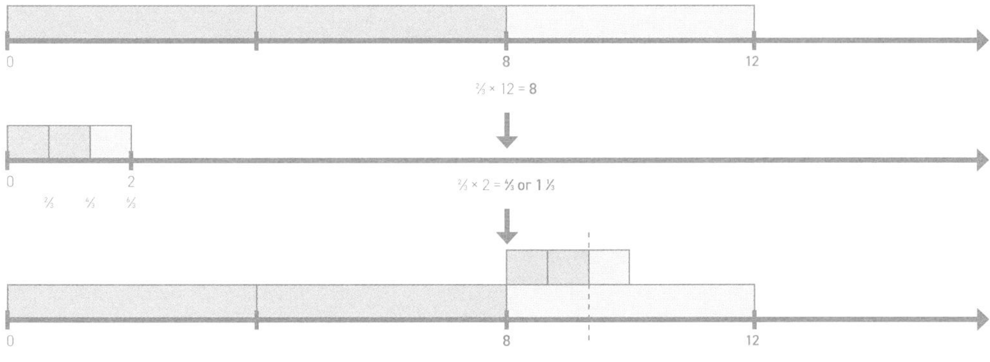

⅔ × 14 = ⅔ × (12 + 2) = ⅔ × 12 + ⅔ × 2 = 8 + 1 ⅓ = 9 ⅓

Figure 6.30: ⅔ × 14 is the same as (⅔ × 12) + (⅔ × 2).

NEGOTIATING FRACTIONAL SCALE FACTORS AND MULTIPLICATIVE UNITS

Let's consider the last problem I posed at the beginning of our dive into multiplication involving fractions: ⅔ × 4/5. Would you believe that we have already covered most of what's needed to solve this problem in the first two problems?

PAUSE AND PONDER

Take a moment to reflect on how the role of the fraction is different in the problems $6 \times \frac{8}{9}$ and $\frac{2}{3} \times 12$.

Use this information to think about how you might use these ideas to solve $\frac{2}{3} \times \frac{4}{5}$.

Would you believe that one of the first two problems we discussed is analogous to $\frac{2}{3} \times \frac{4}{5}$? Ahh! The suspense is killing you, right? Let's dig in!

The multiplicative unit in this problem is $\frac{4}{5}$. Let's start by creating a length to represent this unit. As I had you do earlier to create the multiplicative unit, you need to first know the length of a unit of 1 (*one*). Then, you would partition the unit of 1 (or whole unit) into 5 equally sized lengths that each represent a length of $\frac{1}{5}$ (1 *fifth*). A length of $\frac{4}{5}$ is four times as long as a length of $\frac{1}{5}$ ($4 \times \frac{1}{5} = \frac{4}{5}$). Now, because the scale factor is $\frac{2}{3}$, you need to partition a length of $\frac{4}{5}$ into 3 equally sized pieces, but that's messy! Let's use our equal exchange superpower to create a quantity and size of unit that is easily partitioned into 3 equally sized lengths. Let's see—a length of 4 *fifths* is the same as a length of 8 *tenths*. Will that work? ($8 \div 3 =$ **2 ⅔**, not very nice!) Nope! Not that one! How about 12 fifteenths? ($12 \div 3 =$ **4**, nice!) Yes, a length of 12 *fifteenths* is the equal exchange ticket because it's mentally easy to partition 12 *fifteenths* into 3 equally sized lengths, 4 *fifteenths*. Since the scale factor is $\frac{2}{3}$, not $\frac{1}{3}$ ($\frac{2}{3} \times \frac{12}{15}$), we need to know the length of 2 of those equally partitioned lengths. This length happens to be 2 groups of a length of 4 *fifteenths*, or 8 *fifteenths*. These actions using the bar–number line representation are shown in figure 6.31.

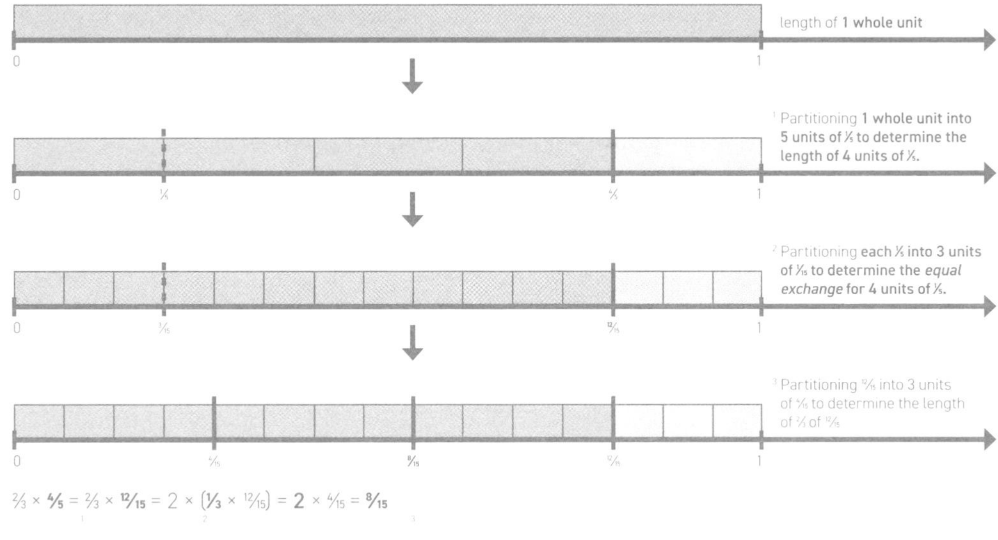

Figure 6.31: Seeing $\frac{2}{3} \times \frac{4}{5} = \frac{8}{15}$.

I want to point out that there was a lot of partitioning happening, but it was happening on different units. The first partitioning action was on the whole unit. This action yielded a length of $\frac{4}{5}$ of 1 whole unit. The second partitioning action was an equal exchange that happened to each $\frac{1}{5}$ in $\frac{4}{5}$, resulting in a length of $\frac{12}{15}$ (the same length as $\frac{4}{5}$ using a different size of unit), and the third partitioning action was on $\frac{12}{15}$, yielding a length of $\frac{8}{15}$.

I liken the way that most of learned how to multiply fractions to starting a car. There is a lot that is happening under the hood. Would you believe all these actions were lying under the hood of multiplying straight across?

Reviewing More Analogous Multiplication Problems

Before we move on, I want to point out one more thing that I primed you to think about earlier. Would you believe that $\frac{2}{3} \times 12$ and $\frac{2}{3} \times \frac{12}{15}$ are analogous problems? In this instance, we are performing the same scale factor actions (that is, partitioning the multiplicative unit into 3 equally sized lengths to determine the length of 2 of those lengths) on 12 different unit lengths. Notice that the product of $\mathbf{\frac{2}{3} \times 12}$ is **8** and the product of $\mathbf{\frac{2}{3} \times \frac{12}{15}}$ is $\mathbf{\frac{8}{15}}$. In the first instance, the unit length is 1, and in the second instance, the unit length is $\frac{1}{5}$. Generalizing this idea, $\frac{2}{3} \times 12$ of *any unit* results in 8 of *any unit.*

Let's talk about one more type of analogous problem by comparing the whole-number multiplication problem 6×83 to $6 \times 8\frac{3}{4}$. Knowing the power of the distributive property of multiplication over addition will take you places!

PAUSE AND PONDER

Take a moment to reflect on how the multiplication problems 6 × 83 and 6 × 8 ¾ are considered analogous problems.

Reflect on how you could use the distributive property to mentally compute both of these problems.

The work illuminating why 6 × 83 and 6 × 8 ¾ are analogous problems is shown in figure 6.32.

6 × 83	6 × 8 ¾
6 × (80 + 3)	6 × (8 + ¾)
(6 × 80) + (6 × 3)	(6 × 8) + (6 × ¾)
480 + 18	48 + 18⁄4

Figure 6.32: "Seeing" the structure of two analogous problems.

Multiplying Decimals

OK, do you feel like you have a handle on multiplication involving fractions? Let's jump to multiplication problems involving decimals. There's not much new to talk about, especially if you're comfortable with analogous problems, because decimals are fractions, and unlike many fractions, the equal exchanges involve 10 of a unit. I will be brief, but let's take a quick look at three problems that involve the same familiar multiplication fact, 6 × 8 = 48.

- 6 × 0.8
- 0.8 × 6
- 0.8 × 0.6

The multiplication problem is 6 × 0.8 or 6 × 8 *tenths* or 48 *tenths*. We already know the 8 aligns with the tenths place, so the answer is 4.8. Or, using an equal exchange, 40 *tenths* is 4 *ones*, so 48 tenths is 4 *ones* and 8 *tenths* (4.8). The multiplication problem 0.8 × 6 will have the same answer as 6 × 0.8 (4.8) because of the commutative property of multiplication. Since we already know that 8 × 0.6 is 4.8, then 0.8 × 0.6 is going to involve an adjustment of each quantity to the next smaller size of unit, since 0.8 is one size of unit lesser than 8. That is, 4 ones become 4 tenths, and 8 tenths become 8 hundredths, or 0.48. Boom! Done! We covered multiplication involving decimals in one paragraph.

Folding Back

I want to make once final point about multiplication. While not explicitly stated, we've been using multiplicative relationships from the very beginning. For example, a number such as 358 can be expressed as the sum of three multiplicative relationships, (3 × 100) + (5 × 10) + (8 × 1). Likewise, a fraction like ⅝ is also a multiplicative relationship, 5 × ⅛. Since I can write all numbers in terms of multiplicative relationships, it truly underpins the operations before multiplication. For example, the addition problem 50 + 40 can be rewritten, using the distributive property, as (5 × 10) + (4 × 10) = (5 + 4) × 10 = 9 × 10 = 90 or even (2 × 25) + (2 × 20) = 2 (25 + 20) = 2 × 45 = 90. Multiplicative relationships are everywhere!

As these examples illustrate, a dynamic understanding of multiplication problems in which one or both numbers are fractions or decimals requires awareness and flexibility with the following five ideas.

1. The language to interpret a multiplication problem (for example, *number of groups*, *action fraction*, *scale factor*, and *multiplier* are all language that represents the first number in a multiplication problem)
2. Fluency with multiplication facts
3. An understanding of the role of unit and the ability to coordinate those units
4. The dual meaning of fractions (that is, representing an action and a unit)
5. An awareness of analogous problems to whole-number multiplication problems

My final thought is that all this work supports students' ability to reason multiplicatively. Take a moment to reflect on how you might use these understandings and the language you have learned to reason about a multiplicative reasoning task like 10 × 6 = 5 × 12.

Shown in figure 6.33 is a language-focused solution and a visual solution utilizing a bar–number line model to solve the problem.

"The only way for 10 groups of 6 and an unknown number of groups of 12 to be the same whole is if the number of groups is halved because the size of the group doubled. This means the unknown number of groups is half of 10 or 5."

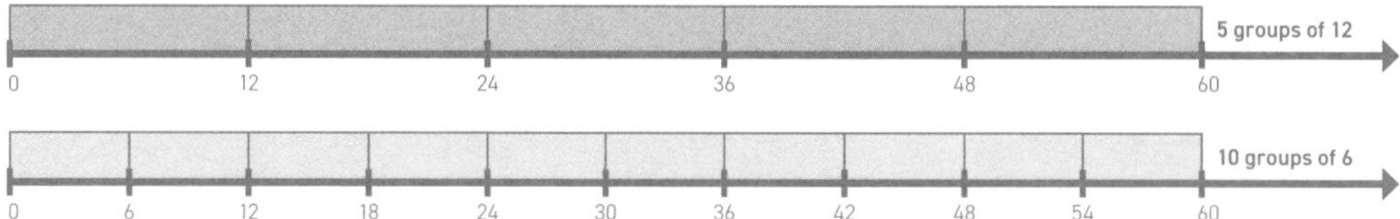

Figure 6.33: Two solutions to the problem 10 × 6 = 5 × 12 that involve multiplicative reasoning strategies.

PAUSE AND PONDER

As a result of reading this chapter, how are you thinking differently about multiplication?

After reading this chapter, what one or two instructional shifts are you planning to make in how you teach multiplication?

Key Points

Before proceeding, please take a moment to review the following takeaways from this chapter.

- Make sure students' initial experiences with multiplication involve a representational progression moving from connectable blocks representing composite units (for example, 8 groups of *six*) to those same blocks being arranged into discrete rectangular arrays (for example, 8 rows by 6 columns) to continuous rectangular arrays to bar–number line models. Each illuminates a different multiplicative structure that students need to "see" as the complexity of problems increases.

- This representation progression also involves a shift in the language. Initially, the numerals in a multiplication problem are described using "groups of" language in which the unit is explicit. For example, in the problem 8 × 14, the first number represents the number of groups (8), and the second number represents the size of the group, or multiplicative unit (1 *ten* and 4 *ones*). As students progress in their understanding of units, this notation can be removed for the standard notation 8 × 14 to make properties such as distributivity more visible [8 × 14 = 8 × (10 + 4)]. As bar–number line models are introduced to teach multiplication involving fractions, the language can be added to include a scalar interpretation of multiplication. For example, 8 × 6 can be interpreted as a length of 6 units that is repeated 8 times. In other words, a length of 48 is 8 times larger than a length of 6.

- There are multiple types of analogous multiplication problems. For example, 8 × 6 of *any size of unit* is analogous to the whole-number problem 8 × 6. Likewise, $\frac{2}{3}$ of 12 of *any size of unit* is analogous to the problem $\frac{2}{3}$ × 12.

The key points in this chapter emphasize the progression of representations and language as well as the connections necessary for helping students develop a dynamic and flexible understanding of multiplication. The application guide for this chapter reflects this progression and will support your efforts in developing these understandings among your students.

Chapter 6 Application Guide

Chapter Concepts	How Can I Incorporate This Into My Teaching Practice Moving Forward?
Seeing, Saying, and Symbolizing Multiplication (Part 1) **Decomposing groups of composed units into decimal units (for example, *tens* and *ones*)**	Provide opportunities for students to do the following. 1. Use connectable blocks to create groups of the same size of composed unit (for example, 4 groups of six). 2. Physically decompose those units into units of ten and one (2 tens and 4 ones). 3. Use "groups of" language to communicate the number of groups and size of groups (for example, "4 groups of a unit of six is 2 tens and 4 ones). 4. Write the multiplication problem represented by these actions first by making the units explicit (4 groups of six is 2 tens and 4 ones) and then by using formal notation (for example, $4 \times 6 = 24$).
Seeing, Saying, and Symbolizing Multiplication (Part 2) **Creating multiple groups of equally sized units (commutative, associative, and distributive properties of multiplication)**	Have students do the following. 1. Use individual blocks to create discrete rectangular arrays. 2. Horizontally or vertically partition those arrays into equal groups using stir straws. 3. Repeat steps 3 and 4 from the previous row. 4. Extend the size of the arrays from known facts to one to two additional columns or rows. Use the stir sticks to partition the array at the known number fact. 5. Repeat steps 3 and 4 from the previous row. 6. Transform those rectangular arrays into other rectangular arrays (for example, halving and doubling). 7. Using continuous rectangular array models, extend the process to two-digit numbers.
Seeing, Saying, and Symbolizing Multiplication (Part 3) **Partitioning of multiplicative units**	1. Using bar-number line models (or paper strips), partition the given multiplicative unit in a way that results in whole unit lengths (for example, ⅔ of 12 or ¾ of 12). 2. Ask students to write the multiplication problem that corresponds with these actions. 3. Provide a less-than-whole-unit length (that is, 4 fifths) and ask them to create this length from a whole unit. 4. Give them different scale factors, asking them which equal exchanges of the multiplicative unit would be easier to mentally compute the measure of the partitioning actions.
Seeing Connections **Analogous multiplication problems**	1. Ask students to reflect on and generate both fraction and decimal multiplication problems that are analogous to whole-number multiplication problems. 2. Press them to explain why, making sure the units are explicit, these problems are analogous.

The illiterate of the 21st century
will not be those who cannot read and write,
but those who cannot learn, unlearn, and relearn.

—Alvin Toffler

CHAPTER 7

Division

In chapter 3 (page 47), I presented a focused and connected way to introduce the *F* word of elementary mathematics, *fractions*. Fraction concepts were introduced in terms of measures (that is, quantities of sizes of units) that enabled explicit connections to be made between already developed whole-number ideas, such as place value and equal exchanges. My hope was that by explicitly and intentionally forging connections between concepts that seemed disjointed, I would leave you thinking differently about fractions by the end of the chapter. If you previously had negative associations with fractions, ideally this way of thinking about fractions would remove those negative associations and provide you with the tools to teach your students in a way that limits the potential for these negative associations with fractions gaining a foothold. The hope is that by the time students reach division, they will have developed strong fraction-as-measure conceptions.

Through the first four chapters of the book, a measurement conception of fractions was the only conception that was needed. In chapter 5 (page 91), an action conception of a fraction was added (for example, $\frac{2}{3} \times 12$) that technically involved the same partitioning actions you learned in chapter 3, but on various composite units (for example, a unit of 12) instead of only a unit of 1 (*one*). In this chapter, we will add another conception: *fractions as division*.

Indeed, it's time to deal the *D* word of elementary mathematics, *division*. For whatever reason, out of all the four operations, division is the one operation that students and adults find most challenging. I understand why—because the operation of division is connected to the *F* word, *fractions*. In the pages that follow, we'll look at different interpretations of division, the ability to see division, how to solve division problems leveraging what we already know, long division, the partial quotient algorithm, divisions involving fractions, and the "why" behind "keep, change, flip." Then we'll cover how to see division as addition and subtraction, a connection to whole-number division, flexibility with interpretations, and, finally, division involving both mixed numbers and decimals.

Different Interpretations of Division

Up to this point, I've resisted using contextual problems unless it helped illuminate an idea. In many cases, contextual problems shed tremendous light on the nature of student thinking. While I'm a big believer in the power of contextual problems, through the first three operations, I wanted to focus attention on the mathematical structure underlying the operation while also emphasizing the size of unit. However, with division, the focus shifts a bit because contextual problems help illuminate the two different interpretations of division.

PAUSE AND PONDER

Unleash your inner student and consider how a student, using concrete objects, might solve the following problems.

Problem 1: *Keisha has 18 chocolates. She wants to share them equally with her 3 friends. Assuming Keisha gives all her chocolates away, how many chocolates will each friend receive?*

Problem 2: Keisha has made 18 chocolates. She wants to place them in gift bags that have 3 chocolates each. How many gift bags can she make?

On initial inspection, you might think that the problems I've presented in the Pause and Ponder are the same because the answers are the same. However, think about the actions that you performed to solve both problems. In the first problem, you moved 18 physical objects into 3 groups using some strategy. Maybe you moved two at a time to each group, two more, and then one more, until there were no more objects to move into the 3 groups. In the second problem, you counted out sets of 3 objects and continued to make groups of 3 objects until there were no more objects.

These two problems exemplify the two different interpretations of division problems: *sharing* (partitive) and *measurement* (quotative). The difference between a sharing and a measurement interpretation is what is known and unknown. In a sharing division problem, the number of groups is known (that is, sharing them equally with 3 friends), and the size of the group is what is to be determined by the question (that is, how many chocolates will each friend receive?). Figure 7.1 exemplifies the work of a student who completed three sharing actions to use all the chocolates to create three equal groups.

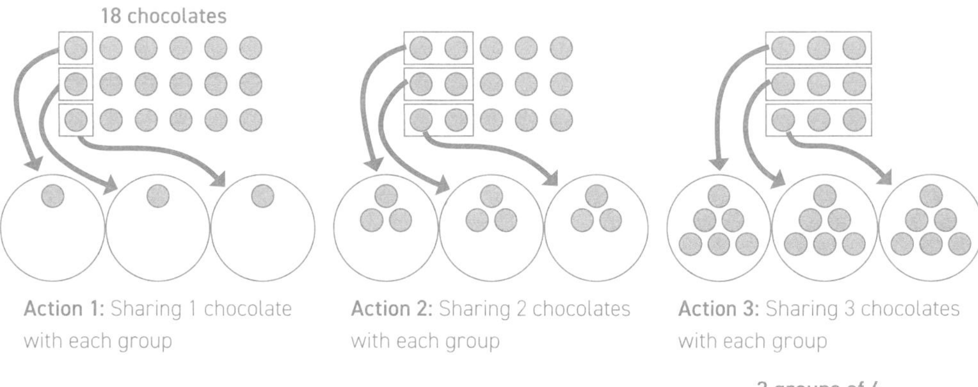

Figure 7.1: Student work reflecting a sharing interpretation of division.

In a measurement division problem, the size of the groups is known (that is, gift bags have 3 chocolates), and the number of groups (that is, how many gift bags can she make?) is what is to be determined by answering the question. This is shown in figure 7.2. The whole of 18 chocolates is partitioned into groups of 3 until all the chocolates are used.

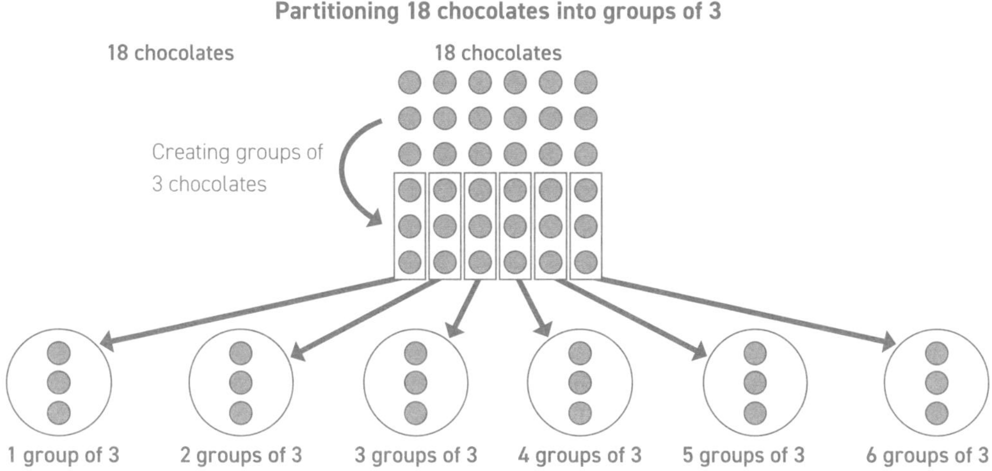

Figure 7.2: Student work reflecting a measurement interpretation of division.

The difference between the sharing and measurement perspectives are summarized in figure 7.3. Awareness of these two different interpretations will help you to create contextual problems that exemplify each interpretation. A dynamic understanding of division involves knowing each of these interpretations and flexibility to determine which situations are more easily understood with one interpretation over the other.

Multiplication Number of Groups × Size of Groups = Whole	
Number of Groups	Known
Size of Groups	Known
Whole	**Unknown**

Sharing Division Whole ÷ Number of Groups = Size of Groups	
Number of Groups	Known
Size of Groups	**Unknown**
Whole	Known

Measurement Division Whole ÷ Size of Groups = Number of Groups	
Number of Groups	**Unknown**
Size of Groups	Known
Whole	Known

Figure 7.3: Contrasting the two interpretations of division and why there are two.

The Ability to See Division

The beauty of division is that students with a dynamic understanding of multiplication are well positioned to develop a strong understanding of division. Understanding the language and structures of multiplication and the representation involving them forms a strong foundation. For example, the implied question to solve the whole-number division problem 20 ÷ 4 using a measurement interpretation is "How many groups of 4 can be created from a whole of 20?" Figure 7.4 reflects the actions to solve the problem utilizing each representation that we used with multiplication. In this problem, the whole is partitioned into 5 groups of 4.

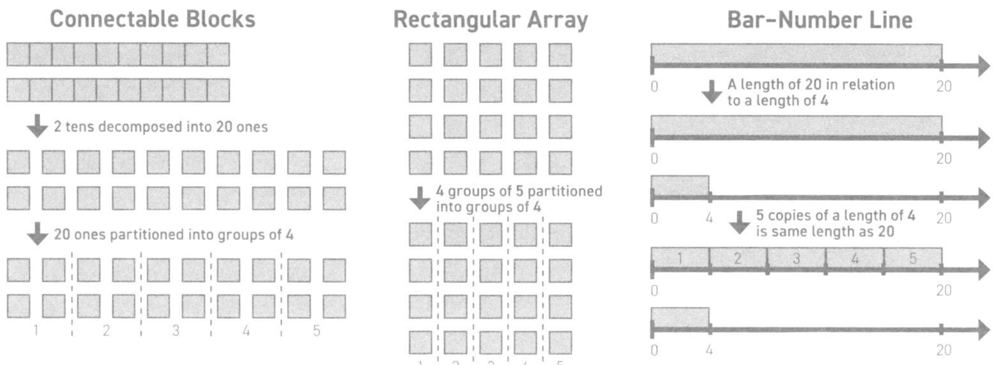

Figure 7.4: Seeing solving the division problem 20 ÷ 4 using three different representations.

Let's suppose that we change the whole to 22 while keeping the size of the group the same, creating the division problem 22 ÷ 4. Remember the question that we're answering by solving the problem is "How many groups of 4 can be created from a whole of 22?" Both the connectable block model and the bar–number line model enable a partial group of 4 to be seen, but the rectangular array model requires a little multiplicative thinking to reason about the number of groups of 4. We know that we could create 5 groups of 4 from the whole of 20. Now the whole is 22, which leaves 2 left over. How would we describe this using "groups of" language? We have ½ of a group of 4. This is shown multiple ways in figure 7.5 using the same three representations as before.

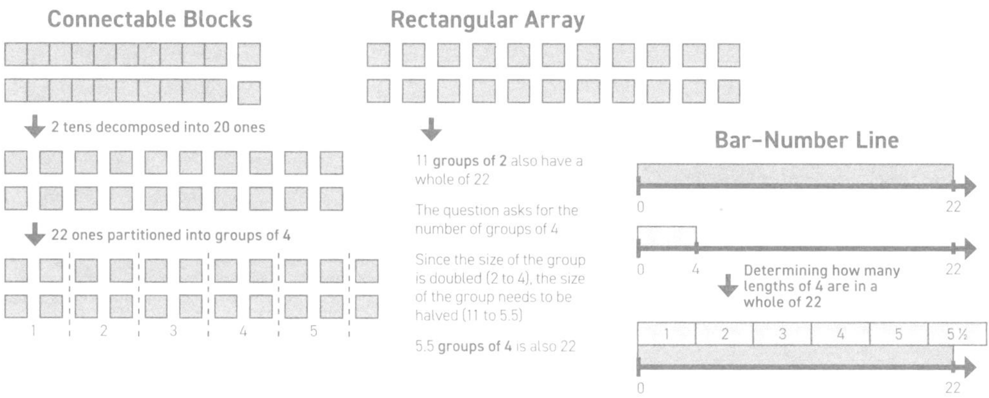

Figure 7.5: Seeing solving the division problem 22 ÷ 4 using three different representations.

There comes a point in which concrete models, as they did with multiplication, become too cumbersome to use to model division problems. Either the numbers become too large to represent with the model, or the model is unable to represent needed units (for example, *thousandths*). This is true for both connectable block models and rectangular arrays. The bar–number line has the greatest potential for handling division problems involving larger numbers or units less than one.

PAUSE AND PONDER

Suppose that you have 3 one-dollar bills and you're going to share all of the money equally with 4 friends. The only exchanges you can do are for dimes and pennies. Reflect on the actions you would take to ensure that each friend receives the same amount.

Same question, but now instead of 3 one-dollar bills, you have 3 one-hundred-dollar bills. Reflect on what is similar or different about solving this problem compared to the first problem.

How to Solve Division Problems Leveraging What We Already Know

Let's now consider two different types of division problems that students are typically asked to solve, 300 ÷ 4 and "Convert the fraction ¾ to a decimal." Both problems require activating our superpowers—specifically, our number-unit-name and equal exchange superpowers. We are going to look at each of these division problems using a sharing interpretation. The implied sharing question in the problem 300 ÷ 4 is "Assuming each group receives the same amount, how much will each of the 4 groups receive from a whole of 300?" Now, let's focus on the quantity and size of unit represented by the whole of

300 (3 *hundreds*). Can you equally share 3 *hundreds* with each of the 4 groups? Nope! You have only a quantity of 3 of the unit *hundreds*. But we can equally exchange 3 *hundreds* for 30 *tens*! We can now share 7 *tens* with each of the 4 groups (4 × 70 = 280). This leaves us with 2 *tens* to share between the 4 groups. Equally exchanging 2 *tens* for 20 *ones*, we can share 5 *ones* with each of the 4 groups (4 × 5 = 20). Each of your friends receives 7 *tens* and 5 *ones*, or 75 (4 × 75 = 300). These actions are modeled using a pictorial representation of connectable blocks in figure 7.6. Would you believe that the algorithm that you learned to solve division problems involved these same actions? They were just hiding under the hood! Compare the standard division algorithm, also shown in figure 7.6, with the actions to solve the problem illustrated with the pictorial model.

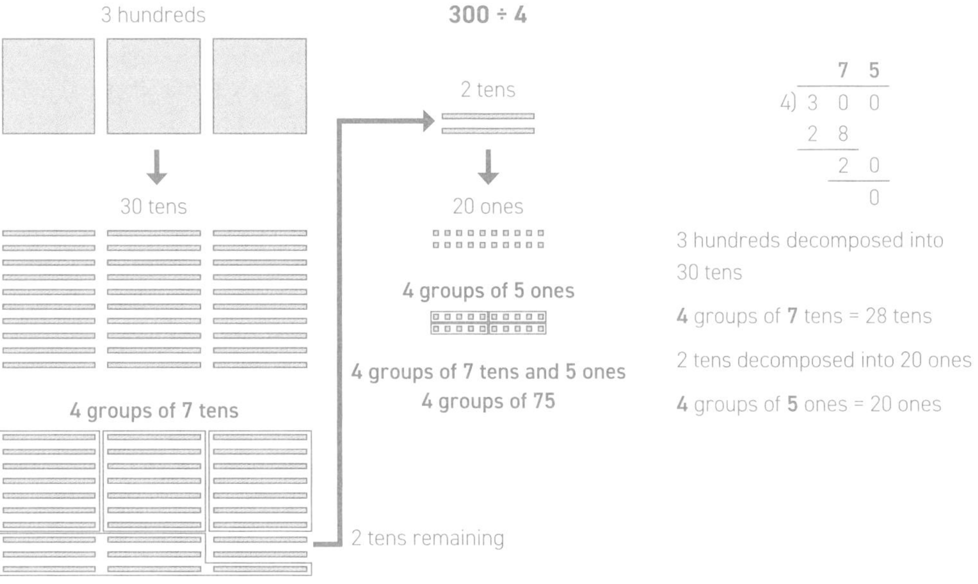

Figure 7.6: Seeing the decomposing of units to solve 300 ÷ 4.

Did you realize that you solved this problem already in the Pause and Ponder prior to this? Did you realize that you also solved the second problem, convert ¾ to a decimal, in the Pause and Ponder? Did you realize they were analogous problems? Table 7.1 illustrates why these two problems are analogous.

Table 7.1: Connecting the Actions of Solving "Different" Problems That Both Involve Division

300 ÷ 4	Convert ¾ to a decimal
1. Decompose 3 *hundreds* into 30 *tens*.	1. Decompose 3 *ones* into 30 *tenths*.
2. Determine how *tens* can fit equally into 4 groups (4 groups of 7 tens).	2. Determine how many *tenths* can fit equally into 4 groups (4 groups of 7 tenths).
3. Decompose remaining 2 *tens* into 20 *ones*.	3. Decompose remaining 2 *tenths* into 20 *hundredths*.
4. Determine how many *ones* (20) can fit equally into 4 groups (4 groups of 5 ones).	4. Determine how many *hundredths* (20) can fit equally into 4 groups (4 groups of 5 hundredths).

continued →

5. Determine total number in each of the 4 groups (4 groups of 7 *tens* and 5 *ones*).	5. Determine total number in each of the 4 groups (4 groups of 7 *tenths* and 5 *hundredths*).
7 *tens* and 5 *ones* = 75	**7 *tenths* and 5 *hundredths* = 0.75**

Long Division

Like fractions and timed multiplication tests, long division is another often-cited topic among college students in conversations about what took them out of the mathematics game. As I suggested in the previous chapter, Siri or Alexa can perform these calculations quicker than we can write the problem. Our students have the answers at their fingertips to any long division problem in their textbook. The goal is no longer just to be proficient with using the algorithm to obtain answers but to understand the why behind the algorithm and why that answer makes sense. In other words, because of technology, the "proficiency of" has changed from utilizing to interpreting.

There are three understandings that we want students to have related to division problems involving more challenging numbers, or long division. First, students need to be able to determine a reasonable estimate so that they can discern whether the technology is giving them a reasonable answer. Remember the technology is only as accurate as the person entering the data! We have probably all learned this lesson! Second, students need to understand why what they are doing makes mathematical sense. This supports their ability to find a way through when they aren't sure what to do. And third, students need opportunities to see it and say it before symbolizing it. In this chapter, we'll cover all three of these ideas.

Let me take a moment to illustrate what I mean. We could start out the lesson on long division writing the problem 2,470 ÷ 8 on the board and explaining the process to students using terms like *dividend*, *divisor*, *quotient*, and *remainder*. But why? While those words have mathematical meaning, are they helpful to students first learning the concept? I made the same argument earlier in the book with the terms *numerator* and *denominator*. I think you know where I stand on this issue. Remember the importance of being sensitive to our adult brains knowing the concept language versus the student first learning the concept language. Contrast the first approach with one in which students are given a contextual problem, "There are 2,470 candy bars, and we're going to place them equally into 8 boxes. How many boxes will be needed?" A lot of candy bars! Big boxes! A little contrived, I know, but hang with me!

PAUSE AND PONDER

Does the candy bar problem represent a sharing or measurement interpretation of division? How do you know?

Write a similar division problem that uses the same numbers, but with the other interpretation of division.

I gave this problem to a student who I knew had a dynamic understanding of multiplication. They hadn't even been taught the long division algorithm yet. The first thing they did was decompose 2,470 into 2,400 and 70. They knew that 8 groups of 300 (3 *hundred*) was 2,400 and 8 groups of 8 (8 *ones*) was 64, leaving 6 remaining candy bars. They knew that 6 remaining candy bars would need to be broken apart, and each of the 8 boxes would receive ¾ (75 *hundredths*) of another candy bar. The result would be that each of the 8 boxes would be filled with 308 ¾ (3 *hundreds* and 8 *ones* and 75 *hundredths*) candy bars. I often find that students can reason about contextual division problems but struggle when they are presented in a form without context, 2,470 ÷ 8. The reason is that students have not made associations between the actions involved in solving a contextual problem and interpreting those same actions in a noncontextual problem. Part of a conceptually consistent understanding is seeing the same ideas in different representation forms as well as seeing the same language. To illustrate this point, consider solving the same problem,

2,470 ÷ 8, using the long division algorithm. The recording of the algorithm is shown in figure 7.7. Also shown is a contrast between the language we often, internally or externally, speak while working through a long division problem and a shift in language that makes the unit and equal exchanges explicit.

```
   308.75
8)2470
  24
   070
    64
     60
     56
      40
      40
       0
```

Long Division Algorithm	Units and Equal Exchanges Made Explicit
8 does not go evenly into 2, but it does go into 24, **3** times	2 *thousands* is decomposed into 20 *hundreds* so that there are now 24 *hundreds* 8 groups of **3** ***hundred*** is 24 *hundred*
Subtracting 24 from 24 is 0	24 *hundred* − 24 *hundred* = 0
Bring down the 7; 8 does not go into 7; place a zero in tens place; but it does go into 70, 8 times	7 *tens* is decomposed into 70 *ones* 8 groups of **8** ***ones*** is 64 *ones*
Subtracting 64 from 70 is 6	70 *ones* − 64 *ones* = 6 *ones*
Bring the 6 down; 8 does not go into 6, but it does go into 60, 7 times	6 *ones* is decomposed into 60 *tenths* 8 groups of **7** ***tenths*** is 56 tenths
Subtracting 56 from 60 is 4	60 *tenths* − 56 *tenths* = 4 *tenths*
Bring the 4 down; 8 does not go evenly into 4, but it does go into 40, 5 times	4 *tenths* is decomposed into 40 *hundredths* 8 groups of **5** ***hundredths*** is 40 *hundredths*
Subtracting 40 from 40 is 0	40 hundredths − 40 hundredths = 0

Figure 7.7: Using the long division algorithm to solve 2,470 ÷ 8.

PAUSE AND PONDER

Reflect on the strategy that the student, not knowing the long division algorithm, used to solve the problem "There are 2,470 candy bars, and we're going to place them equally in 8 boxes. How many candy bars will be needed?"

Carefully study the recording of the use of the long division algorithm shown in figure 7.7. Compare the student's strategy and the long division algorithm. What is similar? What is different?

Did you notice how closely aligned the student's reasoning, not knowing the long division algorithm, aligned with the actual recording of the use of the algorithm? The student decomposed the whole of 2,470 into the parts 2,400 and 70 and determined how many groups of 8 were in each. That is, 8 groups of 300 and 8 groups of 8 and 8 groups of ¾ or, making the units explicit, 8 groups of 3 *hundred* and 8 groups of 8 *ones* and 8 groups 75 *hundredths*. Do you see 8 of each of those three quantities of units anywhere in figure 7.7? Where do you see the 300 and 8 and 0.75 in the long division algorithm? The point I want to make is that this student, using a dynamic understanding of multiplication, was using the long division algorithm without knowing that they were! Give students the right tools and problems that give them the opportunity to reason, and they'll surprise you with the thinking they can do!

Partial Quotient Algorithm

Aside from the typical unit and equal exchange hiding language (that is, "goes into" and "bring down") used to teach the long division algorithm, there is one other issue I have with it. It requires that students have mastery of their 0–9 multiplication facts. Some of our students will not have this mastery before they are introduced to long division. I wish this weren't the case, but that's the reality. Most of us have had the experience of beginning to teach long division knowing that we have students who have not yet developed automaticity with their multiplication facts. There must be a way to help them be successful with long division despite this limitation. Welcome to the power of the *partial quotient algorithm*!

Unlike the traditional long division algorithm, the partial quotient algorithm gives students the flexibility to choose the multiplication relationships that they are most comfortable using. It gives them the flexibility to use the multiplicative facts that they know. Let's return to the earlier problem, 2,470 ÷ 8, to examine how the partial quotient algorithm works. The implied question, using a sharing perspective, is "Given a whole of 2,470 and 8 equal-sized groups, what will be the size of each of those groups?" Let's imagine that we're working with a frustrated student who has struggled with their multiplication facts beyond 5. Do they know 8 groups of 1? Sure! How about 8 groups of 100? They do, if they see 8 groups of 1 and 8 groups of 100 as analogous problems. Let's leverage this known fact to remove 8 groups of

100 from 2,470. So far, we have 8 groups of **100** (800) and there is 1,670 left in the whole (2,400 – 800). Can we remove 8 groups of 100 again? Actually, we can remove 8 groups of **100** (1,670 – 800 = 870) and 8 groups of **100** again (870 – 800 = 70). The student knows that 8 groups of **5** is 40 (70 – 40 = 30) and 8 groups of **1** is 8 (30 – 8 = 22), which they use again, 8 groups of **1** (22 – 8 = 14), and again, 8 groups of **1** (14 – 8 = 6). This results in 8 groups of **308** (100 + 100 + 100 + 5 + 1 + 1 + 1) with 6 remaining. It may take a little work to get them to think about 8 groups of__ = 6, but possibly leveraging 8 groups of 1 is 8 and 8 groups of 0.5 is 4, the student may be able to reason that 8 groups of **0.75** is 6. This means there are 8 groups of a size of 308.75 in a whole of 2,470 (8 × 308.75 = 2,470).

It may seem like more work than using the long division algorithm, but remember the goal is to help students develop a dynamic understanding of division relying heavily on their understanding of multiplication at whichever level that might be. The choice of the size of the groups is guided by the students' understanding of their multiplication facts and the multiplicative relationships they see. In other words, they get to choose the route to reach the same destination. That is the beauty of the partial quotient algorithm—the student chooses what to see along the journey! The journey of three different students to reach a destination of 308.75 from the starting point of 2,470 ÷ 8 is shown in figure 7.8.

Student 1

0.75	
1	
1	
1	
5	
100	308.75
100	
100	
8) 2470	
800	8 × 100 = 800
1670	
800	8 × 100 = 800
870	
800	8 × 100 = 800
70	
40	8 × 5 = 40
30	
8	8 × 1 = 8
22	
8	8 × 1 = 8
14	
8	8 × 1 = 8
6	8 × 0.75 = 6

Student 2

0.75	
8	308.75
300	
8) 2470	
2400	8 × 300 = 2400
70	
64	8 × 8 = 64
6	8 × 0.75 = 6

Student 3

0.75	
3	
5	308.75
100	
200	
8) 2470	
1600	8 × 200 = 1600
870	
800	8 × 100 = 800
70	
40	8 × 5 = 40
30	
24	8 × 3 = 24
6	8 × 0.75 = 6

Figure 7.8: A recording of three different students' work using the partial quotient algorithm.

As I mentioned earlier, long division provides another great opportunity to build students' estimation powers. For example, an instructional strategy I like to use is, before they are shown a a strategy that will yield an exact answer, to ask students to "reasonably guess" as to how much each person would receive, using the numbers from the Try It, if \$3,444 is shared equally with 6 people. When a student provides an estimate (for example, \$500), it is "tested" (for example, $6 \times 500 = 3{,}000$). The rest of the class—pardon the Goldilocks and the Three Bears reference—responds "too much," "too little," or "just right," and adjustments are made to the estimate until an answer that is close is determined.

TRY IT
Use the partial quotient algorithm to solve the division problem 3,444 ÷ 6 three different ways.
Give your students a contextual division problem like 3,444 ÷ 6 and observe the strategies they use. Do any of their strategies connect to the three ways you used the partial quotient algorithm?

Division Involving Fractions

When working with a class of fifth graders, I posed the following problem: "A zookeeper has 4 cups of frog food. His frog eats ⅓ cup of food each day. How long can he feed the frogs before the food runs out?" (Empson & Levi, 2011). I watched as each group drew pictures to represent the problem and successfully solved the problem. The most common strategy used by multiple groups is shown in figure 7.9 (page 160).

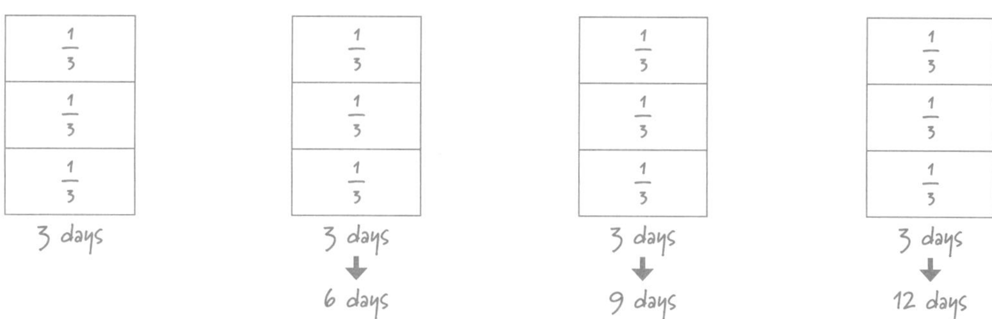

Figure 7.9: Example of the reasoning students used to solve the frog problem.

Since they already had experiences with division, I asked them to present the division problem 4 ÷ ⅓ as a warm-up the following week. As a class, the students were unsure how to reason about the problem. This is despite the fact that the previous week they had all shown that they were able to reason about the conceptual underpinnings of the same problem presented contextually. As I stated earlier, students often don't see those conceptual underpinnings when the problem is presented without context.

So what do we want students to "see" and "say" when given a division problem like 4 ÷ ⅓? Using a measurement interpretation, we want them to "say" the implied question, "How many groups of size ⅓ can be made from a whole of 4?" Second, we want them to "see" that the problem will have the same answer as the division problem 12 ÷ 1. Let's explore the language that supports what we want them to "see" as they look through a division problem and why both of these division problems have the same answer.

Students need a language beyond "keep, change, flip" to make sense of what they're doing to solve division problems involving fractions. Remember! Getting answers is no longer the destination. They have technology available that will do that for them. The language they need, as I shared, is a way to describe the question that is being asked by 4 ÷ ⅓. I'm going to adjust the implied question to make the unit explicit: "How many groups of size 1 *third* can we make from 4 *ones*?" I am going to adjust the implied question one more time using an equal exchange: "How many groups of size 1 *third* can we make from 12 *thirds*?" Yep! The division problem 4 ÷ ⅓ is analogous to the whole-number problem 12 ÷ 1!

If you take another look at the student work shown in figure 7.8 (page 158), these adjusted questionss can be seen in their work. They partitioned each *one* into 3 groups of 1 *third* and determined that there were 3 *thirds* in each *one*, so there would be 12 *thirds* in 4 *wholes*, and since the frog eats 1 *third* of a cup each day, they determined it would take 12 *days* (12 ÷ 1) for the frog to finish 4 cups of food. The symbolic recording of their work could be 3 + 3 + 3 + 3 = 12, or 4 groups of 3 is 12. "Wait!" you might be thinking. "Addition? Multiplication? I thought we were doing division." More on that in a moment!

The Why Behind "Keep, Change, Flip"

In order to help us translate the traditional language of "keep, change, flip" into student-friendly terminology and ultimately deepen students' understanding, let's take a moment to see for ourselves what is meant by the language associated with the common algorithm used to solve division problems and how the actions of this algorithm are seen in the group's work shown in figure 7.8 (page 158). Using the "keep, change, flip" language to solve the division problem 4 ÷ ⅓, the first number is "kept," the operation is "changed" to multiplication, and the second number is "flipped," creating the multiplication problem **4 × 3**. Remember the first number is the whole, 4 *ones*, and the second number is the size of the group, 1 *third*. How many 1 *thirds* are there in 1 whole? (3). So, using a little multiplicative reasoning, if 1 whole (or *one*) has 3 *thirds* (1 × 3), then 4 wholes (or *ones*) have **4 × 3** *thirds*. As shown in figure 7.10, the "flipping" action is about determining how many of a quantity of units (1 *third*) are in 1 whole (for example, **3** *thirds*) and then multiplying together the number of wholes (4) and the number of that unit in 1 whole (4 × 3 = 12).

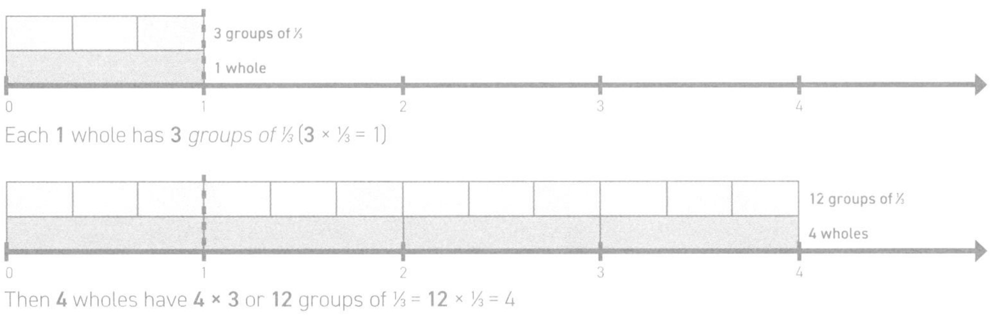

Figure 7.10: Seeing the why underpinning "keep, change, flip."

A lot of units to coordinate! The actions to think about a familiar division problem, 4 ÷ ⅓, and a related problem, 4 ÷ ⅔, in terms of multiplication are shown using a bar–number line model in figure 7.11. Notice what happens to the number of groups as the size of the group doubles from ⅓ to ⅔.

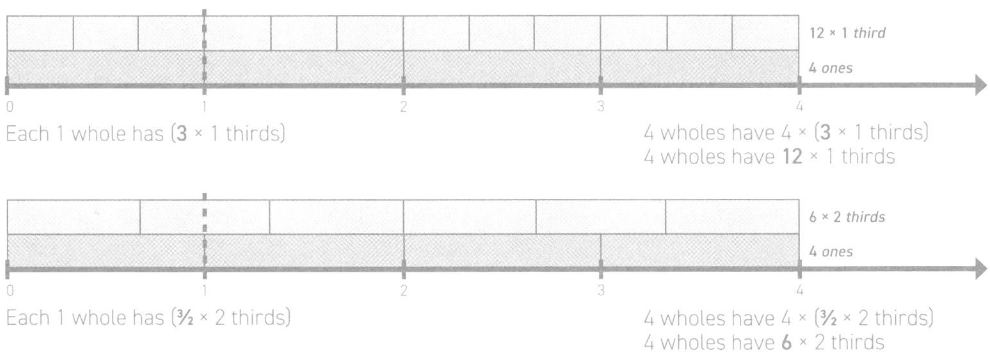

Figure 7.11: Seeing 4 ÷ ⅓ and 4 ÷ ⅔ in terms of 4 × 3 and 4 × $\frac{3}{2}$.

A dynamic understanding of division involves the ability to use the conceptual language of division to make sense of related problems. For example, if a student sees why 4 ÷ ⅓ is 12 and knows the conceptual language to interpret the problem, then reasoning about why the answer to 4 ÷ ⅔ is 6 should not be a challenge. That is, the size of the group has doubled from ⅓ to ⅔ while the whole remained the same, which means the number of groups is half (12 to 6).

How to See Division as Addition and Subtraction

As alluded to earlier, I have been in classrooms in which students have solved the frog food problem (4 ÷ ⅓) using different operations. Some students repeatedly added groups of ⅓ together, realizing that there are 3 groups of ⅓ in 1 whole. They multiplied by 4 (4 × 3) to determine that there were 12 groups of ⅓ in 4 wholes. Other students subtracted groups of ⅓ from 4 wholes until there were no more groups of ⅓ to remove. Oftentimes, the pictorial models look similar, so it's essential that students have opportunities to symbolically record their thinking so that you know exactly how they are thinking.

PAUSE AND PONDER

Create a pictorial model to solve the following two problems.

Problem A: *You have 9 brownies. You want to make bags with 4 brownies each. How many bags with 4 brownies can you make? (Be sure to include partial whole bags.)*

Problem B: *Your breakfast meal involves ¾ of a whole cup of oatmeal. The only clean measurer is ⅓ whole cup measurer. How many times will you have to fill your measurer to obtain the correct amount of oatmeal for your morning breakfast? (Be sure to include partial fills.)*

If it's appropriate, share these two problems in tandem with your students. Observe the strategies they use and any reasoning barriers that they may face in solving these problems.

A Connection to Whole-Number Division

I can imagine a group of students using physical objects to model solving problem A by creating 2 groups of 4 with 1 object left over. Problem B would be a little more challenging for them. To solve the problem, students would need a way to determine how many groups of 1 *third* would be in 3 *fourths*. The problem, as has been the case many times before, is that the units are not the same. However, as has also been the case many times before, equal exchanges to the rescue! The group size of 1 *third* can be equally exchanged for 4 *twelfths*, and 3 *fourths* can be equally exchanged for 9 *twelfths*. Do the quantities 9 and 4 look familiar? Yes, indeed! Those are the same quantities that were used in problem A. And I know what you're thinking—problems A and B are analogous! Let that sink in for a moment. The whole-number division problem **9** ÷ **4** is an analogous problem to the fraction division problem ¾ ÷ ⅓, or **9⁄12** ÷ **4⁄12**. Solving both problems results in **2 ¼** groups of 9 of a unit. The actions to solve each problem are shown using a bar–number line in figure 7.12. One of the important aspects of division is attending to, or coordinating, the size of the groups or units. In the first problem, 9 ÷ **4**, units of length 4 were created. The remaining 1 is interpreted in relation to the group size of **4**. That is, 1 is ¼ of another unit of **4**. Likewise, in the second problem, 9⁄12 ÷ **4⁄12**, the remaining 1 *twelfth* is represented not in terms of the whole of 12 *twelfths* but as a part of a unit of 4 *twelfths*, since that is the size of the group. That is, 1 *twelfth* is ¼ of another unit of ***4 twelfths***.

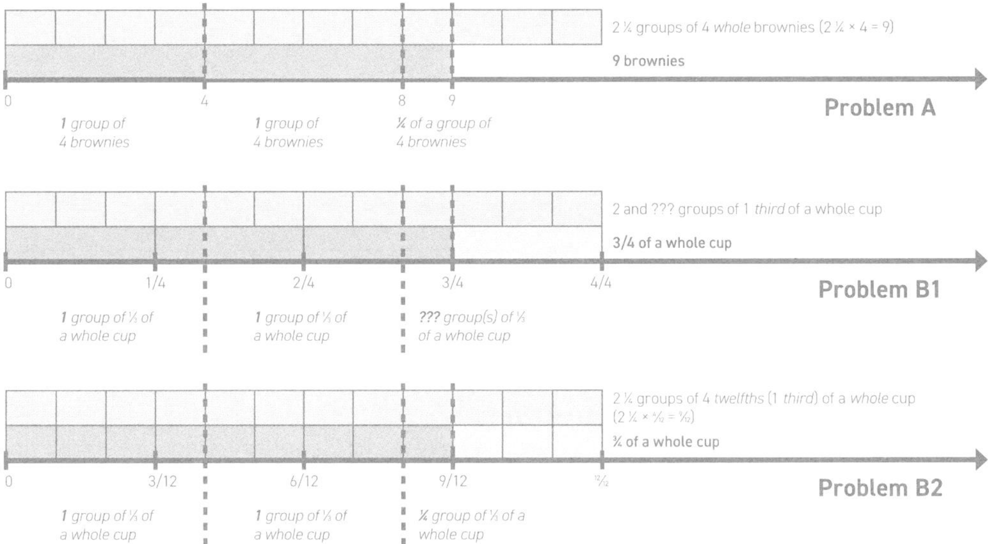

Figure 7.12: Modeling the solution to the analogous division problems 9 ÷ 4 and ¾ ÷ ⅓.

Create an analogous whole-number division problem to ⅔ ÷ ¼. Use a bar–number line to model the solution to both.

Any division problem of the form *whole number ÷ unit fraction* can easily be transformed into an analogous whole-number division problem. Convince yourself of this. Which understanding(s) of division underpins your reasoning?

As we discussed in chapter 4 (page 73), the phrase "getting a common denominator" is typically associated with the action of adding fractions. This makes sense since adding is a combining action that requires the size of the units to be the same. As you just experienced, this idea can be used to turn any fraction division problem into a whole-number division problem. Using a measurement interpretation of division, the implied question is, How many groups of a particular size can be created from a given whole? The analogous whole-number division problem can be created by making sure the whole and the size of the group have the same size of unit. For example, consider the division problem $\frac{15}{16} \div \frac{1}{2}$, or, making the units explicit, 15 *sixteenths* ÷ 1 *half.* Using an equal exchange, the problem is recomposed into 15 *sixteenths* ÷ 8 *sixteenths*, which is now in a form that is analogous to the whole-number division problem 15 ÷ 8.

A few years ago, I shared this idea with a group of construction management foremen at a technical college symposium. One of the construction foremen slammed his tape measure down on a desk and quite angrily exclaimed, "You mean all these years I could have simply solved fraction division problems with a common denominator? Why was I never taught that?" It was right in front of him the whole time! He expressed to me that knowing this would have made the real-world division he does so much easier.

Flexibility With Interpretations

The reality of division is that some problems are more easily understood using a measurement interpretation (for example, 4 ÷ ⅔) while others are more easily understood using a sharing interpretation (for example, ⅔ ÷ 4). Let's consider the implied question of the problem 4 ÷ ⅔ from a sharing interpretation: How much of 4 wholes can we share with ⅔ groups? Sounds funny, right? Now consider the implied question from a measurement interpretation: How many groups of ⅔ can be created from 4 wholes? In this case, it makes more sense to reason from a measurement interpretation of division. That is, there are 12 thirds in 4 whole. So we can make 6 groups of 2 thirds with 12 thirds.

The implied question that the solution to the division problem ⅔ ÷ 4 is answering using a sharing interpretation is, How much will be in 4 equal groups if the whole is ⅔? Using a measurement interpretation, the implied question is, How many groups of a 4 whole units can be created from ⅔ of a whole unit? I am sharing a contextual division problem of ⅔ ÷ 4 using both interpretations. Take a moment to reason through each problem.

Problem A: *You have ⅔ of a pound of ground beef. You want to make ground beef patties to feed 4 friends. Using all the ground beef, how much will each friend receive? (Sharing)*

Problem B: *You have ⅔ of a pound of ground beef. There are 4 pounds of ground beef in each package. What part of a whole 4-pound package is ⅔ of a pound of ground beef? (Measurement)*

Did you feel the sharing interpretation problem, problem A, aligning with the reasoning we have used on other division problems? Were you able to imagine partitioning a whole of 2 *thirds* into 4 equally sized groups as shown in figure 7.13 easier than you could determining which part of a whole 4-pound package is ⅔ of a pound of ground beef?

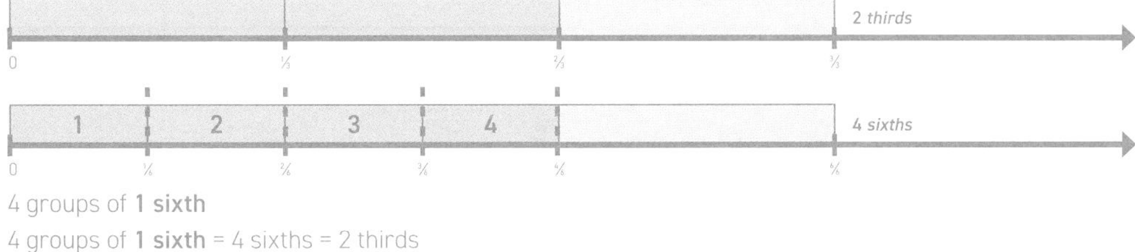

4 groups of **1 sixth**

4 groups of **1 sixth** = 4 sixths = 2 thirds

4 × (⅙) = 4/6 = ⅔

Figure 7.13: Seeing ⅔ ÷ 4 from a sharing interpretation of division.

The measurement interpretation problem feels more like a proportion problem in which two quantities are bound together (1 whole package to 4 pounds), and that idea is used to determine what part of a whole package is ⅔ of a pound. We'll save this for the next chapter.

PAUSE AND PONDER

Consider the division problem $\frac{2}{3} \div 4$. Write the implied question that solving the problem is answering using both sharing and measurement interpretations of division.

Which interpretation seems to make more sense? Or do they seem equally sensible?

Division Involving Mixed Numbers

Complete the following four division problems. Take note of your reasoning so you may compare it to that of your students.

PAUSE AND PONDER

Using the dynamic understanding of division that you have developed over the course of reading this chapter, use your mental arithmetic superpowers to reason through the following four division problems.

- $4\frac{1}{2} \div \frac{1}{2}$

- 4 ¼ ÷ ⅛

- 4 ¼ ÷ 2 ⅛

- ¾ ÷ 3

If it is appropriate, engage your students in a number talk or two involving these four problems.

A significant part of unleashing mental arithmetic superpowers with division involves four elements: (1) understanding the implied question that is being asked using the appropriate interpretation; (2) seeing flexibility with equal exchanges; (3) having an awareness of whole-number analogous problems; and (4) leveraging multiplicative relationships. Figure 7.14 shares two mental arithmetic strategies to solve each of the problems you completed in the Pause and Ponder, so you can imagine the possibilities of how students with a dynamic understanding of division might reason about those same problems.

Problem	Mental Strategy 1	Mental Strategy 2
4 ½ ÷ ½	1. There are 2 groups of 1 *half* in each 1 *whole*, so there are 8 groups of 1 *half* in 4 *wholes*. 2. There are 2 groups of 1 *half* in 1 *whole*. 3. There is a total of **9** groups of 1 *half* in 4 wholes and 1 *half*.	1. An equal exchange of 4 *wholes* and 1 *half* is 9 halves. 2. There are 9 groups of 1 *half* in 9 *halves*.

continued →

4 ½ ÷ ⅛	1. There are 8 groups of 1 *eighth* in each 1 *whole*, so there are 32 groups of 1 *eighth* in 4 *wholes*. 2. An equal exchange for 1 *half* is 4 *eighths*. 3. There are 4 groups of 1 *eighth* in 1 *half*. 4. There is a total of **36** groups of 1 *eighth* in 4 *wholes* and 1 *half*.	1. The number of groups in the previous problem was 9. 2. The size of the unit in this problem as compared to the previous problem is 4 times lesser, and the whole is the same, so the number of groups must be 4 times greater or 4 × 9 = **36**.
4 ½ ÷ 2 ¼	1. The sum is 4 *wholes* and 1 *half*. 2. An equal exchange for 4 *wholes* and 1 *half* is 4 *wholes* and 2 *fourths*. 3. There are **2** groups of 2 *wholes* and 1 *fourth* in 4 *wholes* and 2 *fourths*.	1. An equal exchange for 4 *wholes* and 1 *half* is 18 *fourths*. 2. An equal exchange for 2 *wholes* and 1 *fourth* is 9 *fourths*. 3. The answer is the same as the analogous whole-number problem 18 ÷ 9 = 2.
3 ¾ ÷ 3	1. 3 *wholes* partitioned into 3 equal groups is 1 hole. 2. 3 *fourths* of a whole portioned into equal groups is 1 *fourth*. 3. 3 *wholes* and 3 *fourths* partitioned into 3 equal groups is **1** *whole* and **1** *fourth*.	1. An equal exchange of 3 *wholes* and 3 *fourths* is 15 *fourths*. 2. 15 *fourths* partitioned into 3 equal groups is 5 *fourths* or 1 *whole* and 1 *fourth*.

Figure 7.14: Imagining the possibilities for students with a dynamic understanding of division.

Division Involving Decimals

The beauty of division problems involving decimals is that they can easily be turned into analogous whole-number division problems. As mentioned earlier, all that is needed is an ability to create equal exchanges in which both the whole and the size of groups are the same size of unit.

PAUSE AND PONDER

Using the dynamic understanding of division that you have developed over the course of reading this chapter, use your mental arithmetic superpowers to reason through the following three division problems.

- 6 ÷ 0.8

- 0.6 ÷ 0.08

- 0.28 ÷ 0.07

If it is appropriate, engage your students in a number talk involving these three problems.

Now consider how the three problems that you just reasoned can be turned into analogous whole-number division problems using equal exchanges in which both the whole and size of group are represented using the same size of unit. The first problem, 6 ÷ 0.8, or 6 ÷ 8 *tenths*, can be transformed, using an equal exchange, into **60** *tenths* ÷ **8** *tenths*. Likewise, the next problem, 0.6 ÷ 0.08, or 6 *tenths* ÷ 8 *hundredths*, can be transformed again, using an equal exchange, into the same whole-number division problem, **60** *hundredths* ÷ **8** *hundredths*. The last problem, 0.28 ÷ 0.07, or **28** *hundredths* ÷ **7** *hundredths*, doesn't even need an equal exchange to be seen in terms of an analogous whole-number division problem.

Students' abilities to unleash their mental arithmetic superpowers with division problems involve two decimals proficiencies: (1) a flexibility with equal exchanges and (2) an awareness of whole-number analogous problems. Both proficiencies are underpinned by an awareness of the units and the relationship between the quantities and units in equal exchange transformations.

PAUSE AND PONDER

As a result of reading this chapter, how are you thinking differently about division?

After reading this chapter, what are one or two instructional shifts that you are planning to make in how you teach division? What will be the biggest challenge to implementing those shifts?

Key Points

Before proceeding, please take a moment to review the following takeaways from this chapter.

- The numerals in a multiplication problem (for example, 6 × 8) can be interpreted as a quantity or number of groups or a scale factor, 6, and a multiplicative unit or size of a group, 8 units of *one* or 1 *eight*. The whole is the result of performing this operation. Since division is the undoing of multiplication, division problems can be interpreted in terms of either a number of groups (sharing) or the size of the groups (measurement). For example, the division problem 48 ÷ 6 can be interpreted contextually as either "Given 6 groups and 48 objects, how many objects can be equally placed in each group?" (sharing) or "Given groups of 6 and 48 objects, how many groups can be created?" (measurement).

- As multiplication involves recomposing units, division involves decomposing units. For example, in a problem such as 42 ÷ 8, there are not enough tens, 4, to place them equally into 8 groups. The 4 *tens* and 2 *ones*, using an equal exchange of 10 *ones* for 1 *ten*, can be decomposed into 42 *ones*. This enables the partitioning action to occur so that 8 groups of 5 *ones* can be created. The remaining 2 *ones*, using another equal exchange (10 *tenths* for 1 *one*), can be decomposed into 20 *tenths*. This enables another partitioning action to occur, creating 8 groups of 2 *tenths*. The remaining 4 *tenths*, using another equal exchange (10 *hundredths* for 1 *tenth*), can be decomposed into 40 *hundredths* so that 8 groups of 5 *hundredths* can be created. The result of the actions to determine the size of the 8 equal groups given a whole of 42 (42 ÷ 8) is 5 *ones* and 2 *tenths* and 5 *hundredths*. In other words, 8 groups of 5.25 can be created from a whole of 42.

- All division problems, whether they involve fractions or decimals, can be represented by an analogous whole-number division problem. For example, the fraction division problem ⅝ ÷ ¼, or, making the size of the units explicit, 5 *eighths* ÷ 1 *fourth*, can be transformed into a problem with the same size of unit. In this case, 5 *eighths* ÷ 1 *fourth* is transformed into the analogous problem 5 *eighths* ÷ 2 *eighths*, which can be transformed into the whole-number division problem 5 ÷ 2.

- The partial quotient algorithm is a great alternative to the traditional long division algorithm because it relies on multiplication relationships with which the student is familiar. Unlike the traditional long division algorithm, the student gets to choose which multiplicative relationship to use.

As was the case with the three previous operations, the key points of division emphasize "seeing" the size of the unit and making connections to analogous division problems. What is unique about division is that noncontextual problems can be interpreted two different ways, sharing and measurement. The application guide in this chapter provides ideas that will support you as you work to develop a dynamic and flexible understanding of division in your own students.

Chapter 7 Application Guide

Chapter Concepts	How Can I Incorporate This Into My Teaching Practice Moving Forward?
Seeing Division	Provide opportunities for students to do the following. 1. Solve contextual problems using concrete objects to create equal-sized groups (measurement) or move objects into a fixed number of groups (sharing). 2. Solve division problems using base 10 blocks, placing an emphasis on decomposing units and making connections to the symbolic form of the division problem. Have students record these actions making sure the unit name is made explicit. 3. Solve division problems using the bar–number line model, placing an emphasis on partitioning the whole into equal-sized groups. Start with the bar–number line model and provide both the length of the whole and the size of the group. 4. For 1 through 3, have them perform the actions, and as they become more proficient, have them write the symbolic division problem modeled by those actions.
Saying Division (Sharing and Measurement Interpretations)	1. Communicate the implied question of noncontextual division problems using either one or both interpretations. 2. Use conceptual language to describe equal exchanges. 3. Describe the actions involved in solving division problems, making sure the units are made explicit. 4. Use conceptual language to describe the relationship between the whole, size of groups, and number of groups in pairs of division problems (for example, $4 \div \frac{1}{3}$ and $4 \div \frac{2}{3}$).
Seeing Division Through Multiplication **Partial Quotient Algorithm**	1. Solve contextual division problems involving larger numbers using the strategy of their choosing. 2. Use their own strategies to solve division problems using the partial quotient algorithm that rely on the multiplication facts they are comfortable using. 3. Compare their solution strategies without a known algorithm to the partial quotient algorithm.
Seeing Connections **Analogous Problems**	1. Identify and create whole-number division problems that are analogous to division problems involving fractions and decimals.
Seeing and Saying Connections **Mental Arithmetic Superpowers**	1. Use mental arithmetic strategies to solve problem strings of division problems involving fractions (for example, $4\frac{1}{2} \div \frac{1}{2}$, $4\frac{1}{4} \div \frac{1}{8}$, $4\frac{1}{4} \div 2\frac{1}{8}$, $\frac{3}{4} \div 3$) and problem strings of division problems involving decimals (for example, $6 \div 0.8$, $0.6 \div 0.08$, $0.28 \div 0.07$). 2. Communicate, making the units explicit and specifying the strategies used.

Math: the only place
where you have to figure out
the ratio of red candy to blue candy
when all you're thinking about
is eating them.

—Unknown

CHAPTER 8

Ratios, Proportions, and Percentages, Oh My!

Before diving into ratios, proportions, and percentages, let's spend a few moments reflecting on our journey up to this point. We started with early number concepts and passed through place value, fractions, and the four basic operations. One of my overarching goals is to provide you with the tools to help you develop in your students a dynamic understanding of numbers and operations. Can you believe that this can be done by cultivating four superpower understandings in your own students? These understandings are as follows.

1. **Numbers should be seen in terms of both quantities and sizes of units**. For example, 134 is 1 hundred and 3 tens and 4 ones, and 1 ¾ is 1 whole (or one) and 3 fourths. Related is the idea that the same string of numerals can represent different quantities and sizes of units. For example, the string 134.0 represents 1 *hundred* and 3 *tens* and 4 *ones*, or 13 *tens* and 4 *ones*, or 134 *ones*, or 1,340 *tenths*.
2. A quantity of a size of a unit can be equally exchanged for other quantities of different-sized units. An **equal exchange** is a fair trade of one quantity and size of a unit for another. For example, 1 one can be equally exchanged for 6 sixths, or 4 fourths, or 10 tenths, or 100 hundredths.
3. A fraction can be viewed through several different lenses (that is, part-whole relationship, action, division, and measure) but the most important, consistent with seeing fractions as numbers, is as a measure. A **unit fraction** (formed by

partitioning a whole unit into equally sized lengths and identifying 1 of those lengths in relation to the whole) is the foundation from which all other fractions of the same unit are derived. For example, a measurement interpretation of $\frac{5}{8}$ is a length of 5 groups of a length of 1 eighth of a whole unit.

4. There are many problems that are **analogous problems** of each other. Analogous problems are problems that involve the same quantities but different units. For example, the problem 0.27 + 0.69 (27 *hundredths* + 69 *hundredths*) is analogous to the whole-number addition problem 27 + 69; the problem $\frac{3}{4} \div \frac{1}{3}$ (9 *twelfth* ÷ 4 *twelfths*) is analogous to the whole-number division problem 9 ÷ 4; and the multiplication problem $6 \times \frac{8}{5}$ (6 × 8 *fifths*) is analogous to the whole-number multiplication problem 6 × 8. They are everywhere!

These superpower understandings, coupled with the connector understandings for operations, empower students with the tools to mentally reason about a wide range of problems. These overarching understandings bind together each of the four operations. *Connector understandings* are those overarching understandings that underpin each operation and enable connections to be made among different types of numerical and algebraic expressions. For example, a connector understanding for addition and subtraction is that quantities can be combined (addition) or removed (subtraction) *only* if the size of the unit is the same.

The connector understanding for multiplication and division is the language to differentiate the role of each number in the problem. That is, the first number in a multiplication problem represents the "action," or number of groups, and the second number represents the multiplicative unit, or size of the groups. The result of performing the multiplying action is to determine the whole amount represented by the number of groups of a particular size. Likewise, the first number in a division problem is the whole, or available amount, and the second number can be interpreted as either a number of groups (sharing) or a size of a group (measurement). The result of performing the dividing action on a whole is to determine either the size of the group (sharing) or the number of groups (measurement). With these understandings in their back pockets, students have the tools necessary to move beyond numbers and operations and to tackle a new idea that sometimes looks and feels like a number but isn't: ratios.

Moving forward, we'll first introduce a new interpretation of fractions, as a ratio, and differentiate this interpretation from one that we already know, as a measure. Then, we'll explore equivalent ratios, ratio comparison, proportion, the trouble with the cross multiplication method, and percentages—which will lead us into how to figure out a tip, how to solve a different type of percentage problem, and a final mental arithmetic strategy for the road.

But before diving into ratios, let me lighten the mood a bit, as you've been working hard so you need a good laugh. Like my story that opened the book, this anecdote has to do with my grandma Edna—who was sneaky for an old woman! She knew I loved chicken wings. One time she asked me whether I wanted chicken wings for dinner. At the time, I was only eight years old, and up to that point, anything she made for me had been kissed by the gods. If not for her cooking, there would be a lot less of me today! Now, I must admit when she brought out a plate of these "alleged" chicken wings, they looked a little different, but it was my grandmother. She had yet to lead me astray! As I started working my way through my third wing, she informed me that it wasn't actually a wing at all, but *a leg*. A frog leg, to be precise! Sneaky Grandma! She somehow managed to use that same ploy again to introduce me to other culinary delights—squirrel and beef tongue. She could make anything taste good! She grew up during the Great Depression, which I guessed meant she learned to cook and eat a lot of different stuff! What I didn't know was that she was once again giving me a means for seeing mathematics, as you're about to find out.

Ratios: Same Fraction Notation, Different Interpretations

Ratios are like frog legs! (Bet you didn't see that coming!) They may look, smell, and taste like a fraction, but they act differently! Using the same notations for both fractions and ratios makes understanding these different, but related, ideas difficult for many students.

PAUSE AND PONDER

The two problems that follow illuminate this difficulty. Take a moment to answer the two problems shown.

Problem 1: *Suppose that you ate 13⁄16 of a whole pan of brownies and 3⁄4 of another whole pan of brownies. You were hungry! Assuming both pans are the same size, how much of a whole pan of brownies did you eat?*

Problem 2: *You took two quizzes in a class. On quiz 1, the teacher wrote 13⁄16 at the top of the page. On quiz 2, the teacher wrote 3⁄4 on it. What is your overall quiz grade?*

Did you get two different answers? If you did, take a moment to consider why the answers to these problems are different. If you aren't sure, there is no need to worry because we'll spend some time unpacking the why.

The two problems involve the same pair of "fractions," but are they really both "fractions"? These problems exemplify the difference between two different interpretations of fractions: *fraction-as-measure* and *fraction-as-ratio*. Through the first seven chapters of the book, I've relied heavily on a fraction-as-measure interpretation because the first operations that students encounter (addition and subtraction) require this interpretation to make sense of combining and breaking apart quantities of the same size of unit. This interpretation means seeing the fraction in terms of numbers, as quantities of a size of unit. For example, the fraction ¾ is interpreted as a quantity, 3, of a size of unit, 1 *fourth*, or *fourths*. It's important to note that a different interpretation of fractions (that is, *fraction-as-action*) is used to make sense of some multiplication problems (for example, mentally computing ⅔ × 9), and another interpretation (that is, *fraction-as-division*) is used to make sense of many different division problems (for example, converting ¾ to a decimal). In this chapter, we'll rely heavily on another interpretation of fractions: *fraction-as-ratio*.

FRACTION-AS-MEASURE INTERPRETATION

Let's return to the two earlier problems to compare the difference between *fraction-as-measure* and *fraction-as-ratio* interpretation. Problem 1 involves a fraction-as-measure interpretation because both fractions are viewed as numbers in terms of a quantity and size of unit in relation to the same size of whole. That is, the fractions 13⁄16 and ¾ are interpreted as making the size of the units explicit, as 13 *sixteenths* and 3 *fourths*. The question was, How much of a whole pan of brownies did you eat? Answering this question involves adding the measures together, but this action cannot be performed until the sizes of the units are the same. Using an equal exchange, 3 *fourths* are transformed into 12 *sixteenths*. Now the two measures (13 *sixteenths* and 12 *sixteenths*) can be combined to determine how much of a whole pan of brownies you ate (13 *sixteenths* + 12 *sixteenths* = 25 *sixteenths* = 1 *whole* and 9 *sixteenths*). Don't worry! It was after school Friday, and those calories don't count; plus, the pans were not that big! That rationalizing behavior is a nice segue into problem 2.

FRACTION-AS-RATIO INTERPRETATION

Problem 2 involves a *fraction-as-ratio* interpretation. There is a quantity representing a part, the points you received for correct answers, and a quantity representing the whole, the total number of points.

A *ratio* is merely a comparison between two quantities. This is the fundamental difference between a fraction-as-measure and fraction-as-ratio interpretation. In this case, the fractions $\frac{13}{16}$ and $\frac{3}{4}$ represent a part-whole comparison involving two quantities, points correct and total points. In this instance, there are no sizes of units, *sixteenths* or *fourths*. The denominators of the fractions represent the quantity of total points. One way to determine the overall grade is to combine the quantity represented by the two parts (13 + 3 = 16) and the quantity of two wholes (16 + 4 = 20) to determine that you have received 16 points correct out of a total of 20 points. A bar–number line model and a table showing the solution to each problem is shown in figure 8.1.

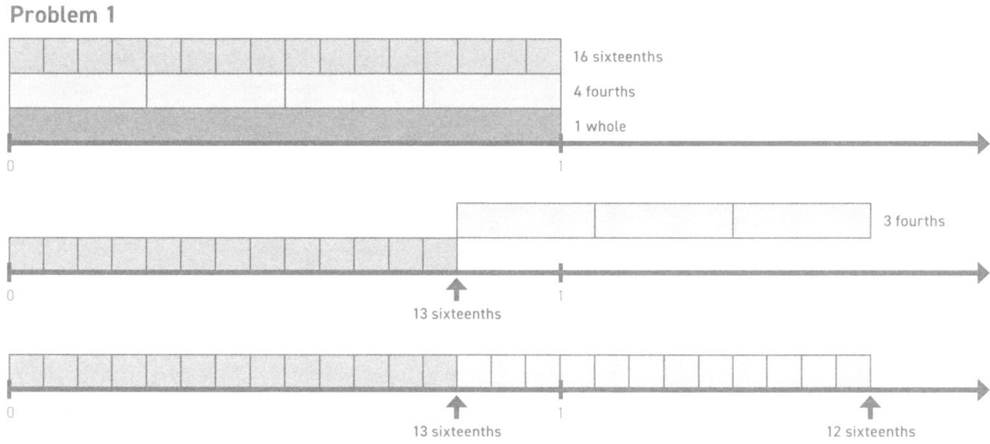

13 sixteenths + **12** sixteenths = **25** sixteenths

Problem 2

	Quantity of Points Correct	Quantity of Total Points
Quiz 1	13	16
Quiz 2	3	4
Total	16	20

Figure 8.1: Comparing *fraction-as-measure* and *fraction-as-ratio* interpretations.

The key takeaway from this discussion is this. As you may remember from chapter 3 (page 47), it is important not to use the standard fraction notation (for example, $\frac{5}{8}$) to introduce fraction-as-measure conceptions because it doesn't illuminate the size of the unit. And many students don't see the numeral in the denominator of a fraction as a unit because their experiences up to this point have been that numerals represent quantities, not units. It's almost like they have developed fraction-as-ratio conceptions before fraction-as-measure conceptions, which is a problem. Once ratios are introduced to students, there is another problem with fraction notation. As the discussion of the solutions to problems 1 and 2 illustrates, determining which interpretation is required, a fraction-as-measure or fraction-as-ratio conception, can be a little confusing for less experienced elementary students to sort out. Just like those frog legs, you'd better know what you're eating before you take a bite!

Equivalent Ratios

There is significant power in not only recognizing equivalent ratios, but also "seeing" the multiplicative relationships that exist between them. In this section, I am going to avoid using the traditional fraction notation to represent ratios to make these multiplicative relationships more visible. I would like to start by having you reflect upon a familiar situation.

PAUSE AND PONDER

A 16-ounce bottle of a particular brand of soda has 60 grams of sugar. Imagine you poured a quarter of the 16-ounce bottle of soda into a cup. Would you expect the remaining soda to be more, less, or just as sugary as when the bottle was full? How many ounces of soda are in the cup? How many grams of sugar would the soda in the cup have?

Suppose you poured three 16-ounce bottles of the same soda into a large container. Would you expect the soda in the large container to taste more, less, or just as sugary as a 16-ounce bottle of the same soda? How many ounces of soda would be in this larger container? How many grams of sugar would the soda in the container have?

Let's suppose that you have a strip of paper and you labeled the strip as I did in figure 8.2 using a bar–double number line.

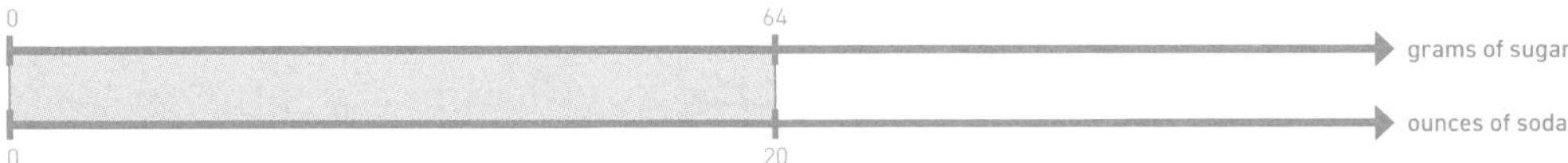

Figure 8.2: Using a bar–number line to model the relationship between 20 ounces of soda and 64 grams of sugar.

Now partition, by folding, the strip of paper into four equally sized pieces. Determine the numbers that correspond with the question marks shown in figure 8.3.

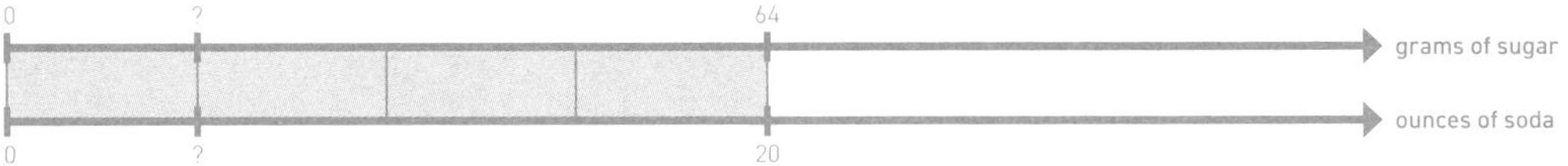

Figure 8.3: Using a bar–number line to partition the whole unit of 20 ounces of soda to 64 grams of sugar into four equally-sized pieces.

The Pause and Ponder before this primed you to begin thinking about ratio rationships. Let's check your work using the following figure 8.4 and use that as a foundation to discuss those two multiplicative relationships.

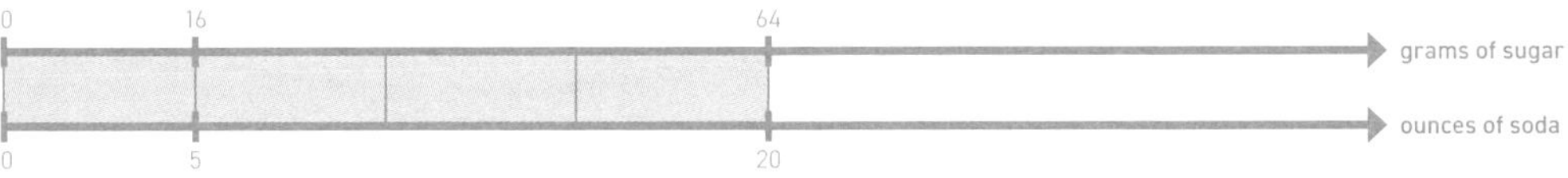

Figure 8.4: ¼ of 64 grams of sugar is 16 and ¼ of 20 ounces is 5.

With every key concept discussed in this book, introducing a concept to students involves helping them "see" the important understandings that underpin the concept first and use conceptual language related to (or "say") what they are seeing. The foundational concept of this chapter is *equivalent ratios*. Equivalent ratios are required for the concepts we're going to explore in this chapter (that is, comparing ratios, proportions, and percentages). Equivalent ratios are bound together by two multiplicative relationships that exist between them. As we discussed earlier, a ratio is a comparison between two quantities. Think of both quantities in a ratio as measured spaces. For example, in the problem that we just explored, the two measured spaces are grams of sugar and ounces of soda. Both the quantity of sugar and the quantity of soda were measured using a particular form of measurement unit, grams (weight), and ounces (technically fluid ounces, which is a measurement unit of liquid volume). There is a multiplicative relationship that exists *between* the two measured spaces of equivalent ratios and a multiplicative relationship that holds *within* the same measured spaces of equivalent ratios (Vergnaud, 1988). Let's take a moment to examine each type of multiplicative relationship.

WITHIN-MEASURED-SPACES

More than likely, the values that you replaced the question marks with in figure 8.3 were 16 and 5. You recognized that each value in its respective measured space (grams of sugar and ounces of soda) would be ¼ of the given value, and you determined that the corresponding values would be ¼ of 64 grams of sugar, or 16 grams of sugar, and ¼ of 20 ounces of soda, or 5 ounces or soda. In other words, you multipled each quantity *within* each measured space by ¼ to determine an equivalent ratio.

I tried to get you in this mindset in the Pause and Ponder. As you did in chapter 4 (page 73) to determine ¼ of a whole unit, you partitioned the whole unit into 4 equally sized pieces and found the length of 1 of those pieces. You did the same thing in the Pause and Ponder, except you were acting on both quantities (20 and 64), which represent a composed unit (20:64). In this case, you more than likely divided both 20 and 64 by 4, which is the same as multiplying them both by ¼. This is an example of a *within-measured-spaces* multiplicative relationship. You more than likely multiplied by a different number to answer the second Pause and Ponder situation, 3 groups of the ratio 64 grams of sugar to 20 ounces of soda is 192 grams of sugar (3 × 64 = 192) and 60 ounces of soda (3 × 20 = 60). Both of these within-measured-spaces multiplicative relationships are shown in figure 8.5 using a bar–number line and a *ratio table*.

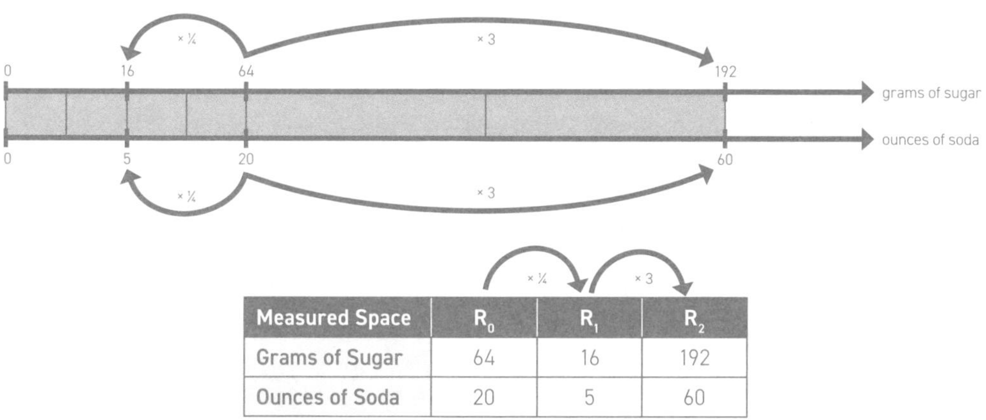

Measured Space	R_0	R_1	R_2
Grams of Sugar	64	16	192
Ounces of Soda	20	5	60

Figure 8.5: Within-measured-spaces multiplicative relationship of equivalent ratios.

BETWEEN-MEASURED-SPACES

The second multiplicative relationship, *between-measured-spaces*, describes a function relationship *between* the quantities represented in the two measured spaces. You have done this many times before to calculate a unit rate. Use a calculator to compute the following: 64 ÷ 20, 16 ÷ 5, and 192 ÷ 60. The result you obtained represents the multiplicative relationship between the two measured spaces. If you were given any quantity of ounces of soda, you could multiply 3.2 times that quantity to determine the quantity of grams of sugar. Or, using the reciprocal of 3.2, or 0.3125, if you were given any quantity of grams of sugar, you could multiply by 0.3125 to determine the quantity of ounces of soda. Both 3.2 and 0.325 represent unit ratios, as 3.2 represents 3.2 grams of sugar to 1 ounce of soda and 0.325 represents 0.3125 ounces of soda to

1 gram of sugar. In the context of this particular problem, the unit ratios, or technically *unit rates* (that is, different units of measure) in this case, describe the measure of the sugariness of the soda. Think back to the Pause and Ponder. Did you expect the pouring actions that I asked you to perform would result in the quantity of soda tasting the same? If so, then you already intuitively knew that each had the same level of sugariness, right? The within-measured-spaces multiplicative relationships represented in figure 8.6 using a bar–number line model and ratio table describe a relationship between the two measured spaces (grams of sugar and ounces of soda) that describe a measure of sugariness (ratio of grams of sugar to ounces of soda).

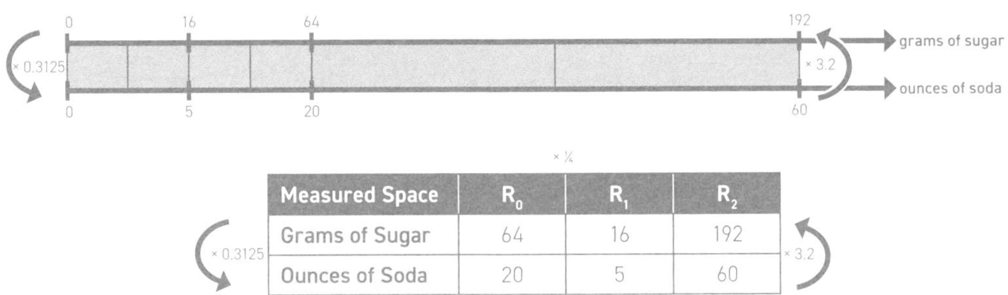

Measured Space	R_0	R_1	R_2
Grams of Sugar	64	16	192
Ounces of Soda	20	5	60

Figure 8.6: Between-measured-spaces multiplicative relationship of equivalent ratios.

The between-measured-spaces and within-measured-spaces multiplicative relationships of equivalent ratios represent the *connector understanding* of ratios. "Seeing" these two multiplicative relationships as they work with problems that involve equivalent ratios provides students with the tools to flexibly solve a multitude of problems involving ratios, proportions, and percentages.

PAUSE AND PONDER

Suppose students are given a ratio that describes the relationship between grams of sugar and ounces of soda (60 grams of sugar in a 16-ounce soda) and are asked to determine how many grams of sugar are in a 20-ounce soda. Take a moment to consider a few of the strategies students might use.

If appropriate, ask your students the same question and reflect on the strategies they use. (*Note: If they have never done this before, I have found it helpful to pour a beverage into different-sized cups.*)

Similar to the partial quotient algorithm for long division, the beauty of giving students a ratio and part of a target ratio provides them the opportunity to use the multiplicative relationships that they see to engage in proportional reasoning without knowing that they're engaging in proportional reasoning. More on that later. Shown in figure 8.7 is a recording of a few students' reasoning to solve the same problem as the one given in the Pause and Ponder. Student A utilized multiple within-measured-spaces multiplicative relationships involving different composite units, student B utilized one within-measured-spaces multiplicative relationship and added quantities of the two ratios together, and student C estimated until they found the correct between-measured-spaces multiplicative relationship for the given ratio and applied it to determine the unknown quantity.

Student A	Student B	Student C
½ group of (60:16) is (30:8)	¼ group of (60:16) is (15:4)	4 × 16 = 64 (too high!)
½ group of (30:8) is (15:4)	(60:16) + (15:4) = (**75**:20)	3 × 16 = 48 (too low!)
5 groups of (15:4) are (**75**:20)		3.5 × 16 = 54 (too low!)
		3.75 × 16 = 60 (just right!)
		3.75 × 20 = **75**

Figure 8.7: Student work showing use of between-measured-spaces and within-measured-spaces multiplication relationships to solve a problem.

As mentioned previously, the *connector understandings* of ratios are the two multiplicative relationships that exist between equivalent ratios, between-measured-spaces and within-measured-spaces. It is important to utilize representations (for example, bar–double number line and ratio tables) and language that provide students with the best opportunity to see these two relationships.

Ratio Comparison

Understanding the multiplicative relationships between and within equivalent ratios also provides students with the tools to compare ratios. Often, in real life, we are asked to compare the relationship that exists between two or more ratios.

PAUSE AND PONDER

Take a moment to reflect on how you would solve the following problem: The ratio of an orange juice mixture is 3 cans of orange juice to 4 cans of water. Let's call this mix A. A student decides to add 1 can of orange juice and 1 can of water to the mixture. Let's call this mix B. Which mixture will be juicier? Or will both mixtures be the same juiciness?

If it's appropriate, pose the same question to your students. Reflect on the strategies they used to make sense of the problem and what you would need to do instructionally to move their thinking forward.

Comparing ratios, as was the case with fractions, challenges students to shift from seeing additive relationships, which are often more visible, to seeing multiplicative relationships. I posed a similar question to my college students as the question I posed in the Pause and Ponder. The results were slightly higher than the percentage of students who indicated that the fractions $\frac{5}{6}$ and $\frac{7}{8}$, a fraction comparison problem from chapter 4 (page 73), were equal. *Over 30 percent of my students indicated that mix A and mix B were the same juiciness.* They were seeing additive relationships when they needed to see multiplicative relationships.

It seems natural for students to see the ratio of 3 parts juice to 4 parts water (mix A) as being the same as the ratio of 4 parts juice to 5 parts water (mix B). Oftentimes, what is most visible, especially with discrete models like the one shown in figure 8.8, is that it takes 1 more part of orange juice in each mixture to have the same amount of water (3 + **1** = 4, 4 + **1** = 5).

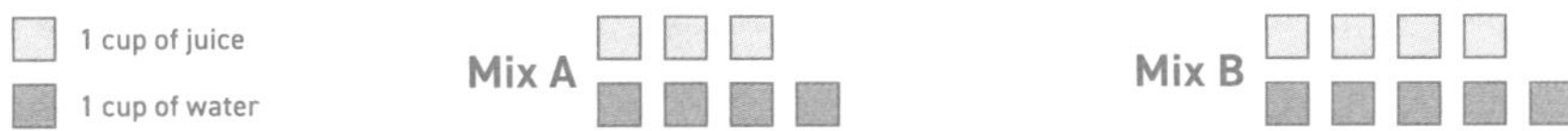

Figure 8.8: Both mixtures have 1 more cup of water than OJ.

Since these two ratios are not easily compared, we need a way of standardizing, or *norming* (Lamon, 1994), the two ratios so they can be compared. Norming means we need to strategically create equivalent ratios for one or both ratios with the goal of making sure one of the quantities in each ratio is the same. Shown in figure 8.9 is a ratio table in which a few norming possibilities are shown so that the two ratios can be easily compared. Comparing the juiciness of mix A and mix B can be done easily using ratio 1, 2, or 3 because the quantities of water in both mixtures are the same. Since the quantities of water have been normed, the comparison can easily be made by comparing the quantity of orange juice.

Mix A ($R_0 \times 5 \rightarrow R_1$, $R_1 \times 5 \rightarrow R_2$, $R_2 \times \frac{1}{100} \rightarrow R_3$)

Measured Space	R_0	R_1	R_2	R_3
Orange Juice (Cups)	3	15	75	0.75
Water (Cups)	4	20	100	1

Mix B ($R_0 \times 5 \rightarrow R_1$, $R_1 \times 5 \rightarrow R_2$, $R_2 \times \frac{1}{100} \rightarrow R_3$)

Measured Space	R_0	R_1	R_2	R_3
Orange Juice (Cups)	4	16	80	0.80
Water (Cups)	5	20	100	1

Figure 8.9: Using norming to determine which mixture is juicier.

There are three brief points I want to make. In some instances, the within-measured-spaces multiplicative relationship is more visible than the between-measured-spaces multiplicative relationship—that is, unless one of the ratios generated in the ratio table is a unit ratio. A unit ratio makes this between-measured-spaces multiplicative relationship more visible. For example, in figure 8.9, ratio R_3 in mix B can be interpreted using the between-measured-spaces multiplicative relationship as for any given quantity of cups of water there are 0.80 times the amount of orange juice. The other ratios of mix B have this same between-measured-spaces multiplicative relationship.

The second point is I can imagine students using a calculator to compute 3 ÷ 4 and 4 ÷ 5 and returning with the answers 0.75 and 0.80, respectively. I can also imagine them reasoning which mixture is juicier, saying "point 80 is greater than point 75." When pressed a bit, they might say, "80 *hundredths* is greater than 75 *hundredths*." The problem we are solving, however, is a ratio comparison involving two quantities, not a number comparison involving a quantity and size of unit. We are talking not about a size of unit, *hundredths*, but about a quantity that has been normed to another quantity, 100. The correct interpretation would be a ratio of a part of 80 cups of orange juice to another part of 100 cups of water is juicier than a ratio of a part of 75 cups of orange juice to another part of 100 cups of water. It is also important to note that 0.75 and 0.80 could be interpreted as a quantity of lemon juice in relation to a quantity of 1 cup of water. I know, but if we want students to communicate exactly the relationship that exists between the two ratios, we need to make that distinction. And we definitely do not want students "mixing up," pun intended, *fraction-as-measure* and *fraction-as-ratio* interpretations.

The part-part business takes me to my third point. Some relationships between quantities can be expressed as either *part-part* ratios or *part-whole* ratios. We interpreted the mixture problem using a part-part ratio (part orange juice and part water). The two parts must combine to create the whole. A part-whole ratio comparison (cups of orange juice to total cups) of the same mixture problem is shown in figure 8.10. Which mixture is juicier doesn't depend on whether we use part-part or part-whole ratios to make the comparison—each type just tells their own story, but in a slightly different way.

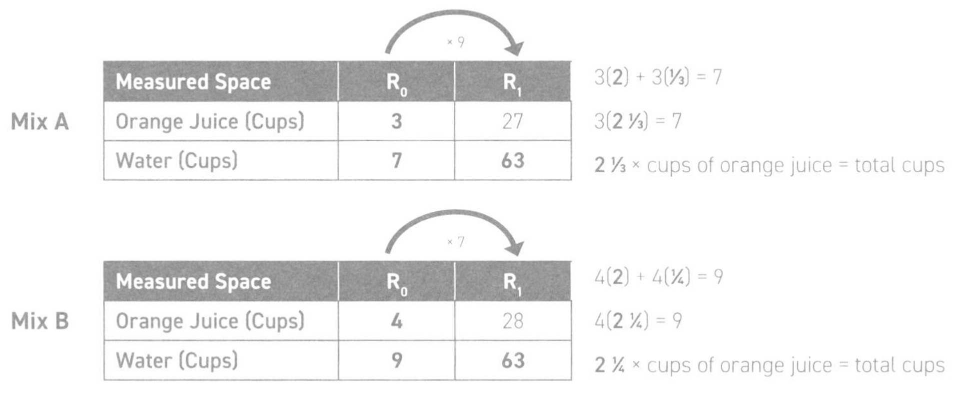

Mix A

Measured Space	R_0	R_1
Orange Juice (Cups)	3	27
Water (Cups)	7	63

Mix B

Measured Space	R_0	R_1
Orange Juice (Cups)	4	28
Water (Cups)	9	63

Figure 8.10: Using a part-whole ratio to compare mixtures.

What About Proportions?

Nothing new to report here! Recall that a *ratio* is a relationship, or comparison, between quantities (for example, 3 cups of orange juice to 7 total cups). If the same multiplicative relationship exists between two ratios, then these ratios are considered to be *proportional* to each other. For example, the two ratios of mix A in figure 8.10, 3 cups of orange juice to 7 total cups and 9 cups of orange juice to 21 total cups, are proportional because in each ratio there are 3⁄7 the quantity of cups of OJ as there are total cups. Equivalent ratios are inherently proportional to each other, so if students have had opportunities to use the multiplicative relationships (that is, within- and between-measured-spaces) to generate equivalent ratios, then they have already been engaging in proportional reasoning. Solving proportion problems merely involves determining an unknown quantity of another equivalent ratio to the one that is given. For example, referring again to mix A in figure 8.10, if the ratio of orange juice to total cups is 3:7 and you want to create the same mixture with 35 total cups, how many cups of orange juice would you need? To solve this problem, you could either take 3⁄7 of 35 (15) or multiply the quantity of cups of orange juice of the initial ratio by 5 (3 × 5 = 15).

Introducing proportional reasoning to students gives me another opportunity to play the "What Do You Know?" game. This helps my students "see" and utilize these multiplicative relationships to generate equivalent ratios to solve proportion problems. I'm going to challenge my students by giving them a scenario that involves a scale drawing in which the ratio is 2 actual feet of room length for every ¼ inch on a scale drawing of the room length. We aren't converting between units in the same measurement system (for example, 12 inches = 1 foot) or different measurement systems (1 inch = 2.54 cm) either. These are all ratio relationships as well. In this case, we have established a ratio relationship to compare the length or distance shown in scale drawing (measured in inches) to the actual length or distance (measured in feet) of the room, 2 feet : ¼ inch).

Depending on my students' skill levels, I give them a ratio relationship that I'm confident they can handle (for example, 2 actual feet to ¼ of an inch) and ask, "What do you know?" over and over. We record them in a ratio table or, depending on the level of the students, a bar–double number line, and I ask them to describe the multiplicative relationship they're using. I do this because I want to know whether they're using between-measured-spaces or within-measured-spaces multiplicative relationships, as well as the composite unit or units they're using. For example, a student might say "Using the given ratio, R_0, I know that 1 foot of length of actual drawing is ⅛ of a whole inch on the scale drawing because I halved both quantities." This student's reasoning has indicated to me that they utilized a within-measured-spaces multiplicative relationship.

Another student might say, "Using R_1, I know that a quantity of 1 is 8 times greater than a quantity of ⅛. So I know that 32 actual feet corresponds with 4 inches on the scale drawing because it is 8 times greater." This student's reasoning has indicated to me that they utilized a between-measured-spaces multiplicative relationship. As the dialogue progresses, I challenge students to ask questions that will make their peers reason proportionally. For example, "If the actual length of a wall is 10 feet, what would the corresponding measurement be on the scale drawing?"

A recording of students' reasoning that exemplifies the power of this type of activity is shown in figure 8.11.

The class's reasoning shown in Figure 8.11 to create the six ratios exemplifies a flexible use of within-measured-spaces (R_1, R_3, R_6) and between-measured-spaces multiplicative relationships, (R_2, R_4), as well as one more idea that applies to ratios. You can add the quantities of equivalent ratios to create additional equivalent ratios. A student used this idea to create ratio R_5 by adding together the ratios R_0 and R_4.

	R_0	R_1	R_2	R_3	R_4	R_5	R_6
Number of feet (actual length)	2	1	32	4	8	10	30
Number of inches (scale drawing length)	¼	⅛	4	½	1	1 ¼	3 ¾

R_1: "Halving both quantities results in a new ratio of 1 actual foot to ⅛ of an inch on scale drawing."

R_2: "Using R_1, the quantity of feet is 8 times greater than the quantity of inches, so if there are 4 inches on the scale drawing, there will be 8 times 4 equals 32 feet of actual length."

R_3: "Doubling each quantity in R_1 results in a new ratio of 4 actual feet to ⅓ of an inch on the scale drawing."

R_4: "We already know from R_1 and R_0 that there are 8 times as many feet as inches, so if there is 1 inch on scale drawing, then are there 8 actual feet."

R_5: "Combining the quantities in R_4 and R_0, I got 8 plus 2 equals 10 actual feet and 1 plus 1 ¼ equals 1 ¼ inches on the scale drawing."

R_6: "Tripling each quantity in R_5, I got 10 times 3 equals 30 feet and 1 and ¼ times 3 and ¾ inches."

Figure 8.11: Student reasoning to determine equivalent ratios as part of "What do you know?" activity.

The Trouble With Cross Multiplication

The "cross multiplying" strategy is commonly used in classrooms to teach students how to solve problems involving proportions. I believe this is a mistake, because the strategy illustrated in figure 8.12 doesn't illuminate either of the multiplicative relationships discussed in this chapter (Siegler, Carpenter, Fennell, Geary, Lewis, Okamoto, Thompson, & Wray, 2010).

Let's imagine using a cross-multiplication strategy to solve the problem, "A car is traveling at a constant rate of 60 miles per hour. How many hours will it take the car to travel 450 miles?" The work to solve this problem using a cross-multiplication strategy is shown in figure 8.12.

$\frac{\text{miles}}{\text{hours}}$ $\frac{60}{1} = \frac{450}{x}$ → $\frac{60}{1} \; \frac{450}{x}$ "Cross multiply" → $60x = 450$ "solve for x" → $x = \frac{450}{60} = 7.5$

Figure 8.12: Cross multiplying to solve problems involving proportions.

The cross multiplying strategy has the same impact on students' multiplicative ratio reasoning superpowers as Kryptonite has on Superman's powers. It weakens their ability to use those powers. If we want students to stop reasoning about multiplicative relationships (we do not), we show them how to cross multiply. I'm not entirely against students learning at some point how to cross multiply because it's a great strategy to use when solving more complex proportion problems, like those found in geometry involving similar triangles. It just doesn't make sense to share this strategy with students until long *after* you're convinced that they can flexibly utilize multiplicative ratio relationships to solve problems involving proportions.

Here's one more reason to hold off on the cross multiplying strategy—we don't use it to solve the real-life proportionality problems we commonly face. Think about the last time you were at a store and used a cross multiplication strategy to solve a problem. I was on a trip in which I noticed that it took 1 hour and 40 minutes to travel 120 miles. My children, as I am sure yours do, asked, "When are we going to be there?" I am a mathematics guy, so they're getting an answer! We had another 450 miles to go! It wouldn't have been safe while driving to reach for my cell phone or a pad of paper to perform this calculation, so instead I relied on my mental arithmetic ratio superpowers. I started my reasoning with an equal exchange of 100 minutes for 1 hour and 40 minutes. Since we traveled 120 miles in 100 minutes, I knew that we would, assuming a constant rate, travel 360 miles in 300 minutes, 3 groups of the ratio (120 miles:100 minutes), and 480 miles in 400 minutes, 4 groups of the ratio (120 miles:100 minutes). I also reasoned that since 450 miles is closer to 480 miles (400 minutes) than 360 miles (300 minutes), it would take more than 350 minutes, which I estimated, using another proportional relationship (60 minutes in 1 hour), to be about 6 more hours of driving. I shared with them that our drive would be approximately another 6 hours, which stopped the question for another 30 minutes or so! Those of you who have traveled with children know exactly what I am talking about!

Percentages

Let's switch gears. Suppose that you recently took a test that was worth 75 points. At the top of the paper, the teacher wrote that you had received 60 points. What's the next thing that you'd do? In today's world, you would probably find the calculator app on your phone and enter $^{60}/_{75}$, and 0.80 would be returned. Without even thinking, you'd say, "OK, I got an 80 percent."

The technology is programmed in such a way that when you enter $^{60}/_{75}$, it will return 0.80. As we discussed earlier when comparing mixtures, the problem is that the technology doesn't know how to interpret the result. It doesn't know whether to interpret the 0.80 in terms of a measure, 80 *hundredths*, or a ratio, 80 points correct to 100 points total. It is up to us to interpret this output, being mindful of the context of the situation.

A *percentage* is a special type of ratio that involves a specific type of norming. Now, think about the meaning of the word *cent*. How many *cents* in a dollar? Years in a *cent*ury? So, 80 percent (that is, 80%) means 80 out of 100. Since a percentage is a special type of ratio, the multiplicative relationships of equivalent ratios we learned about earlier still hold. We can reason about them in the same way. A percentage, like a unit ratio, is a standardized unit of measure that enables easy comparisons to be made between ratios. Instead of 1, like a unit ratio, the comparison is to 100.

Let's see how these relationships can be used to reason about why a ratio of points correct (60) to total points (75) is in fact 80 percent, or 80:100. Both measured spaces—points on the test and percentages—are part-whole ratios. The respective wholes are 75 (total points) and 100 (total percent). Both whole quantities are represented by the length of 1 whole bar. There are many solution possibilities, but one of those is shown in figure 8.13.

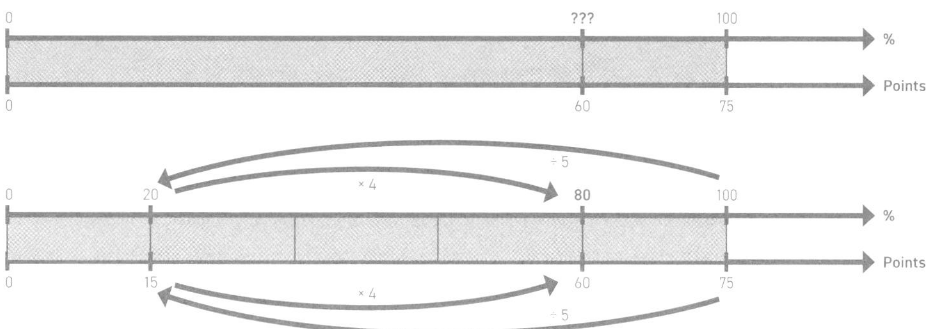

Figure 8.13: Using a bar-double number line to solve a percentage problem.

Using a factor of both 75 and 100, the whole is partitioned into 5 equal parts. This action can be used to determine several equivalent ratios, or composite units, to (75 points:100%), one of which is (15 points:20%). This ratio can be used to determine the desired unknown part (%) of another equivalent ratio with a known part of 60 points, 4 groups of (15 points:20%), or (60 points:**80%**).

How to Figure Out a Tip

When you go to a restaurant, who calculates the tip? Do you get a little nervous when the server hands you the bill and you must calculate the tip? Suppose that you go out for a meal that costs $60. The service was great, so you choose to leave a 22 percent tip. Take a moment to reflect on the strategy you would typically use to do this. Can you give an estimate for the answer? What reasoning did you use to give the estimate?

You may already have the mental arithmetic tools to determine the exact tip. That's awesome! If not, you'll soon have the mental arithmetic superpowers to calculate any tip. Soon you'll have no fear when that bill is handed to you! This type of reasoning is what our students will do with percentages in real life, and we already do, so it is important to introduce this idea to them so they will never fear calculating a tip or determining the percentage off of an item when they are shopping.

10 PERCENT OF A NUMBER

Let's start by activating your mental arithmetic superpowers for percentages. Underpinning this superpower is a specific percentage, 10 percent, that can be utilized to find a great number of other percentages. Let's start by using a multiplicative relationship of equivalent ratios to determine 10 percent of 60. Can we agree that 100 percent of 60 is 60? As we did to solve the previous problem, a composed ratio of 100 percent (100%:60) is an easy place to start. The work to determine both 10 percent of 60 and 1 percent of 60 using the same within-measured-spaces multiplicative relationship is shown in figure 8.14 (page 192). Essentially, determining 10 percent of a number involves partitioning the whole (60) into 10 equally sized lengths and determining the length of 1 of those parts (6).

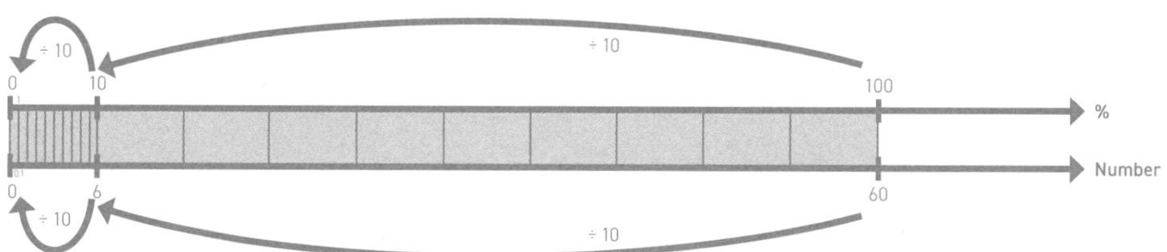

Figure 8.14: Using a double number line to determine 10 percent and 1 percent of 60.

THE WHY BEHIND MOVING THE DECIMAL POINT

Some students will say that 10 percent of 60 is 6 because "you just move the decimal over one place." Unfortunately, when you ask them to explain why, a common response I hear is "I don't know. It's just what I was taught!" There are a couple of additional ways to help students make sense of the why here. One way is to connect this idea to what they've already learned about multiplying fractions. This way requires a little flexibility with fraction interpretations. Ten percent is a part-whole ratio, 10 to 100, which can be transformed into the equivalent ratio 1 to 10, or the fraction $\frac{1}{10}$. Now the problem is $\frac{1}{10}$ of 60 ($\frac{1}{10} \times 60$). The fraction $\frac{1}{10}$ is now an *action* that describes a partitioning action on 6 tens, or 60 ones. This is shown in figure 8.15.

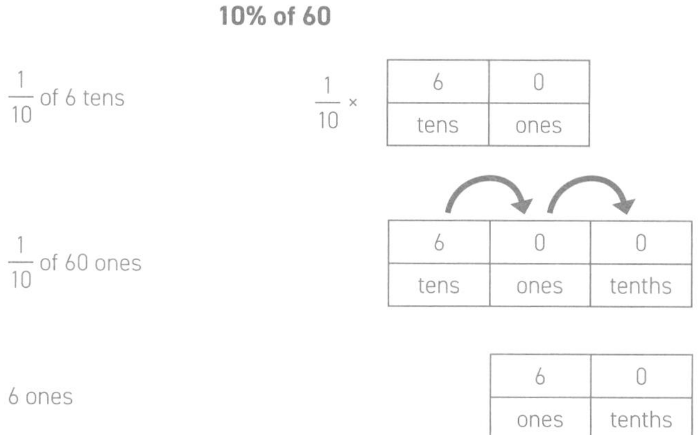

Figure 8.15: Why is 10 percent of 60 equal to 6?

Another way is to think about $\frac{1}{10}$ of 60 in terms of place value. Multiplying a number by $\frac{1}{10}$ has a special power with respect to place value. It keeps the quantities represented in the number the same (that is, 6 and 0) but shifts the size of the units one place value to the right. That is, 6 *tens* and 0 *ones* is transformed into 6 *ones* and 0 *tenths*, or 6.0, or 6. This is also shown in figure 8.15. Knowing 10 percent of a number is like spinach is to Popeye. It unleashes mental arithmetic superpowers! Once that relationship is known, it's easy to jump to other percentages, using those multiplicative ratio relationships we discussed earlier.

Use your newfound mental arithmetic percentage superpower to compute the following problems.

- 1% of 60
- 5% of 60
- 20% of 60
- 60% of 60
- 33% of 60

- 42% of 60

Now you're ready to reason through computing 22 percent of 60. That is, 2 groups of the ratio 10%:6 is **20%:12**, and 2 groups of the ratio 1%:0.6 is **2%:1.20**. Combining those two ratios, (20%:12) and (2%:1.2), yields the desired ratio **(22%:13.2)**. The tip you would leave is $13.20. You got this!

How to Solve a Different Type of Percentage Problem

Students first learning about percentages are expected to solve two different types of problems—(1) those in which the part is unknown and (2) those in which the whole is unknown. The percent problems we've been solving have involved an unknown part. A short version of the mental work to compute another problem (43 percent of 80) in which the part is unknown is shown in figure 8.16. This strategy involves multiple within-measured-spaces multiplicative relationships.

	%	$
	40	32
÷10	4	3.2
÷4	1	0.8
×3	3	2.4

%:$
40:$32
3:$ 2.40
43:**$34.40**

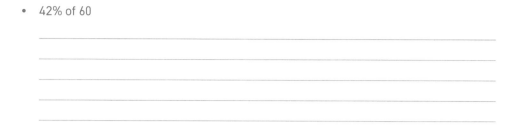

Figure 8.16: Calculating 43 percent of 80.

Now let's examine a problem in which the whole is unknown. An example of a problem of this form is "If 70 percent of a number is 42, what is the number?" In this instance, we don't know what 100 percent (whole) of the number is, or the other whole. In this instance, the length of the part bar representing the ratio (70%:42) is partitioned to create an equivalent ratio that can then be utilized to determine the length of the whole bar representing the ratio (100%:?). Remember—when possible, use the superpower ratio of 10 percent. In this case, the partial ratio (70%:42), as shown in figure 8.17, can easily be partitioned into this ratio (10%:6) since both numbers have a factor of 7. Then, 10 groups of the superpower ratio, a composed unit (10%:6), can be utilized to determine the unknown number representing the number of the whole (100%:**60**). This is an example of the use of a within-measured-spaces multiplicative relationship. It is also possible to solve this problem using a between-measured-spaces multiplicative relationship. In this instance, 70 × 0.**60** is 42, so 100 × 0.**60** = 60. See figure 8.17.

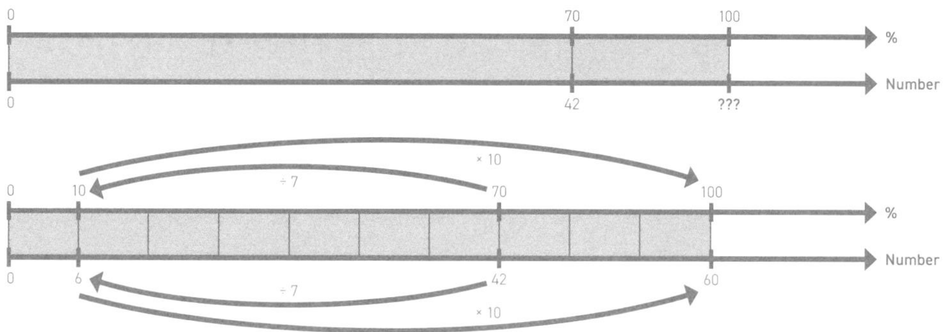

Figure 8.17: 70 percent of 60 is what number?

Once students become proficient in, or see, these multiplicative relationships in ratios, they can begin to use the language, or say, to communicate their reasoning strategies. In a class of fifth graders, I invited students to share the strategies they used to mentally compute a few percentage problems. The first problem was a problem similar to the problem that we just solved but one in which the part is unknown, "70 percent (part) of a 60 (whole) is what number?" The class couldn't come to a consensus as to whether the answer was 4.2 or 42 until a student shared the following reasoning: "We know that 100 percent of 60 is 60 and 50 percent of 60 is 30, so it only makes sense that the answer would be 42." Another student confirming this answer said, "Since 100 percent of 60 is 60, 10 percent of 60 is 6, so the number we get for 70 percent of 60 is seven times greater than the number we had for 10 percent, 7 × 6 = 42." Both students' explanation demonstrated their understanding of within-measured-spaces multiplicative relationships of ratios. To be honest, I may have shed a few tears because it demonstrated such great progress in their reasoning!

The second problem I asked them was "If 5 percent (part) of a number is 30 (part), what is the number?" One student using a within-measured-spaces multiplicative understanding stated, "If 5 percent of a number is 30, then 100 percent of that number is 20 times greater than 30, or 600, so 5 percent of 600 is 30." Meanwhile, another student using a between-measured-spaces multiplicative understanding stated, "We know that 5 percent of a number is 30—the number is 6 times greater than the percentage. Since we want 100 percent of the number, the number is 6 times 100, or 600." Simply asking your students to solve percentage problems that lend themselves to mental arithmetic strategies and listening to their reasoning will give insight into the nature of their ratio superpowers. This superpower will not develop on its own because the technology to perform these computations is at their fingertips. It will have to be cultivated using the models and strategies that have been shared in this chapter. Remember that the goal is not just an answer but to empower students with a why and a way through when, like my student who used a calculator to compute 70 percent of 60 and got an answer of 4.2, they're unsure of the answer the technology returns.

One More Mental Arithmetic Strategy for the Road!

Before we end our journey with percentages, I want to share one more mental arithmetic strategy with you. Some percentage problems are much easier to mentally compute than others.

PAUSE AND PONDER

Take a moment to think about the strategy you would use to mentally compute 84 percent of 25.

Now think about the strategy you would use to compute 25 percent of 84.

Can you believe that both problems have the same answer? You can switch the number and the percentage and get the same answer! Pretty cool, right? Use it to quickly determine 14 percent of 50. This strategy *always* works when taking the percent of a number!

As I have done throughout this book, I want to empower you with the why behind this strategy! Let's look again at 84 percent of 25 and 25 percent of 84. Let's start by mentally reasoning through 84 percent of 25. I think we can agree that 84 percent of 100 is 84. The number in the original problem, 25, is 4 times lesser than 100 (multiply by $\frac{1}{4}$), so the answer to 84 percent of 25 is also 4 times lesser than 84 percent of 100, $\frac{84}{4} = 21$. Now let's mentally reason through 25 percent of 84. Can we agree that 100 percent of 84 is 84? This time, the percentage in the original problem, 25 percent, not the number, is 4 times lesser than 100 percent, so 25 percent of 84, $84/4 = 21$, is also going to be 4 times lesser than 100 percent of 84 (84). Same computation both times! Got to love those multiplicative relationships! This work is shown in figure 8.18.

84% of 25

%	Number
84	21
100	25

× 1/4

25% of 84

%	Number
25	21
100	84

× 1/4

Figure 8.18: 84 percent of 25 is the same as 25 percent of 84.

PAUSE AND PONDER

If appropriate, review your curriculum resources related to ratios and proportions. In what ways does your curriculum incorporate ideas from this chapter?

What are one or two ideas from this chapter that you will use in your classroom?

What will be the biggest challenge to implementing those shifts?

Key Points

Before proceeding, please take a moment to review the following takeaways from this chapter.

1. There is a difference between interpreting a *fraction-as-measure* (for example, 3 fourths) and a *fraction-as-ratio* (for example, 3 shaded circles to 4 total circles). The first represents a number that involves a quantity and size of unit based on a whole unit, while the second represents a relationship between two quantities. It is important to recognize the difference in these two ideas because the same notation (for example, ¾) is often used to represent both situations. It is recommended to avoid using the standard fraction notation to represent fractions until after students have had significant experiences with bar–double number lines and ratio tables.
2. *Equivalent ratios* have two different multiplicative relationships, *within-measured-spaces* and *between-measured-spaces*. For example, consider the ratio of 64 grams of sugar to 20 ounces of soda (R_1), which is equivalent to the ratio of 16 grams of sugar to 5 ounces of soda (R_2). The measured spaces are numbers of grams of sugar and ounces of soda. The *within-measured-spaces* multiplicative relationship is that there are ¼ times as much sugar and ¼ times as much soda, $\frac{1}{4} \times R_1 = R_2$. The *between-measured-spaces* multiplicative relationship is that there are 3.2 times as many grams of sugar as there are ounces of soda.
3. Mentally solving problems involving proportions is about utilizing multiplicative ratio relationships. For example, if you know that 4 packs of soda cost $12, and assuming a constant ratio relationship, you can determine how much 6 packs of soda cost by using a between-ratio multiplicative relationship (that is, 1.5 × 12 = 18) or a within-ratio comparison (that is, 1 pack costs $3, so 6 cost 6 × $3 = 18).
4. Knowing 10 percent of a number is a mental arithmetic superpower that enables you to find a lot of other percentages. For example, 63 percent of 70 can be found knowing that 10 percent of 70 is 7. Once you know that, you know 60 percent of 70 is 42 because it's 6 times more than 10 percent (6 × 7 = 42). You also know 1 percent of 70 is 0.7 because it is 10 times less than 10 percent of 70, which is 7. You also know that 3 percent of 70 is 2.1 because it's 3 times more than 1 percent of 70 (3 × 0.7 = 2.1). So, 63 percent of 70 is 42 + 2.1, or 44.1.

Chapter 8 Application Guide

Chapter Concepts	How Can I Incorporate This Into My Teaching Practice Moving Forward?
Make explicit the difference between a fraction-as-measure conception and a fraction-as-ratio conception.	Before representing ratios using fraction notation, be sure students understand the two multiplicative relationships of equivalent ratios. Model ratios with ratio tables and bar-double number lines first. More than likely, students will obtain decimal answers (for example, 0.80) as they form equivalent ratios. Make explicit the difference between interpreting the decimal as a number (for example, 80 hundredths) and as a ratio (for example, 80 to 100).
See It, Say It, Symbolize It **Understand within-measured-spaces multiplicative relationships and between-measured-spaces multiplicative relationships.**	Progressing from physical paper strip models to enable students to engage in partitioning to bar-double number line models to ratio table models provides opportunities for students to create equivalent ratios. Provide opportunities for them to communicate the composite unit ratio used to create the equivalent ratio and the type of multiplicative relationship (within-measured-spaces or between-measured-spaces).
Use mental strategies based on multiplicative relationships to solve proportion and percentage problems.	Provide opportunities for students to flex their mental arithmetic superpower muscles. For example, engage them in the "What Do You Know?" activity, giving them a ratio (for example, 5 sandwiches cost $20) or a percentage (for example, 10 percent of 80 is 8) and asking them "What do you know?" Then progress to them asking a question that can be answered with the given information (for example, "How much would 15 sandwiches cost?" or "What is 44 percent of 80?").

Final Thoughts

One of my goals in the introduction was that after engaging in this book you would see and say elementary mathematics in a different way—a way that would support you as you engaged your own students in thinking about mathematics differently. My commitment to you from the beginning was that you would, after reading this book, see numbers and operations on those numbers differently. Have I succeeded? While this new way is still about correctness, it's about way more than just getting correct answers. It's about understanding the why behind much of what we have always done, seeing and saying what we have always done in new ways, and reimagining what we have often done so that what once seemed disjointed is now connected.

As I wrote this book, I reflected heavily on one question: What is the least amount I could share with you that, if embraced, would have the greatest transformative impact on your students' mathematics experience? In other words, what could I share with you that would help you keep more students in the mathematics game and stop the tears of frustration and hopelessness? This was boiled down to four superpower understandings. For example, before reading this book, had you ever thought about equal exchanges and analogous problems? As I have illuminated throughout the book, the overarching concepts of equal exchanges and analogous problems have the potential to shift and shape thinking to broader ideas as opposed to simply obtaining an answer.

Bringing the vision of this book into classrooms is going to challenge assumptions related to commonly used curricular resources. First, is a delineation between whole numbers and "decimals" needed? And if so, why? And if not, how can we better connect these ideas so that the bridge between the two is shortened? Second, is there any downside to placing more of an emphasis on quantities and sizes of units by being more explicit about the size of the unit (for example, 364 is 3 *hundreds*, 6 *tens*, and 4 *ones*)? Third, is it possible to narrowly focus attention on initially building fraction-as-measure conceptions only and not shifting until we're certain our students have them? This will have significant implications as to the types of problems and representations that we use to engage students in thinking about fractions.

I also want to re-emphasize the importance of seeing multiplicative relationships. Yes, students' knowledge of single-digit multiplication facts is a significant aspect of seeing those relationships. Though sometimes implicit, those multiplicative relationships underpin most of what we do. For example, single-digit numbers, such as 8, have an implied multiplicative relationship. Say you have 8 snack cakes—that means that you have 8 groups of a unit of one. Those 8 objects (8 groups of 1 one) can be rearranged to show 2 groups of "four" objects in which "four" becomes a composed unit, and the number of 8 objects can be compared multiplicatively to another set of objects. For example, a set with 8 objects has "8 times as many" objects as a set with 1 object.

There are also implied multiplicative relationships moving from larger- or smaller-sized units (that is, place value). For example, the number 364 represents 3 groups of 1 hundred (which is also 10 groups of 1 ten or 100 groups of 1 one), 6 groups of 1 ten (which is also 10 groups of 1 one or even 100 groups of 1 tenth), and 4 groups of 1 one. Likewise, the fraction $3/8$ represents 3 groups of 1 eighth. When we say "three eighths," the unit fraction is hidden (1 eighth), but it's there. What's wild is that multiplication of numbers and ratio relationships, both forms of composite units, are also connected. For example, consider the whole-number multiplication problem $1/4$ group of 64 (16), and scaling a ratio, $1/4$ groups of (64 grams of sugar:20 ounces of soda). In both problems, the number $1/4$ represents the number of groups. As I said before, multiplicative relationships are everywhere! I challenge you to find where they're lurking in your own curriculum.

Well, this is the end of our journey! We covered a lot of ground! My hope is that you see mathematics differently and are imagining possibilities of how you can integrate ideas from this book into your own classroom. Hopefully, you are empowered with the why behind many of the ideas that you were taught as a student. You have also learned some different ways to think about those same ideas and connections between ideas that you may have never known existed. I hope that you see mathematics in a different way and that you will be able to explain it to your own students in a meaningful way—one that enables more students to get it! You have also been given a set of mental arithmetic superpowers that you can pass down to your students! Most importantly, I hope I have empowered you with more tools to help your students thrive. I wish you the best of luck as you embark on your own journey to keep more of your students in the mathematics game! Thank you for taking this trip with me! On a personal note, my grandmother Edna passed away twenty days from her hundredth birthday in October 2021. Before she passed away, I told her of this journey and reminded her that she was the inspiration for this book. It is an honor and a privilege to share this work with you. I hope what you learn helps you inspire others. While my grandmother never had an opportunity to attend college, my hope is that the spark she lit continues to burn in me and, through this book, multiplies into a raging fire that shapes the teaching and learning of mathematics for many others.

Glossary

addition. A mathematical operation that involves combining quantities of the same size of unit. For example, 3 *tens* and 4 *tens* can be combined to form 7 *tens*. Likewise, 3 *eighths* and 4 *eighths* can be combined to form 7 *eighths*. However, 3 *fourths* and 3 *eighths* cannot be combined because the sizes of units are not the same.

additive relationship. Seeing the relationship between two numbers in terms of addition. For example, 9 is 3 more than 6, 6 **+ 3** = 9.

analogous problem. Problems that involve the same quantities, but with different units. Each of the four operations have analogous problems. For example, the addition problem 9 + 6 is analogous to 90 + 60, and the multiplication problem 6 × 90 is analogous to the multiplication problems 6 × 0.9 and 6 × $\frac{9}{5}$.

associative property of addition. A property of addition that involves the regrouping of parts. For example, this property underpins the mental arithmetic strategy of moving a part of a part to a different part to change the addition problem 68 + 26 to another problem with the same whole, 68 + 26 = 68 + (2 + 24) = (68 + 2) + 24 = 70 + 24 = 94).

associative property of multiplication. A property of multiplication that involves regrouping of units. For example, 3 groups of (2 groups of 6), 3 × 12 = 26, is the same as (3 groups of 2) groups of 6, 6 × 6 = 36. This property is most easily seen by using rectangular arrays.

bar–double number line model. A model used to illuminate that ratios are quantities that are bound together around two multiplicative relationships. As the bar–number line model, it supports the portioning and iterating actions on lengths to support the creating of equivalent ratios derived from the within-measured-spaces multiplicative relationship.

bar–number line model. A model used to illuminate that the numbers on a number line are located in relation to the length of the whole unit. Also supports seeing partitioning and iterating actions on lengths to support the placement of additional numbers as well as their relationship to each other.

between-measured-spaces multiplicative relationship. A multiplicative relationship that exists between two equivalent ratios. For example, consider the equivalent ratios involving the measured spaces of dollars and quantity of sandwiches (4 sandwiches:$10) and (20 sandwiches:$50). One of the between-measured-spaces multiplicative relationships is quantity of sandwiches × $2.50 = total cost.

cardinality. An early number concept in which the student understands that the last number in a set counted represents the total number of objects in that set. For example, when a student finishes counting by saying "twelve," there is an acknowledgment that there are 12 objects in the set.

commutative property of addition. A reordering property of addition that involves changing the order of the parts without changing the whole (for example, 8 + 6 = 6 + 8 = 14).

commutative property of multiplication. A reordering property of multiplication in which an array of objects is shifted 90 degrees to transpose the number of rows and columns, which changes what each numeral represents in a multiplication problem but maintains the whole. Also, called the *switcheroo* (for example, 8 groups of 6 is the same as 6 groups of 8. Both have a whole of 48).

compensation. A subtraction mental arithmetic strategy that involves adding the number to the whole and part to be removed. For example, the problem 8 – (–3) can be changed to an "easier" problem to solve mentally by adding 3 to both numbers in the problem: (8 + 3) – (–3 + 3) = 11 – 0 = 11.

composite unit. A group of objects formed to create a larger unit. For example, a dime is the original unit, but 10 of them are composed to form 1 dollar. The nature of the unit is defined by either a mathematical system or the unit that a particular student might be using to make sense of the problem. For example, in the decimal number system, 1 ten is composed of 10 ones, and ⅔ is composed of 2 groups of 1 third. For example, to determine the answer to 8 ⅔, a student is utilizing a composed unit length of ⅔ of a whole unit to count up to 8 whole units.

conceptual subitizing. Seeing the number of objects in an arrangement of objects without having to count each individual object.

connectable block model. A model that enables students to see the composing and decomposing of units in all four operations.

counting on. An early number strategy that involves subitizing a partial set of objects and then utilizing one-to-one correspondence to count the rest of the set. For example, suppose a set of 8 objects was shown. A student would say, "five," and then count the rest of the objects in the set individually, "six, seven, eight."

counting up. A subtraction mental arithmetic strategy that involves counting up from the known part to the whole to obtain the unknown part. For example, the subtraction problem 96 – 68 could be solved by adding 2 to 68 (70), 20 more (90), and 6 more (96), which results in an unknown part of 2 + 20 + 6 or 28.

decimal number system. The number system that we utilize. The same 10 numerals (0–9) are utilized to form all of the numbers in our system, and equal exchanges of decimal size units occur when there is a quantity of 10 of a unit.

decompose. The act of taking 1 of a larger size of unit and equally exchanging it for a quantity of the smaller size of unit. For example, exchanging 1 one-dollar bill for 10 dimes or 1 ten-dollar bill for 10 ones.

denominator. Represents the size of unit of a fraction. For example, in the fraction ³⁄₅ the denominator 5 represents the size of the unit called *fifths*, which is found by partitioning the length of the whole unit into 5 equal lengths. These lengths are called *fifths*.

discrete rectangular array. A representation used to help students see multiplication concepts. The advantage is they make all three aspects of a multiplication problem visible (for example, 6 rows and 8 columns and 48 objects). Also, this representation supports the development of an understanding of the associative, commutative, and distributive properties of multiplication.

distributive property of multiplication over addition. The act of decomposing a unit or quantity into a different quantity or unit while maintaining the whole. Utilized to support students reasoning about larger groups or sizes of units. For example, 7 groups of 7 (49) can be separated using the distributive property into two parts, 5 groups of 7 (35) and 2 groups of 7 (14). Also, 8 groups of 13 is also 8 groups of 10 and 8 groups of 3 ($8 \times 13 = 8 \times (10 + 3) = 8 \times 10 + 8 \times 3 = 80 + 24 = 14$). This can be seen by partitioning a rectangular array either vertically or horizontally.

dividend. A term often associated with division. Refers to the *whole* of a division problem.

division. An operation that involves partitioning a whole into a given size of groups to determine the number of groups (measurement) or separating the whole to ensure that a given number of groups is the same size (sharing). The operation can also be described as multiplication by the reciprocal. For example, the result of 4 ÷ ⅓ is the same as 4 × 3.

divisor. A term often associated with division. Refers to either the *size of the group* (measurement interpretation) or the *number of groups* (sharing interpretation).

equal exchange. Two different quantities and sizes of units that are the same amount or number. We use these all the time when we exchange money. Think about exchanging 10 ones for 1 ten. Numbers inherently have equal exchanges. For example, the symbol string 100 could represent 1 hundred, 10 tens, 100 ones, 1,000 tenths, and so on. A number can also be decomposed, using part-whole relationships, into other equal exchanges. For example, 1 hundred could also represent 9 tens and 10 ones, or 9 tens and 9 ones and 10 tenths. The same is true for fractions. For example, 3 fourths is an equal exchange for 6 eighths.

equivalent fractions. A form of equal exchange involving two fractions that have a multiplicative relationship between quantity and size of unit. For example, the fraction 6 *twelfths* can be equally exchanged for 2 *fourths* because the quantity of units is 3 times greater (2 × 3 = 6), but the size of the unit is 3 times lesser (fourths to twelfths); it takes 3 twelfths to make 1 fourth.

equivalent ratios. Two or more ratios that have both within-measured-spaces and between-measured-spaces multiplicative relationships.

factor. A concept related to whole-number multiplication. In a rectangular array model of multiplication, or area model, it is the possible group size or size of groups for a given whole represented by a whole. For example, if 48 objects were arranged into rectangular arrays, what could be seen is 1 group of 48, 2 groups of 24, 4 groups of 12, 6 groups of 8, 48 groups of 1, 24 groups of 2, 12 groups of 4, or 8 groups of 6. Those numbers represent the factors of 48.

fraction-as-action interpretation. The fraction is interpreted in terms of an action on a multiplicative unit. For example, in the multiplication problem ⅔ × 9, the fraction is interpreted as partitioning 9 into 3 equally sized groups and determining the length, or size, of 2 of those groups.

fraction-as-division interpretation. The fraction is interpreted in terms of division. For example, the fraction ¾ can be interpreted as portioning the whole of 3 into 4 equally sized groups.

fraction-as-measure interpretation. The fraction is interpreted as a number in terms of a quantity and size of unit. For example, the decimal 0.1, a fraction, depending on the context, can be interpreted as 1 *tenth.*

fraction-as-ratio interpretation. The fraction is interpreted in terms of a part and whole. For example, the decimal 0.1, a fraction, depending on the context, can be interpreted as a quantity of 1 part to a quantity of 10 total parts.

gap reasoning. A form of reasoning used by students when comparing fractions that does not attend to the size of unit. It involves reasoning in which the student sees either the "gap" between the numerals of the fraction or, with a pictorial representation, the quantity of missing pieces to complete the whole. For example, students using gap reasoning will indicate that the fractions ⅚ and ⅞ are equal because they have the same number of missing pieces, 1, to make the whole or that 5 + 1 = 6 and 7 + 1 = 8. Also, called *gap thinking* or *benchmark value distance* thinking.

halving and doubling. A mental arithmetic multiplication strategy that involves partitioning a rectangular array, either vertically or horizontally, in half, and moving the objects such that the other dimension is doubled while maintaining the whole. For example, an 8 × 35 array can be partitioned into a 4 × 70 array. Both have a whole of 280.

improper fraction. A fraction in which the quantity of the unit is greater than the quantity of the unit needed to create a whole unit. For example, 9⁄5, 9 *fifths*, is considered an improper fraction because it only requires 5 *fifths* (9 > 5) to create an equal exchange for 1 whole.

iterating. The action of taking a unit length or another composed unit length and copying it to create other lengths. For example, taking a fraction of length 1 sixth and iterating it four times to determine the length of 4 sixths and recognizing that 4 sixths is 4 times greater than 1 sixth.

make a ten. An early number strategy that involves create a composite unit, ten, from a quantity of *ones*. Also, involves an understanding of part-part-whole relationships. For example, a set of 7 ones and 5 ones can be organized into a set of 10 ones and 2 ones to create 1 ten and 2 ones.

measurement interpretation of division. A given whole is partitioned into a given size of groups to determine the number of groups. For example, from a measurement perspective, the implied question in the division problem 2 ÷ ⅓ is, "How many groups of length ⅓ of a whole unit are in 2 whole units?"

mixed number. A number that is described in terms of multiple sizes of units in which one of those units is a fractional unit. For example, 1 $\frac{4}{5}$ is a mixed number because it represents 1 whole (or *one*) and 4 *fifths*.

multiplication. An operation that involves determining the whole of a number of groups of a particular size of unit. This operation often involves decomposing and recomposing a quantity of nondecimal unit into a quantity of one or more decimal units. For example, using connectable blocks to model 6 groups of *eight* is decomposed into 4 groups of *eight* and 2 groups of 8 *ones* and recomposed into 4 groups of *ten* and 8 groups of *one* (48).

multiplicative relationship. Seeing a relationship between numbers in terms of multiplication. For example, 9 is 1.5 times greater than 6 because 6 × **1.5** = 9.

multiplicative unit. The second number in a multiplication problem (for example, 6 × **8**). It is the unit that the multiplier acts upon. Also referred to as the *size of the group*.

multiplier. The first number in a multiplication problem (for example, **6** × 8). Also, called the scale factor, the number of groups, or the action fraction.

norming. The process of creating equivalent ratios to compare two ratios. Converting ratios to a percentage or a unit rate is an example of norming.

number. Represented using numerals. A collection of quantities and sizes of units that express a magnitude when compared to other numbers. For example, the number 356 represents 3 hundreds and 5 tens and 6 ones.

number of copies. A term used, like *groups of*, to describe the multiplicative relationship involving a composite unit. For example, 3 eighths can also be interpreted as 3 copies of 1 *eighth*. The whole-number multiplication problem 5 × 4 can be interpreted as 5 copies of a unit of *four*.

numeral. A symbol used to represent a number or, in the case of the denominator of a fraction, a size of unit.

numeral-unit-name chart. A chart used to record the actions involved in adding or subtracting numbers that makes the size of the unit explicit.

numeral-unit-name notation. A notation used to represent a number to ensure that the size of the unit is visible. For example, $\frac{3}{5}$ is written as 3 *fifths*.

numerator. Represents the quantity of a size of unit of a fraction. For example, in the fraction $\frac{3}{5}$ the numerator "3" represents the quantity of a size of unit called *fifths*.

one-to-one correspondence. Another early number understanding in which the student assigns a number to each object in a set and understands that the quantity of objects in the set is represented by the last number. For example, if there were five objects in a set, a student would say, with or without touching the objects, "one, two, three, four, five" and stop.

open number line. A representation in which students are given the flexibility to determine the size of the unit and order numbers based on their decision. The purpose is to illuminate the need for a unit length of one or another composite and that the location of other numbers is dependent on that length. Also, supports partitioning and iterating activities.

partial product algorithm. An alternative to the traditional multiplication algorithm that is underpinned by the distributive property of multiplication over addition. For example, the multiplication problem 24 × 35 is decomposed into (20 + 4) × (30 × 5) and the four partial products, 20 × 30, 20 × 5, 4 × 30, and 4 × 5, are computed individually and summed.

partial quotient algorithm. An alternative to the traditional long division algorithm that provides students with flexibility to utilize multiplicative relationships that they "see" to solve a division problem.

partial sum algorithm. An alternative to the traditional addition algorithm that involves combining quantities of the same size of unit and recording those individually.

partitioning. The action of taking a whole unit length, or part of a whole unit length, and partitioning it into equally sized pieces to determine partial fraction lengths. For example, partitioning 1 whole unit into 6 equal pieces to create lengths of 1 sixth.

part-part ratio. Ratio in which the quantities in two measured spaces represent subsets of a set. For example, a quantity of red candies and a quantity of green candies, assuming those are the only two colors of candies, represent the total quantity of candies.

part-part-whole relationship. A student who "sees" a set of objects, but also sees them in terms of subsets. For example, a student who sees a whole set of 12 objects also in terms of parts, 7 objects and 5 objects or 2 objects and 10 objects. It underpins a dynamic understanding of operations involving numbers.

part-whole ratio. Ratio in which the quantities in two measured spaces represent a subset of the set and the set. For example, quantity of red candies to quantity of total candies.

percentage. A special type of ratio that involves a norming process in which the whole is always 100. The word is interpreted as "out of 100."

perceptual subitizing. Seeing the number in two sets of objects and using a known number fact to determine how many are in the combined set. For example, seeing 5 objects and 7 objects and knowing that there are 12 total objects.

place value. The size of unit represented by the placement of the numeral. For example, the placement of the 3 in 30 signifies 3 *tens* while the placement of the same numeral in 300 signifies 3 *hundreds*. Moving from right to left, each place value, or size of unit, is 10 times greater. For example, 1 hundred is 10 times greater than 1 ten (that is, 1 hundred = 10 × 1 ten).

quotient. Refers to the answer to a division problem. Represents either the *size of the group* (sharing interpretation) or the *number of groups* (measurement interpretation).

ratio. Comparison of two or more quantities.

ratio table. A representation used to illuminate the multiplicative relationship between equivalent ratios.

reciprocal. A multiplicative relationship between two numbers in which the product is 1. For example, 3 × ⅓ = 1. This means that 3 is the reciprocal of ⅓ and vice versa.

recompose. An equal exchange action that involves taking a quantity of units (depends on the size of the unit) and transforming them into 1 of the next greater size of unit. For example, 5 *fifths* can be recomposed into 1 one (1 whole) or 10 *tens* can be equally exchanged for 1 *hundred*.

residual reasoning. A type of reasoning about fractions that involves considering both the quantity and size of unit from a benchmark. For example, a student comparing the fractions ⅚ and ⅞ will reason that ⅞ is greater than ⅚ because ⅞ is ⅛ away from the whole and ⅚ is ⅙ away from the whole. Since ⅛ is less than ⅙, ⅞ must be the greater number.

sharing interpretation of division. A given whole is separated into a number of equal sized groups to determine the size of the groups. For example, from a sharing perspective, the implied question in the division problem ⅓ ÷ 2 is "A length ⅓ of a whole unit is partitioned into 2 equal sized groups. How much will be in each group?"

size of unit. Refers to the place value of a decimal number (hundreds, tens, ones, tenths, and so on) or the denominator of a fraction (third, fourth, sixth, eighth, and so on).

subitizing. An early number understanding in which the student can determine the number of objects within a set without counting each element in the set. For example, a student playing the dice game immediately says "six" knowing that there are 6 dots on the dice.

subtraction. An operation that involves a "pulling apart" or "separating" action on the whole that involves quantities of the same size of unit. More formally, it is the same operation as "adding the opposite" to the whole. For example, the subtraction problem 8 – (–5) can be thought of in terms of addition by adding the opposite of the known part. In this case, 8 + –5 = 3.

symbol string. A set of symbols. In mathematics, these are numerals and operations organized in a way that has meaning. For example, 267 + 3,580.

unit coordination. The ability of students to create units and maintain their relationship with other units that they contain or constitute. For example, seeing the solution to the problem ⅔ × 9 might involve decomposing the 1 unit of *nine* into 9 units of *one*; partitioning the 9 units of one into 3 equal groups to create a new unit, *three*; and determining 2 groups of 1 *three* to create another unit, *six*.

unit fraction. A measure determined by partitioning a unit length into a number of equal sized pieces to determine the length of 1 of those pieces. For example, a unit fraction, or length of 1 fourth, is determined by partitioning the whole into 4 equally sized lengths and determining the length of 1 of those lengths. The unit fraction is a foundation concept because it forms the multiplicative unit of all other fractions of that particular unit. For example, the length of ¾ of a whole unit is 3 × the length of the unit fraction, ¼.

unit ratio/rate. A ratio or rate in which one of the two quantities in a ratio is 1.

within-measured-spaces multiplicative relationship. A multiplicative relationship that exists between two equivalent ratios. For example, consider the equivalent ratios involving the measured spaces dollars and quantity of sandwiches, ($10:4 sandwiches) and ($50:20 sandwiches). The within-measured-spaces multiplicative relationship is the quantities in the second ratio are 5 times the quantities in the first ratio, (50:20) = 5 × (10:4).

References and Resources

Barmby, P., Harries, T., Higgins, S., & Suggate, J. (2009). The array representation and primary children's understanding and reasoning in multiplication. *Educational Studies in Mathematics, 70*(3), 217–241.

Baroody, A. J. (1987). The development of counting strategies for single-digit addition. *Journal for Research in Mathematics Education, 18*(2), 141–157.

Behr, M. J., Harel, G., Post, T. R., & Lesh, R. (1992). Rational number, ratio, and proportion. In D. A. Grouws (Ed.), *Handbook of research on mathematics teaching and learning: A project of the National Council of Teachers of Mathematics* (pp. 296–333). New York: Macmillan.

Behr, M. J., Harel, G., Post, T. R., & Lesh, R. (1994). Units of quantity: A conceptual basis common to additive and multiplicative structures. In G. Harel & J. Confrey (Eds.), *The development of multiplicative reasoning in the learning of mathematics* (pp. 121–176). Albany: State University of New York Press.

Boaler, J. (2022). *Mathematical mindsets: Unleashing students' potential through creative mathematics, inspiring messages and innovative teaching* (2nd ed.). Hoboken, NJ: Jossey-Bass.

Booth, J. L., & Newton, K. J. (2012). Fractions: Could they really be the gatekeeper's doorman? *Contemporary Educational Psychology, 37*(4), 247–253.

Booth, J. L., Newton, K. J., & Twiss-Garrity, L. K. (2014). The impact of fraction magnitude knowledge on algebra performance and learning. *Journal of Experimental Child Psychology, 118*, 110–118.

Brooks, E. (1873). *The new normal mental arithmetic: A thorough and complete course by analysis and induction*. Philadelphia: Sowers, Potts.

Bruner, J. S. (1966). *Toward a theory of instruction*. Cambridge, MA: Harvard University Press.

Clarke, D. M., & Roche, A. (2009). Students' fraction comparison strategies as a window into robust understanding and possible pointers for instruction. *Educational Studies in Mathematics, 72*(1), 127–138.

Clements, D. H., & Sarama, J. (2020). *Learning and teaching early math: The learning trajectories approach.* New York: Routledge.

Dubé, A. K., & Robinson, K. M. (2018). Children's understanding of multiplication and division: Insights from a pooled analysis of seven studies conducted across 7 years. *British Journal of Developmental Psychology, 36*(2), 206–219.

Ellis, M. W., & Berry, R. Q., III. (2005). The paradigm shift in mathematics education: Explanations and implications of reforming conceptions of teaching and learning. *The Mathematics Educator, 15*(1), 7–17.

Empson, S. B., & Levi, L. (2011). *Extending children's mathematics: Fractions and decimals.* Portsmouth, NH: Heinemann.

Fuson, K. C. (1992). Research on learning and teaching addition and subtraction of whole numbers. In G. Leinhardt, R. T. Putnam, & R. A. Hattrup (Eds.), *Analysis of arithmetic for mathematics teaching* (pp. 53–187). New York: Routledge.

Hackenberg, A. J. (2013). The fractional knowledge and algebraic reasoning of students with the first multiplicative concept. *The Journal of Mathematical Behavior, 32*(3), 538–563.

Hackenberg, A. J., Norton, A., & Wright, R. J. (2016). *Developing fractions knowledge.* Thousand Oaks, CA: SAGE.

Hackenberg, A. J., & Sevinc, S. (2024). Students' units coordinations. In P. C. Dawkins, A. J. Hackenberg, & A. Norton (Eds.), *Piaget's genetic epistemology for mathematics education research* (pp. 371–411). Springer.

Lamon, S. (1994). Ratio and proportion: Cognitive foundations in unitizing and norming. In G. Harel & J. Confrey (Eds.), *The development of multiplicative reasoning in the learning of mathematics* (pp. 89–120). Albany: State University of New York Press.

Lannin, J., Chval, K., & Jones, D. (2013). *Putting essential understanding of multiplication and division into practice in grades 3–5.* Reston, VA: National Council of Teachers of Mathematics.

Leinwand, S., & Milou, E. (2021). *Invigorating high school math: Practical guidance for long-overdue transformation.* Portsmouth, NH: Heinemann.

Leong, Y. H., Ho, W. K., & Cheng, L. P. (2015). Concrete-pictorial-abstract: Surveying its origins and charting its future. *The Mathematics Educator, 16*(1), 1–18.

Lovett, M. C., Bridges, M. W., DiPietro, M., Ambrose, S. A., & Norman, M. K. (2023). *How learning works: Eight research-based principles for smart teaching* (2nd ed.). Hoboken, NJ: Jossey-Bass.

Miller, J., & Warren, E. (2014). Exploring ESL students' understanding of mathematics in the early years: Factors that make a difference. *Mathematics Education Research Journal, 26*(4), 791–810.

Milton, J. H., Flores, M. M., Moore, A. J., Taylor, J. L. J., & Burton, M. E. (2019). Using the concrete–representational–abstract sequence to teach conceptual understanding of basic multiplication and division. *Learning Disability Quarterly, 42*(1), 32–45.

Mitchell, A., & Clarke, D. (2004). When is three quarters not three quarters? Listening for conceptual understanding in children's explanations in a fraction interview. *Mathematics Education for the Third Millennium: Towards 2010, Proceedings of the 27th Annual Conference of the Mathematics Education Research Group of Australasia*, 367–373.

National Governors Association Center for Best Practices & Council of Chief State School Officers. (2010). *Common Core State Standards for mathematics.* Washington, DC: Authors. Accessed at www.corestandards.org/assets/CCSSI_Math%20Standards.pdf on February 6, 2024.

Pape, S. J., & Tchoshanov, M. A. (2001). The role of representation(s) in developing mathematical understanding. *Theory Into Practice, 40*(2), 118–127.

Pearn, C., & Stephens, M. (2004). Why you have to probe to discover what year 8 students really think about fractions. *Proceedings of the 27th annual conference of the Mathematics Education Research Group of Australasia* (Vol. 2, pp. 430–437). Townsville, Australia: MERGA.

Peng, P., Lin, X., Ünal, Z. E., Lee, K., Namkung, J., Chow, J., & Sales, A. (2020). Examining the mutual relations between language and mathematics: A meta-analysis. *Psychological Bulletin, 146*(7), 595.

Pesek, D. D., & Kirshner, D. (2000). Interference of instrumental instruction in subsequent relational learning. *Journal for Research in Mathematics Education, 31*(5), 524–540.

Piaget, J. (1977). *The development of thought: Equilibration of cognitive structures* (A. Rosin, Trans.). New York: Viking.

Pimm, D. (1987). *Speaking mathematically: Communication in mathematics classrooms.* New York: Routledge.

Purpura, D. J., Logan, J. A., Hassinger-Das, B., & Napoli, A. R. (2017). Why do early mathematics skills predict later reading? The role of mathematical language. *Developmental Psychology*, *53*(9), 1633.

Rogers, A. (2014). *Investigating whole number place value in years 3–6: Creating an evidence-based developmental progression* [Doctoral dissertation, RMIT University]. RMIT Research Repository. Accessed at https://researchrepository.rmit.edu.au/esploro/outputs/doctoral/Investigating-whole-number-place-value-in/9921864031901341 on January 29, 2024.

Siegler, R., Carpenter, T., Fennell, F., Geary, D., Lewis, J., Okamoto, Y., Thompson, L., & Wray, J. (2010). *Developing effective fractions instruction for kindergarten through 8th grade: A practice guide* (NCEE 2010-4039). Washington, DC: National Center for Education Evaluation and Regional Assistance, Institute of Education Sciences, U.S. Department of Education. Accessed at https://ies.ed.gov/ncee/wwc/docs/practiceguide/fractions_pg_093010.pdf on January 29, 2024.

Siegler, R. S., Duncan, G. J., Davis-Kean, P. E., Duckworth, K., Claessens, A., Engel, M., et al. (2012). Early predictors of high school mathematics achievement. *Psychological Science*, *23*(7), 691–697.

Siegler, R. S., & Pyke, A. A. (2013). Developmental and individual differences in understanding of fractions. *Developmental Psychology*, *49*(10), 1994–2004.

Siegler, R. S., Thompson, C. A., & Schneider, M. (2011). An integrated theory of whole number and fractions development. *Cognitive Psychology*, *62*(4), 273–296.

Siemon, D., Warren, E., Beswick, K., Faragher, R., Miller, J., Horne, M., et al. (2020). *Teaching mathematics: Foundations to middle years*. New York: Oxford University Press.

Simon, M. A. (2006). Key developmental understandings in mathematics: A direction for investigating and establishing learning goals. *Mathematical Thinking and Learning*, *8*(4), 359–371.

Simon, M. A., Placa, N., Avitzur, A., & Kara, M. (2018). Promoting a concept of fraction-as-measure: A study of the Learning Through Activity research program. *The Journal of Mathematical Behavior*, *52*, 122–133.

Sousa, D. A. (2016). *How the brain learns* (5th ed.). Thousand Oaks, CA: Corwin.

Stafylidou, S., & Vosniadou, S. (2004). The development of students' understanding of the numerical value of fractions. *Learning and Instruction*, *14*(5), 503–518.

Steffe, L. P. (1994). Children's multiplying schemes. In G. Harel (Ed.), *The development of multiplicative reasoning in the learning of mathematics* (pp. 3–39). Albany: State University of New York Press.

Steffe, L. P., & von Glasersfeld, E. (1988). On the construction of the counting scheme. In L. P. Steffe & P. Cobb (Eds.), *Construction of arithmetical meanings and strategies* (pp. 1–19). New York: Springer.

Sullivan, P., & Barnett, J. (2019). Escaping the gap. *Australian Primary Mathematics Classroom*, *24*(4), 25–29.

Sullivan, P. L., Barnett, J. E., & Killion, K. (2023). Beware of "gaps" in students' fraction conceptions. *Mathematics Teacher: Learning & Teaching PK–12, 116*(12), 912–922.

Tall, D., & Vinner, S. (1981). Concept image and concept definition in mathematics with particular reference to limits and continuity. *Educational Studies in Mathematics*, *12*(2), 151–169.

Torbeyns, J., Schneider, M., Xin, Z., & Siegler, R. S. (2015). Bridging the gap: Fraction understanding is central to mathematics achievement in students from three different continents. *Learning and Instruction*, *37*, 5–13.

Van de Walle, J. A., Karp, K. S., & Bay-Williams, J. M. (2023). *Elementary and middle school mathematics* (11th ed.). Hoboken, NJ: Pearson.

Vanluydt, E., Supply, A.-S., Verschaffel, L., & Van Dooren, W. (2021). The importance of specific mathematical language for early proportional reasoning. *Early Childhood Research Quarterly*, *55*, 193–200.

Vergnaud, G. (1988). Multiplicative structures. In M. Behr & J. Hiebert (Eds.), *Number concepts and operations in the middle grades* (pp. 141–161). Mahwah, NJ: Lawrence Erlbaum Associates.

Warren, E., & Miller, J. (2015). Supporting English second-language learners in disadvantaged contexts: Learning approaches that promote success in mathematics. *International Journal of Early Years Education*, *23*(2), 192–208.

Watanabe, T. (2007). Initial treatment of fractions in Japanese textbooks. *Focus on Learning Problems in Mathematics*, *29*(2), 41–60.

Young-Loveridge, J., & Mills, J. (2009). Teaching multi-digit multiplication using array-based materials. In R. K. Hunter & B. A. Bicknell (Eds.), *Crossing divides: MERGA 32 conference proceedings* (pp. 635–643). Wellington, New Zealand: Massey University.

Index

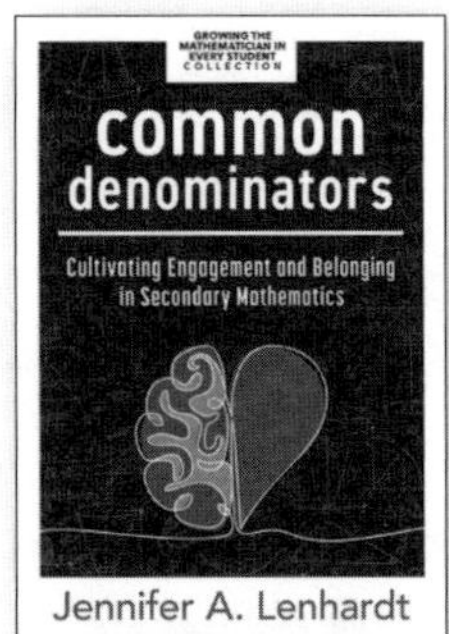

Common Denominators
Jennifer A. Lenhardt
"*Common Denominators* is a collection of stories braided together with research-informed strategies and tools," writes author Jennifer A. Lenhardt. Make sense of student engagement and belonging by using mathematics concepts that illustrate our common humanity and illuminate a clear, sustainable path for honoring and meeting all students' needs.
BKG179

Nurturing Math Curiosity
Chepina Rumsey and Jody Guarino
Gain the educational tools needed for planning, communicating, and representing mathematical ideas to students. This book gives teachers instructional strategies to enhance their students' natural wonder and curiosity toward math concepts.
BKG180

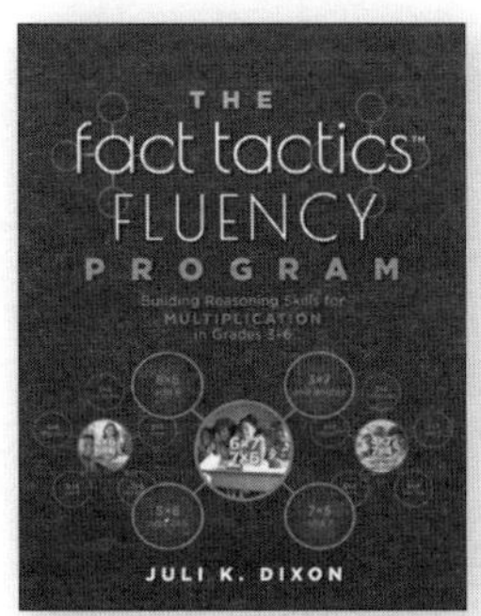

The Fact Tactics™ Fluency Program
Juli K. Dixon
Support students in developing a deep understanding of multiplication by emphasizing procedural fluency to develop automaticity in mathematics. This book will lead you through a 20-week program that utilizes six tactics to promote reasoning over rote memorization.
BKG125

Making Sense of Mathematics for Teaching Girls in Grades K–5
Thomasenia Lott Adams, Taylar Wenzel, Kristopher J. Childs, and Samantha Neff
Close the gender gap in mathematics. Acquire tools, tips, short exercises, and reflection questions that will help you understand the math and gender stereotypes impacting girls' education and eliminate gender bias through effective elementary school math instruction.
BKF816

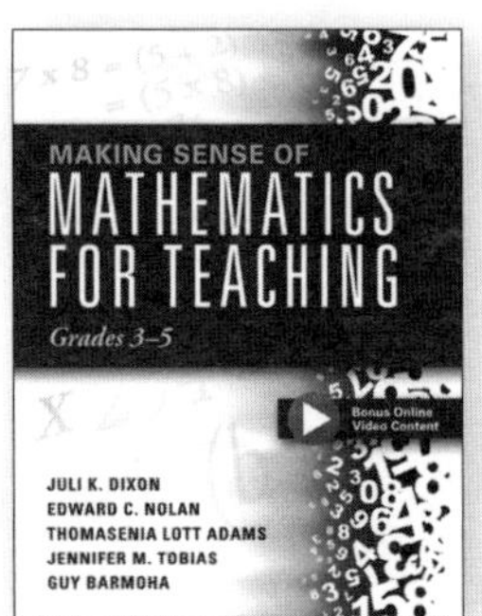

Making Sense of Mathematics for Teaching Grades 3–5
Juli K. Dixon, Edward C. Nolan, Thomasenia Lott Adams, Jennifer Tobias, and Guy Barmoha
Explore strategies and techniques to effectively learn and teach mathematics concepts for grades 3–5 and provide all students with the precise, accurate information they need to achieve success.
BKF696

Solution Tree | Press a division of Solution Tree

Visit SolutionTree.com or call 800.733.6786 to order.